STAR WARS

AGE OF RESISTANCE

HEROES

STAR WARS
AGE OF RESISTANCE

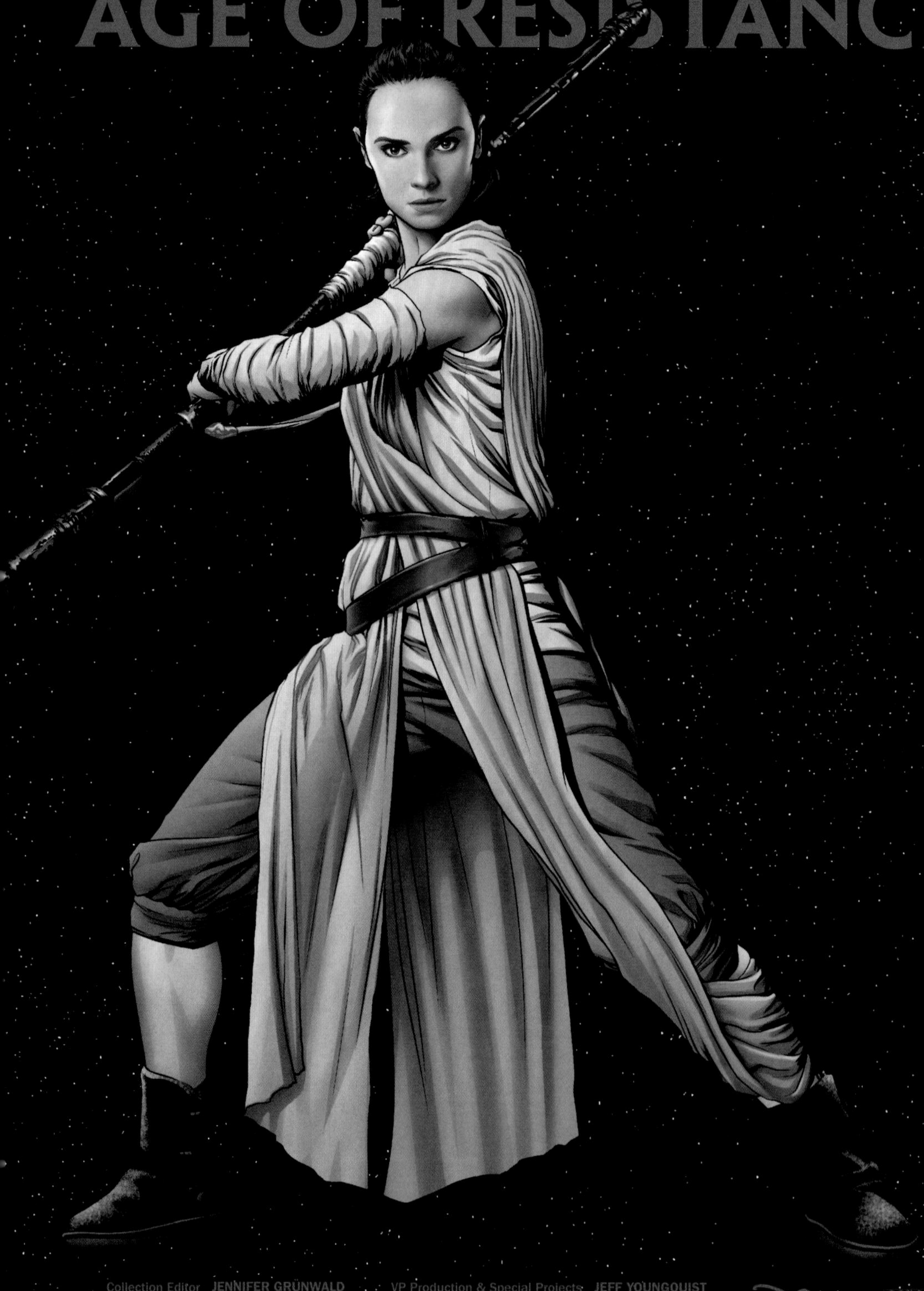

Collection Editor **JENNIFER GRÜNWALD**
Assistant Editor **CAITLIN O'CONNELL**
Associate Managing Editor **KATERI WOODY**
Editor, Special Projects **MARK D. BEAZLEY**

VP Production & Special Projects **JEFF YOUNGQUIST**
SVP Print, Sales & Marketing **DAVID GABRIEL**
Director, Licensed Publishing **SVEN LARSEN**
Book Designer **STACIE ZUCKER** WITH **ADAM DEL RE**

STAR WARS: AGE OF RESISTANCE — HEROES. Contains material originally published in magazine form as STAR WARS: AGE OF RESISTANCE — FINN #1, STAR WARS: AGE OF RESISTANCE — POE DAMERON #1, STAR WARS: AGE OF RESISTANCE — REY #1, STAR WARS: AGE OF RESISTANCE — ROSE TICO #1 and STAR WARS: AGE OF RESISTANCE SPECIAL #1. First printing 2019. ISBN 978-1-302-91712-8. Published by MARVEL WORLDWIDE, INC., a subsidiary of MARVEL ENTERTAINMENT, LLC. OFFICE OF PUBLICATION: 135 West 50th Street, New York, NY 10020.

Printed in Canada. DAN BUCKLEY, President, Marvel Entertainment; JOHN NEE, Publisher; JOE QUESADA, Chief Creative Officer; TOM BREVOORT, SVP of Publishing; DAVID BOGART, Associate Publisher & SVP of Talent Affairs; DAVID GABRIEL, SVP of Sales & Marketing, Publishing; JEFF YOUNGQUIST, VP of Production & Special Projects; DAN CARR, Executive Director of Publishing Technology; ALEX MORALES, Director of Publishing Operations; DAN EDINGTON, Managing Editor; SUSAN CRESPI, Production Manager; STAN LEE, Chairman Emeritus. For information regarding advertising in Marvel Comics or on Marvel.com, please contact Vit DeBellis, Custom Solutions & Integrated Advertising Manager, at vdebellis@marvel.com. For Marvel subscription inquiries, please call 888-511-5480. **Manufactured between 9/20/2019 and 10/22/2019 by SOLISCO PRINTERS, SCOTT, QC, CANADA.**

10 9 8 7 6 5 4 3 2 1

HEROES

Writer **TOM TAYLOR**
Artist **RAMON ROSANAS**
Color Artist **GURU-eFX**

AGE OF RESISTANCE SPECIAL

"MAZ'S SCOUNDRELS"
Writer **TOM TAYLOR**
Artist **MATTEO BUFFAGNI**
Color Artist **CHRIS O'HALLORAN**

"THE BRIDGE"
Writer **G. WILLOW WILSON**
Artist **ELSA CHARRETIER**
Color Artist **NICK FILARDI**

"ROBOT RESISTANCE"
Writer **CHRIS ELIOPOULOS**
Artist **JAVIER PINA**
Color Artist **GURU-eFX**

Letterer **VC'S TRAVIS LANHAM**
Cover Art **PHIL NOTO**
Assistant Editor **TOM GRONEMAN**
Editor **MARK PANICCIA**

Editor in Chief **C.B. CEBULSKI**
Chief Creative Officer **JOE QUESADA**
President **DAN BUCKLEY**

For Lucasfilm:
Senior Editor **ROBERT SIMPSON**
Creative Director **MICHAEL SIGLAIN**
Lucasfilm Story Group **PABLO HIDALGO, MATT MARTIN** &
EMILY SHKOUKANI
Lucasfilm Art Department **PHIL SZOSTAK**

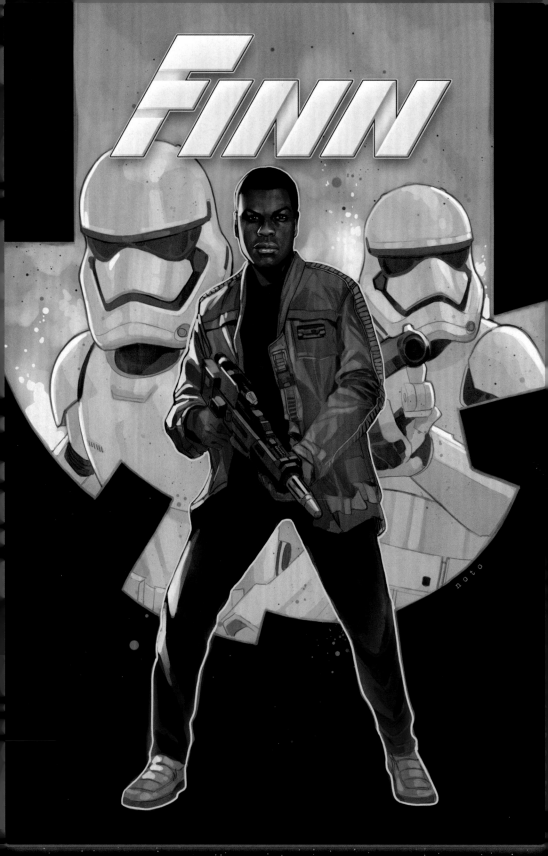

FINN

"INFESTATION"

The Republic maintains peace and order in the galaxy after the fall of the Empire. But the evil First Order, modeled after the old regime, rises in its ashes. And with an untold number of powerful weapons of war and legions of dogmatic stormtroopers at its disposal, the First Order stands poised to overthrow the new galactic government.

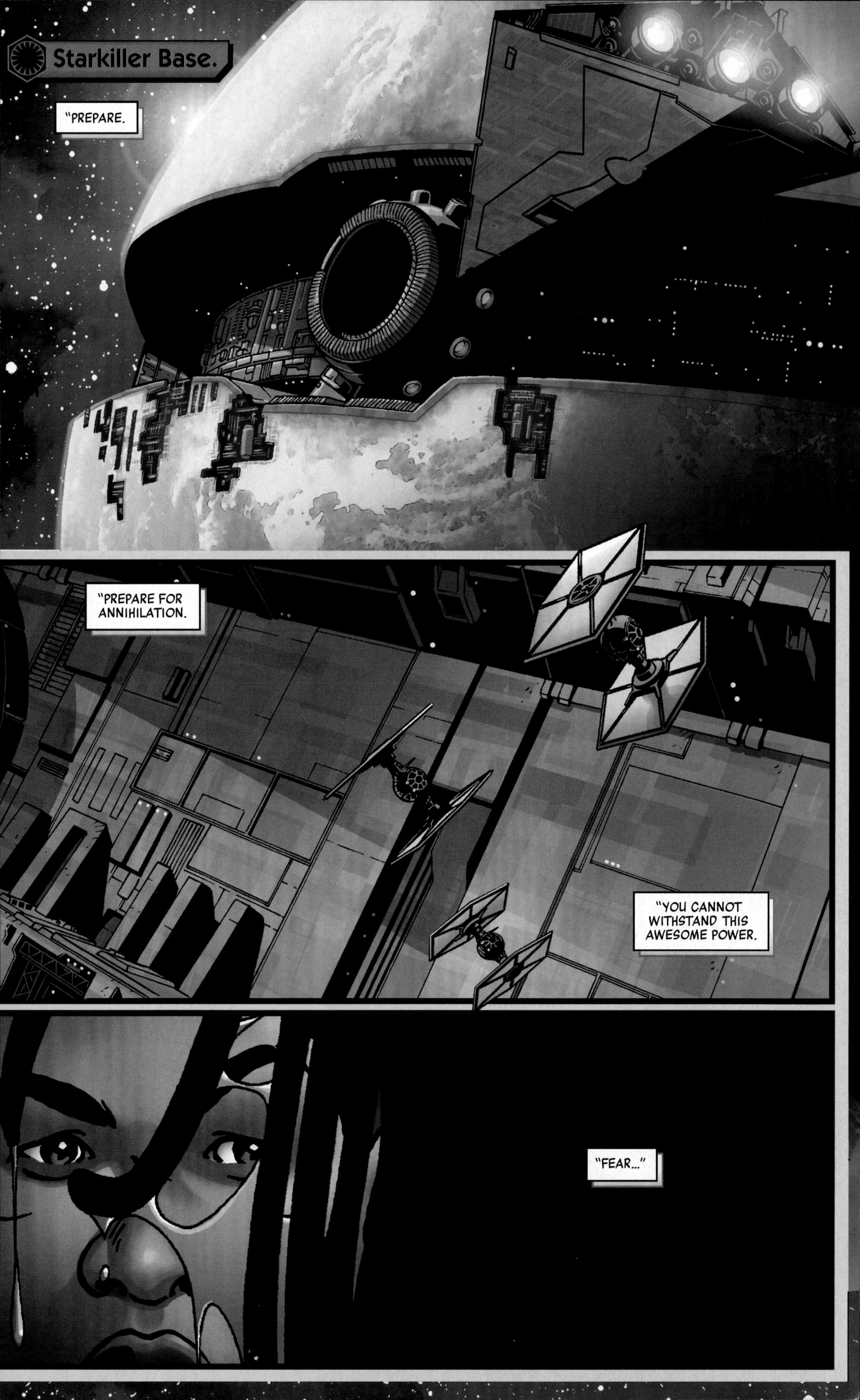
Starkiller Base.
"PREPARE.
"PREPARE FOR ANNIHILATION.
"YOU CANNOT WITHSTAND THIS AWESOME POWER.
"FEAR..."

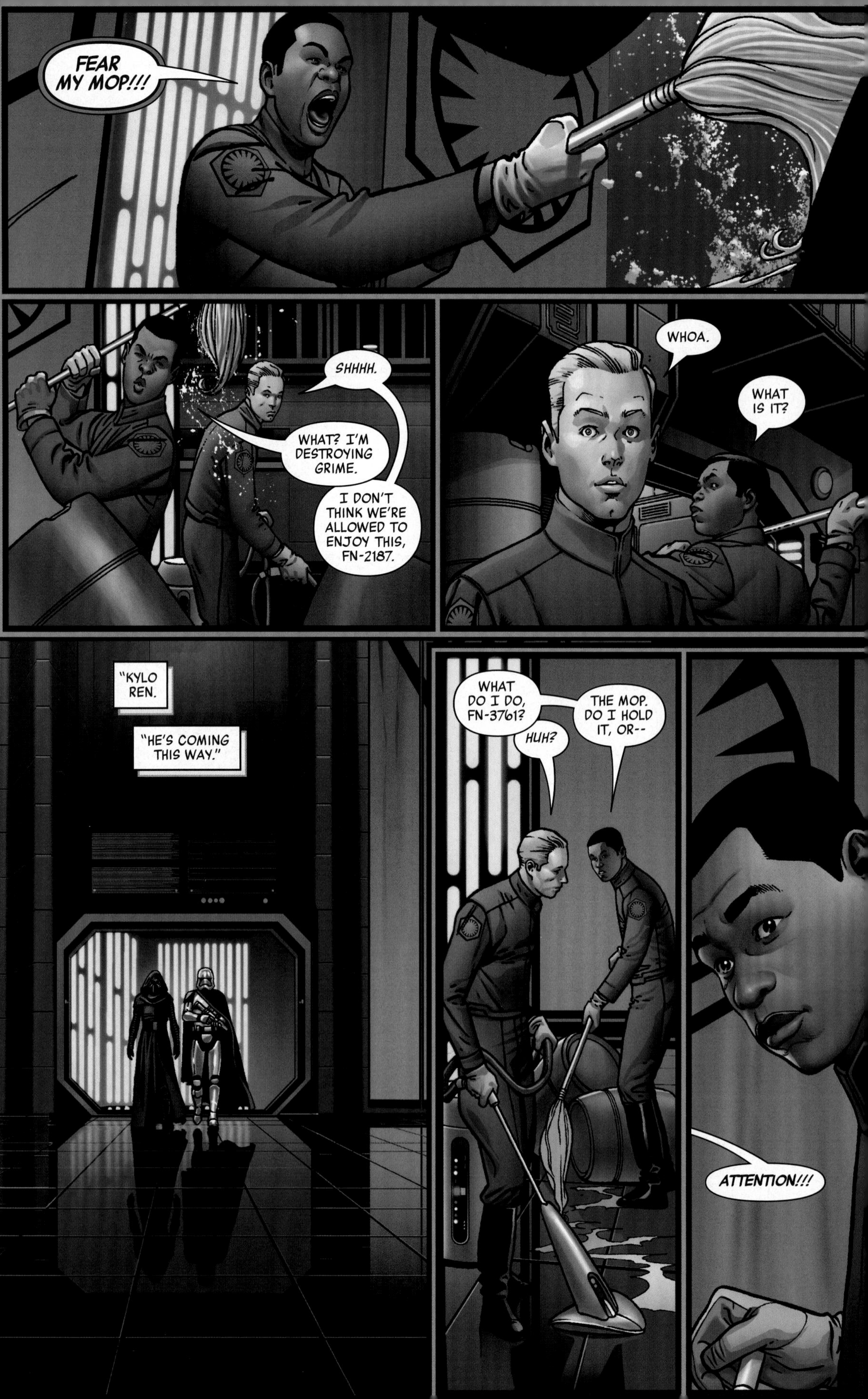
FEAR MY MOP!!!
SHHHH.
WHAT? I'M DESTROYING GRIME.
I DON'T THINK WE'RE ALLOWED TO ENJOY THIS, FN-2187.
WHOA.
WHAT IS IT?
"KYLO REN.
"HE'S COMING THIS WAY."
WHAT DO I DO, FN-3761?
HUH?
THE MOP. DO I HOLD IT, OR--
ATTENTION!!!

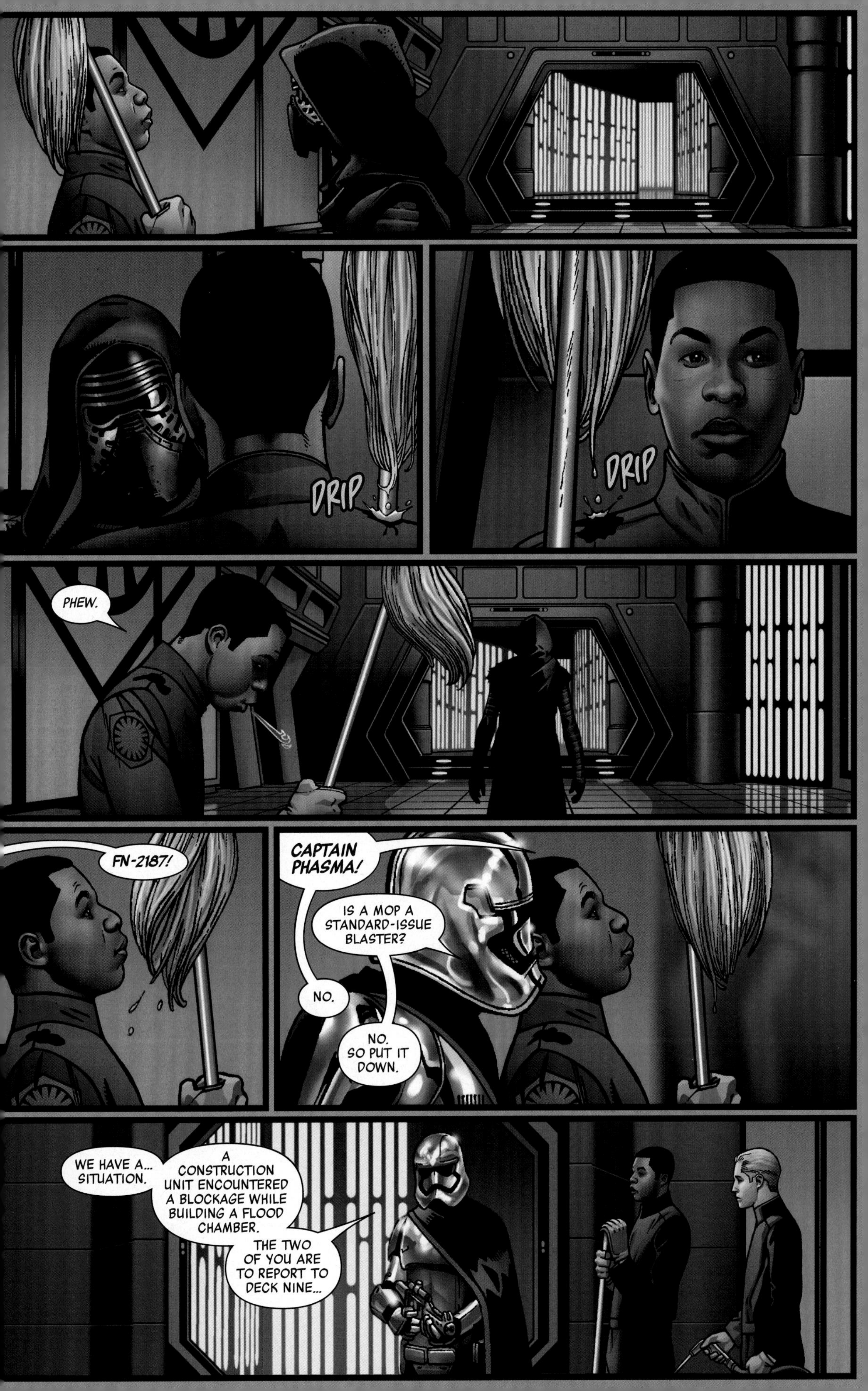
DRIP
DRIP
PHEW.
FN-2187!
CAPTAIN PHASMA!
IS A MOP A STANDARD-ISSUE BLASTER?
NO.
NO. SO PUT IT DOWN.
WE HAVE A... SITUATION.
A CONSTRUCTION UNIT ENCOUNTERED A BLOCKAGE WHILE BUILDING A FLOOD CHAMBER.
THE TWO OF YOU ARE TO REPORT TO DECK NINE...

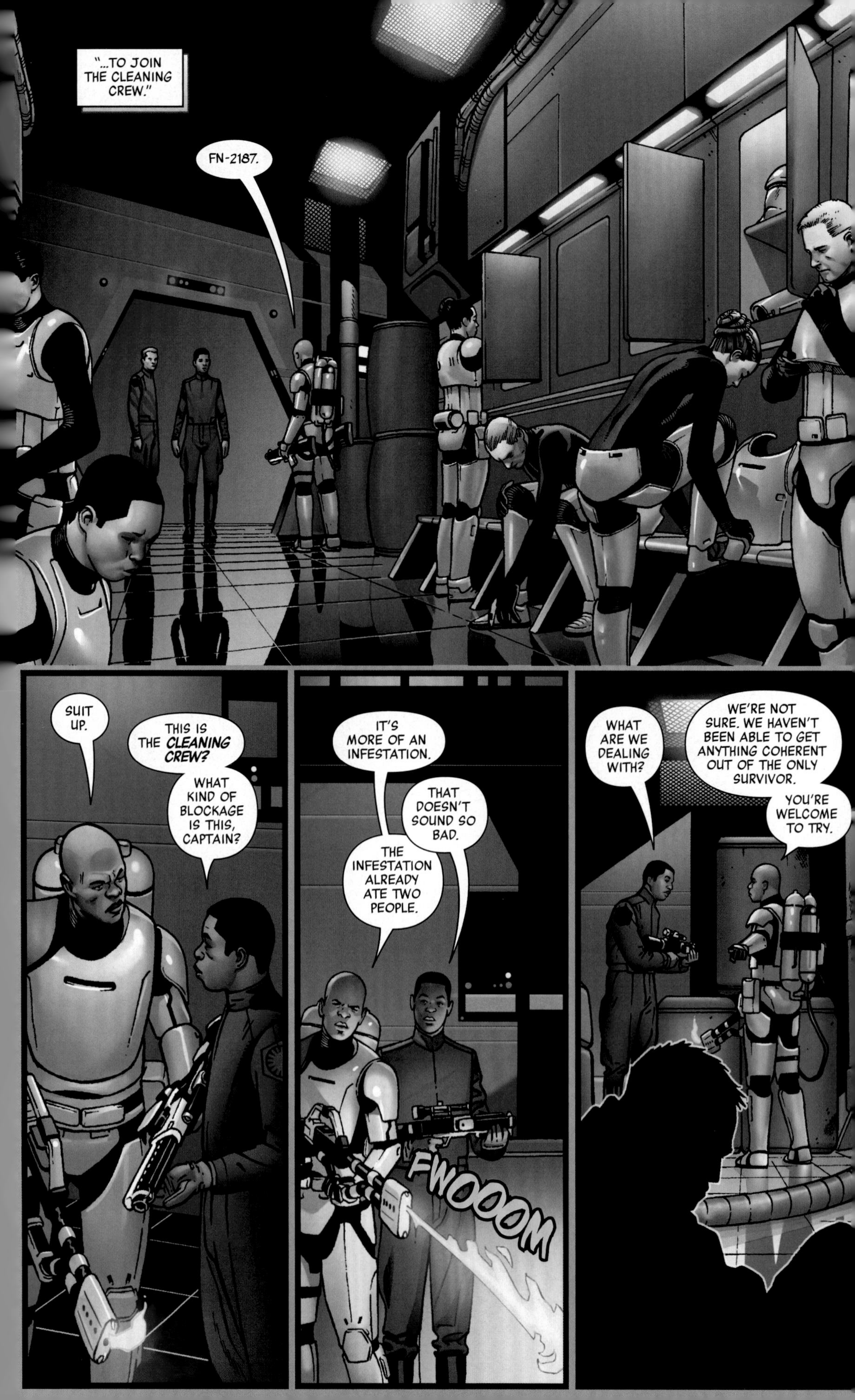
"...TO JOIN THE CLEANING CREW."
FN-2187.
SUIT UP.
THIS IS THE CLEANING CREW?
WHAT KIND OF BLOCKAGE IS THIS, CAPTAIN?
IT'S MORE OF AN INFESTATION.
THAT DOESN'T SOUND SO BAD.
THE INFESTATION ALREADY ATE TWO PEOPLE.
FWOOOM
WHAT ARE WE DEALING WITH?
WE'RE NOT SURE. WE HAVEN'T BEEN ABLE TO GET ANYTHING COHERENT OUT OF THE ONLY SURVIVOR.
YOU'RE WELCOME TO TRY.

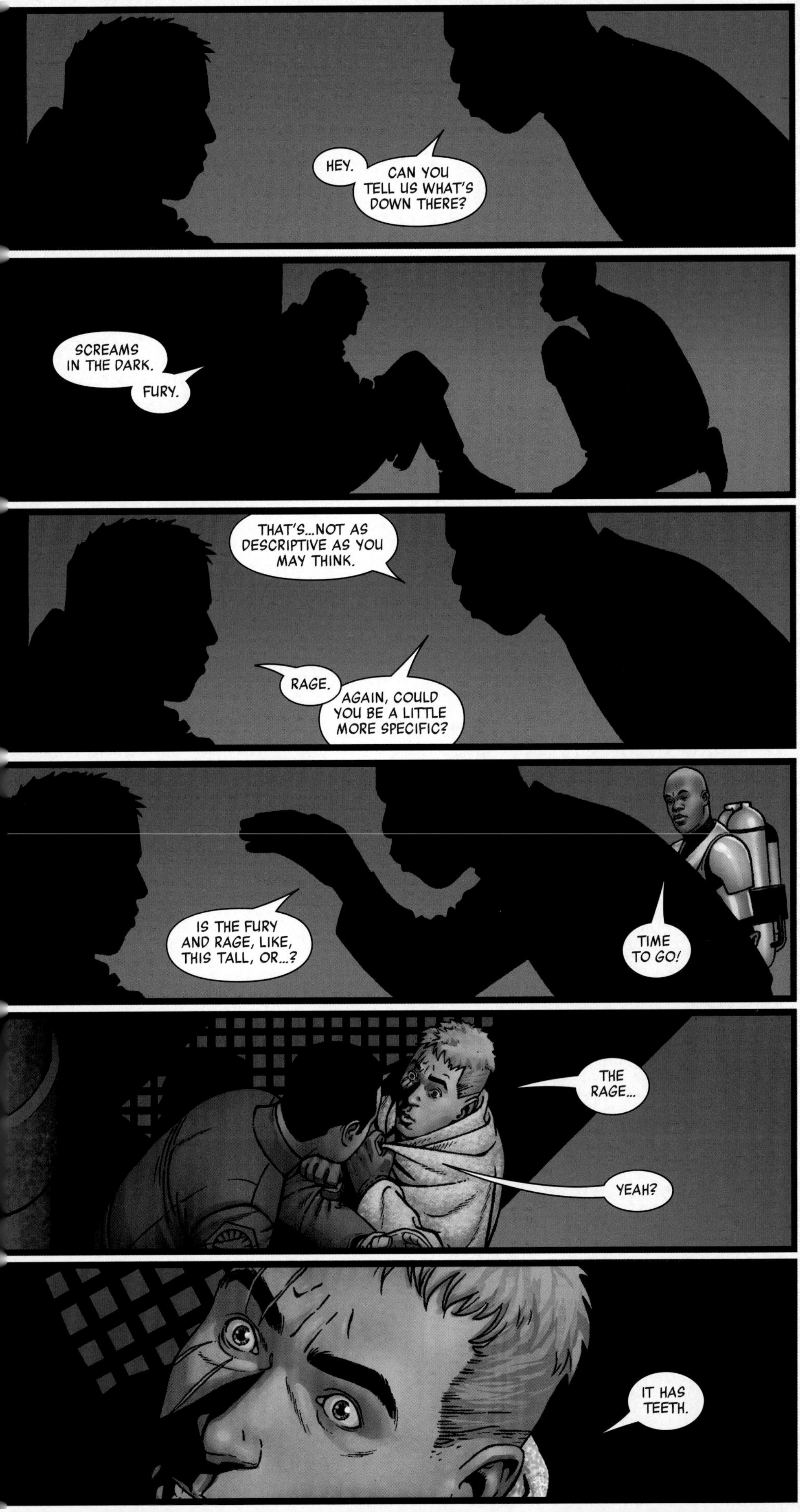
HEY.
CAN YOU TELL US WHAT'S DOWN THERE?
SCREAMS IN THE DARK.
FURY.
THAT'S...NOT AS DESCRIPTIVE AS YOU MAY THINK.
RAGE.
AGAIN, COULD YOU BE A LITTLE MORE SPECIFIC?
IS THE FURY AND RAGE, LIKE, THIS TALL, OR...?
TIME TO GO!
THE RAGE...
YEAH?
IT HAS TEETH.

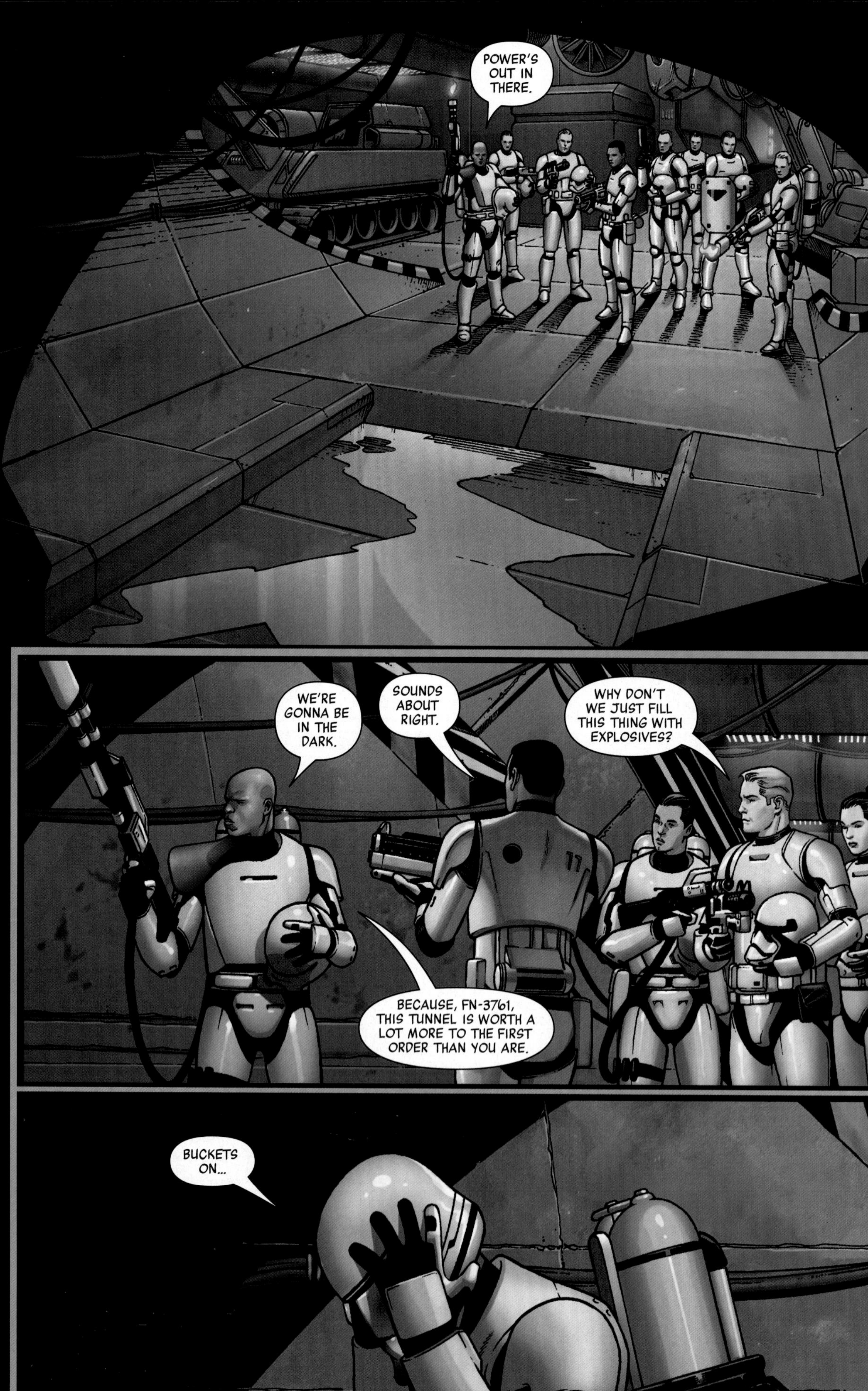
POWER'S OUT IN THERE.
WE'RE GONNA BE IN THE DARK.
SOUNDS ABOUT RIGHT.
WHY DON'T WE JUST FILL THIS THING WITH EXPLOSIVES?
BECAUSE, FN-3761, THIS TUNNEL IS WORTH A LOT MORE TO THE FIRST ORDER THAN YOU ARE.
BUCKETS ON...

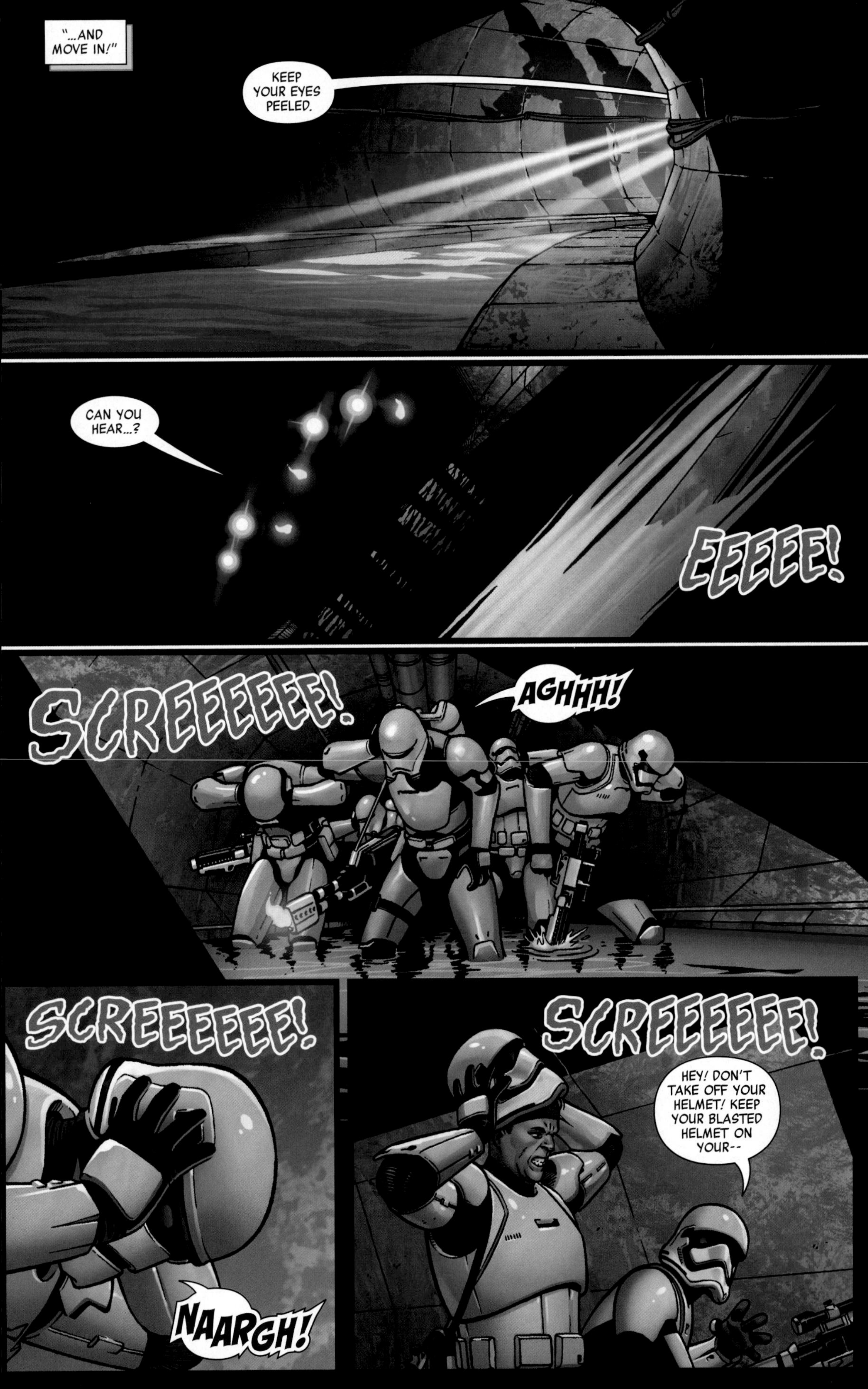
"...AND MOVE IN!"
KEEP YOUR EYES PEELED.
CAN YOU HEAR...?
EEEEE!
SCREEEEEEE!
AGHHH!
SCREEEEEEE!
NAARGH!
SCREEEEEEE!
HEY! DON'T TAKE OFF YOUR HELMET! KEEP YOUR BLASTED HELMET ON YOUR--

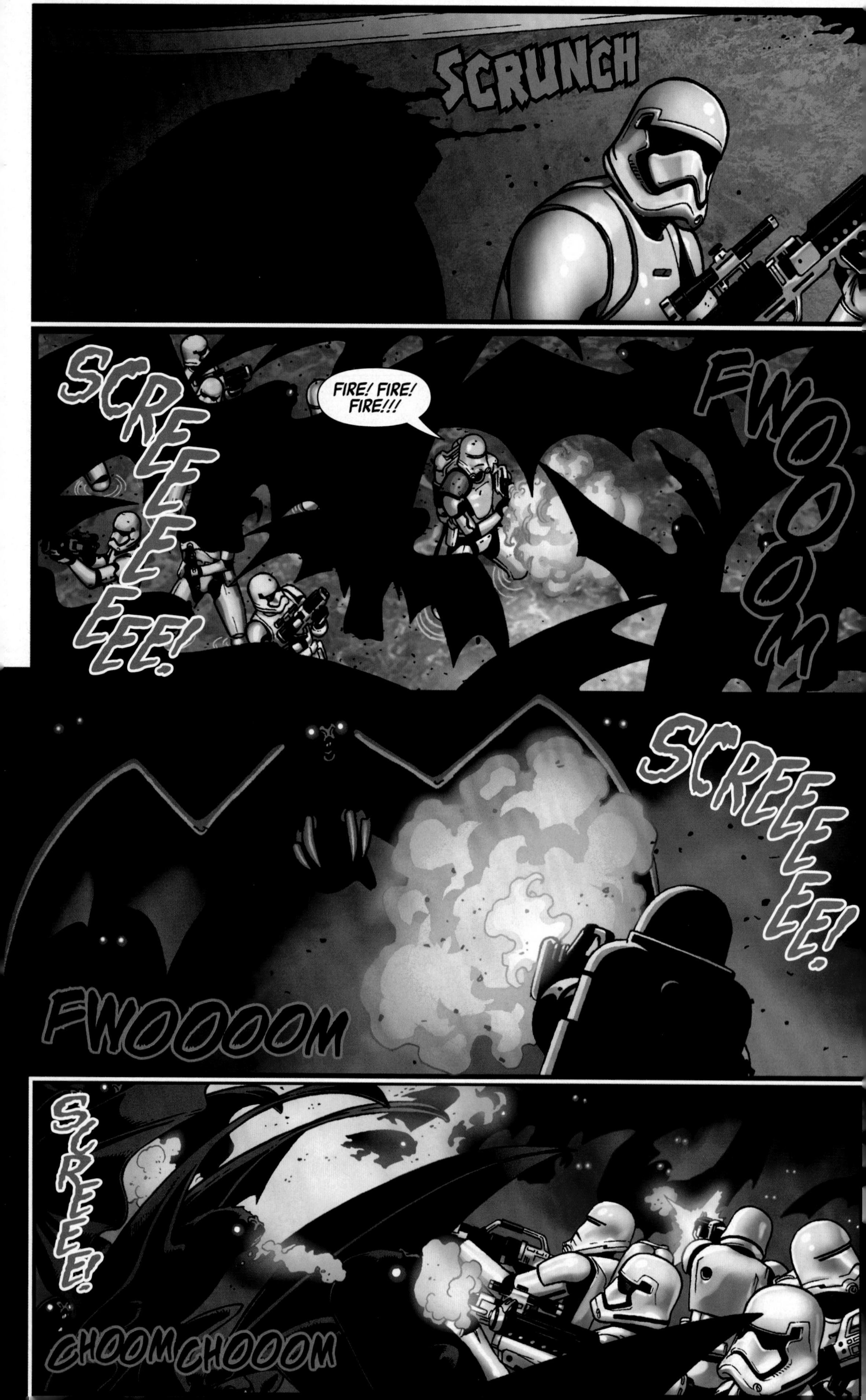
SCRUNCH
SCREEEEEEEE!
FIRE! FIRE! FIRE!!!
FWOOOOM
SCREEEEEE!
FWOOOOM
SCREEE!
CHOOM CHOOOM

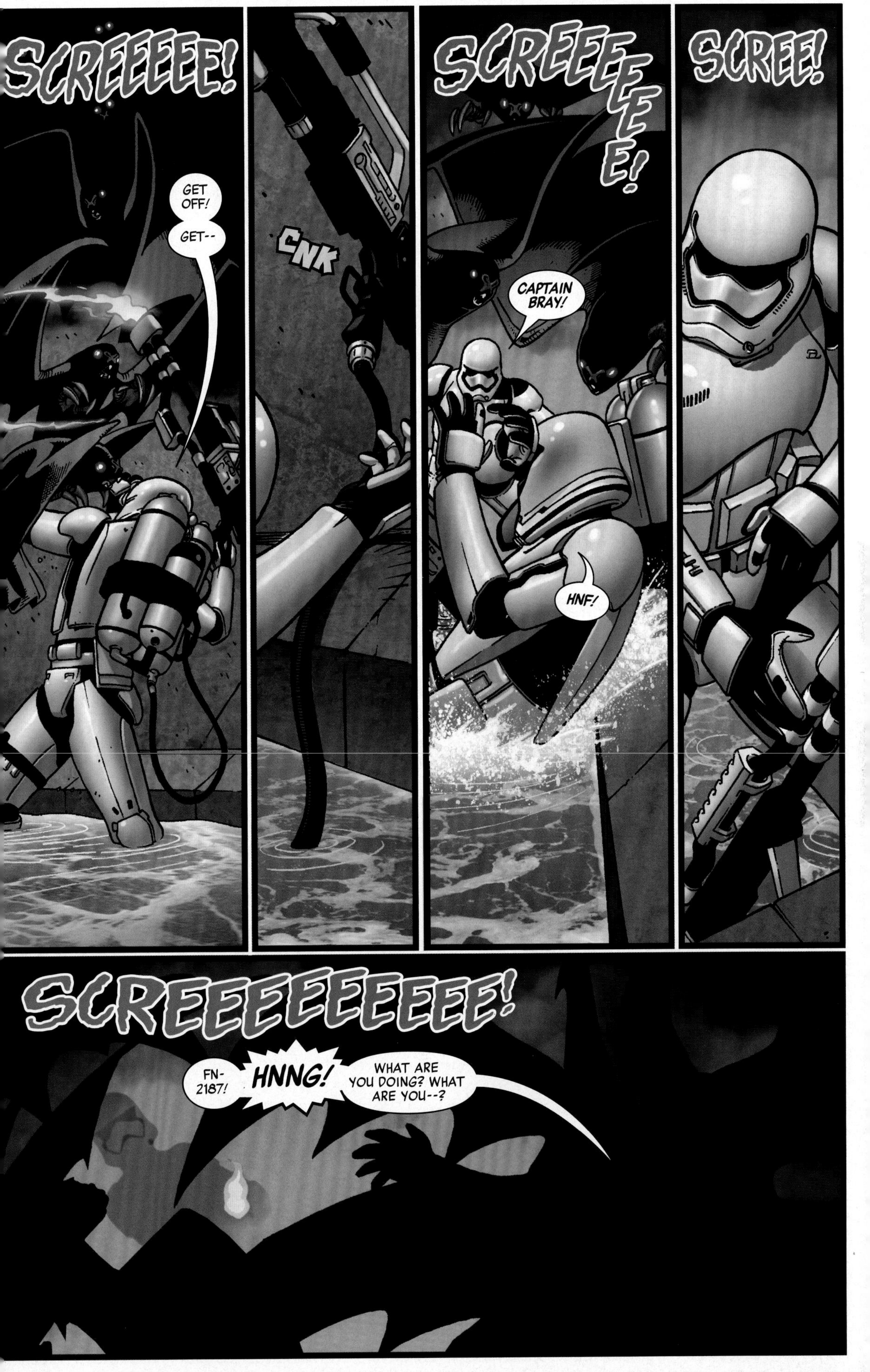
SCREEEEE!
GET OFF!
GET--
CNK
SCREEEEEE!
CAPTAIN BRAY!
HNF!
SCREE!
SCREEEEEEEEEE!
FN-2187!
HNNG!
WHAT ARE YOU DOING? WHAT ARE YOU--?

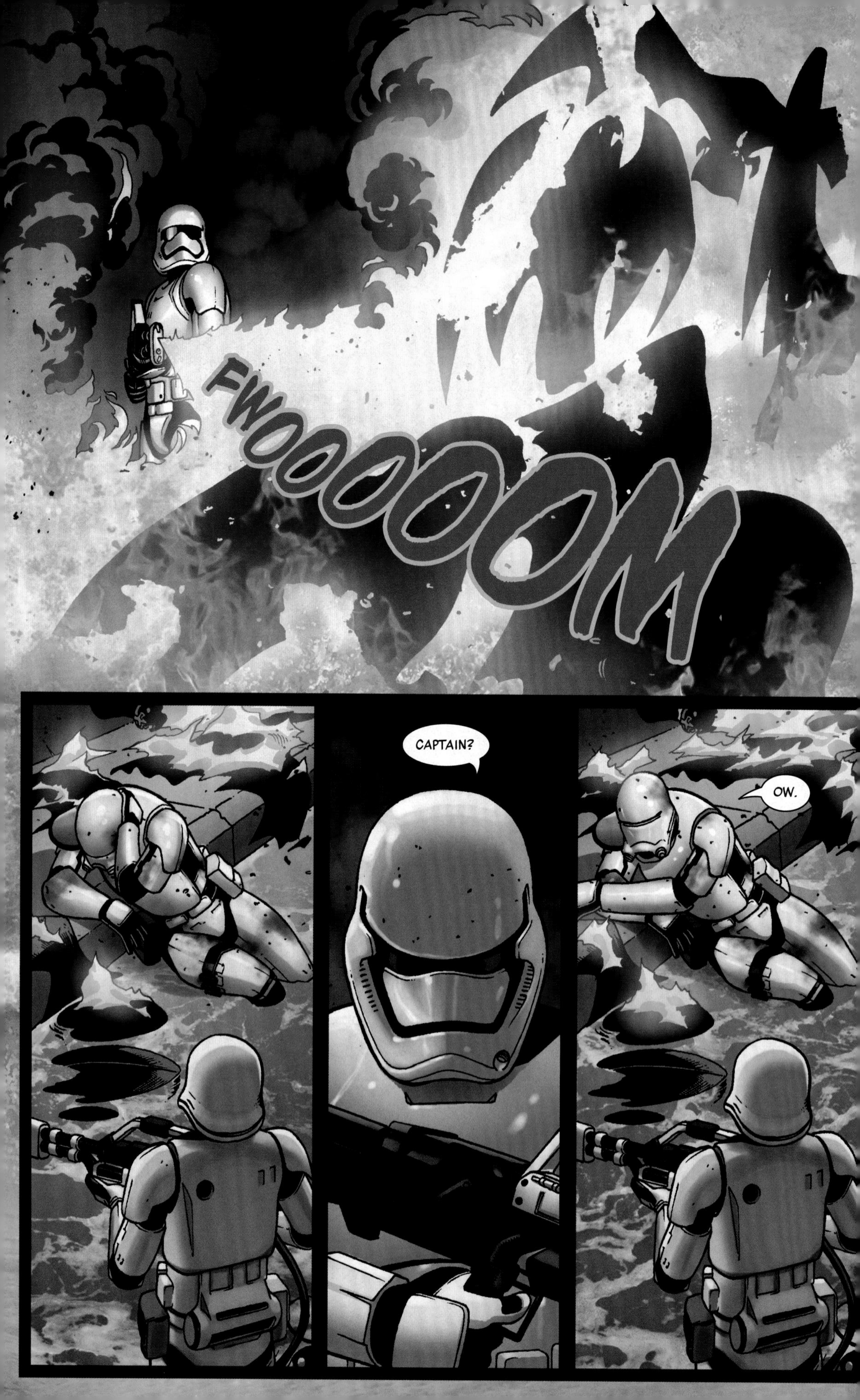
FWOOOOOM
CAPTAIN?
OW.

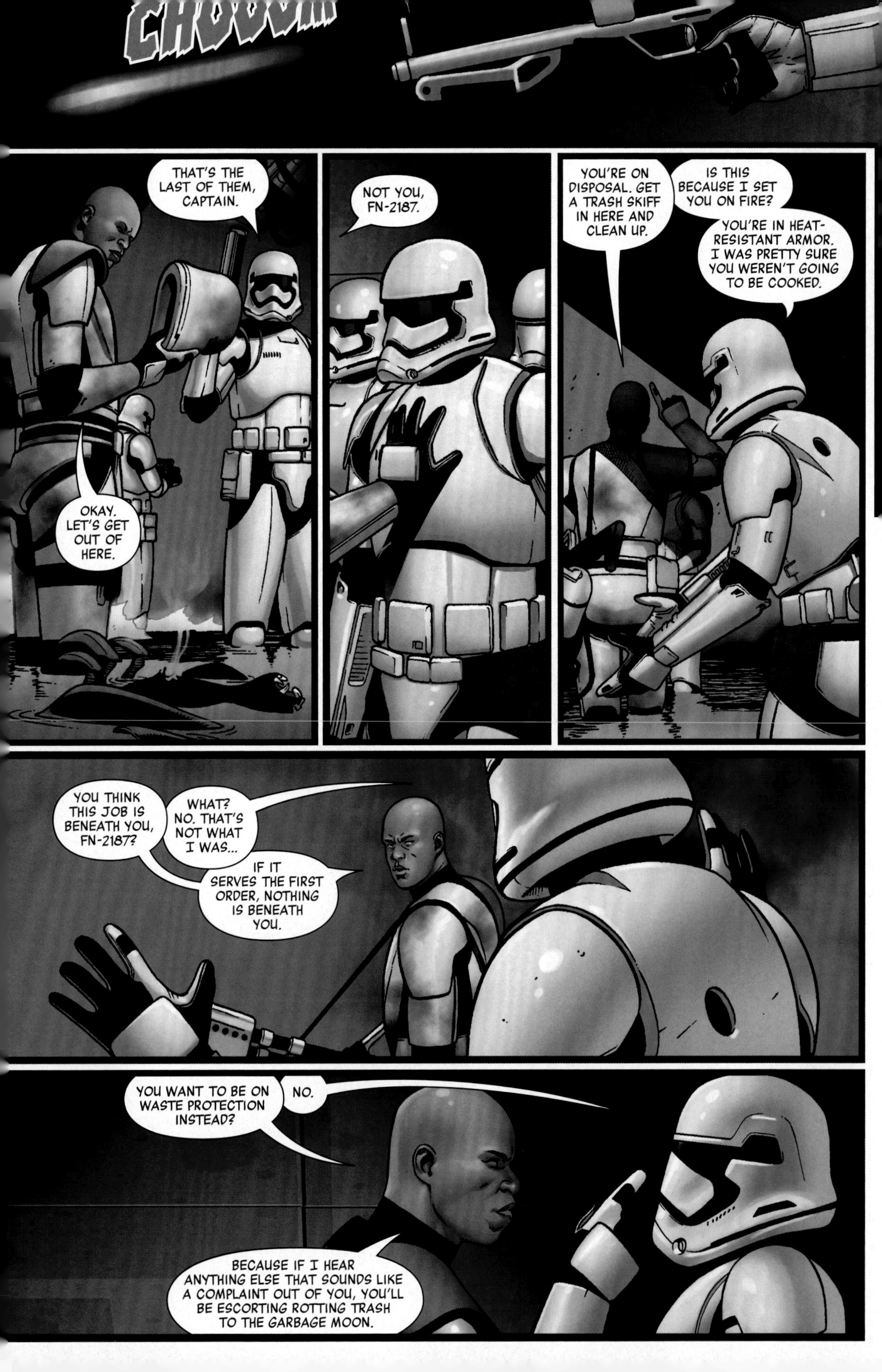
CHOOOM
THAT'S THE LAST OF THEM, CAPTAIN.
OKAY. LET'S GET OUT OF HERE.
NOT YOU, FN-2187.
YOU'RE ON DISPOSAL. GET A TRASH SKIFF IN HERE AND CLEAN UP.
IS THIS BECAUSE I SET YOU ON FIRE?
YOU'RE IN HEAT-RESISTANT ARMOR. I WAS PRETTY SURE YOU WEREN'T GOING TO BE COOKED.
YOU THINK THIS JOB IS BENEATH YOU, FN-2187?
WHAT? NO. THAT'S NOT WHAT I WAS...
IF IT SERVES THE FIRST ORDER, NOTHING IS BENEATH YOU.
YOU WANT TO BE ON WASTE PROTECTION INSTEAD?
NO.
BECAUSE IF I HEAR ANYTHING ELSE THAT SOUNDS LIKE A COMPLAINT OUT OF YOU, YOU'LL BE ESCORTING ROTTING TRASH TO THE GARBAGE MOON.

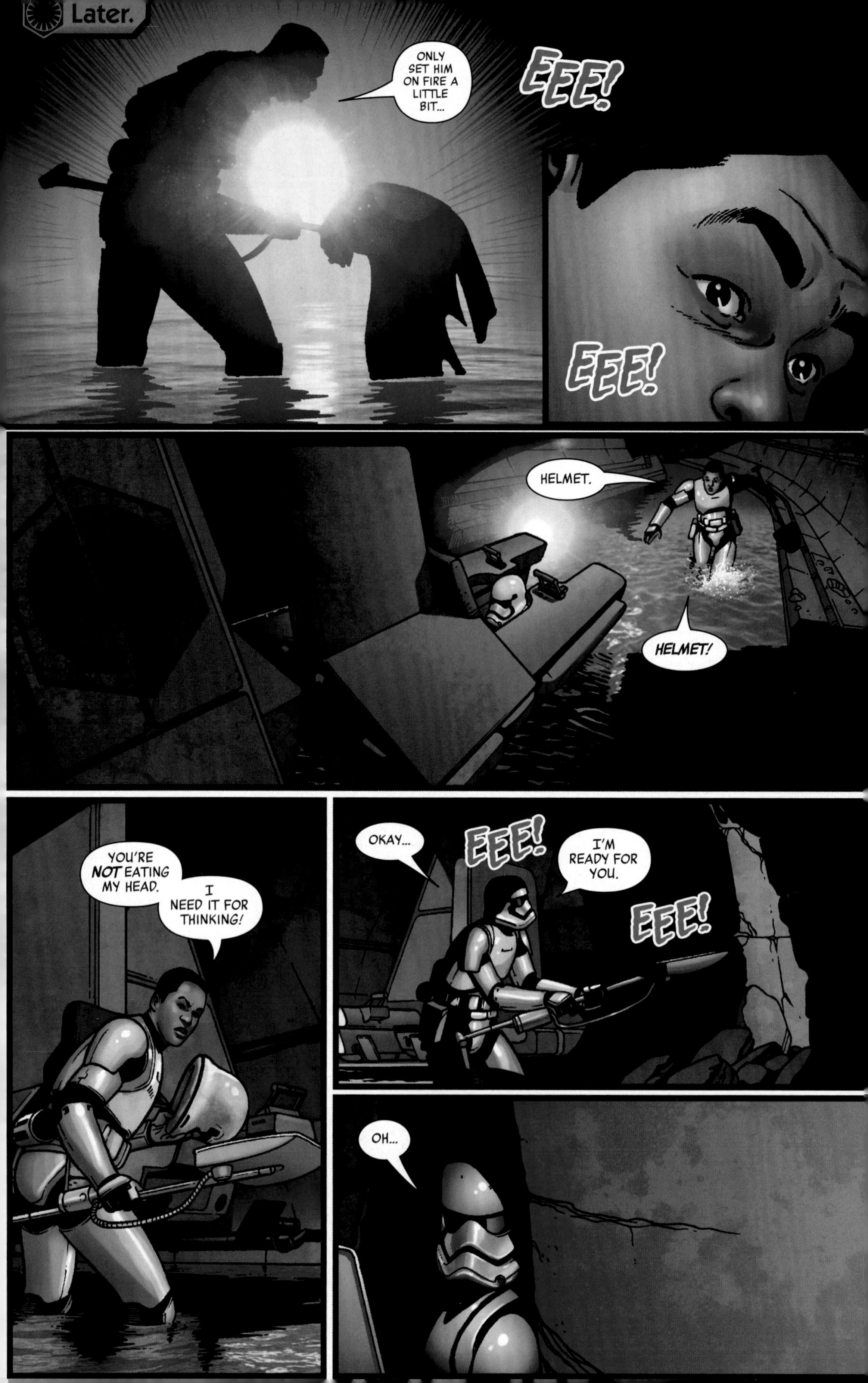
Later.
ONLY SET HIM ON FIRE A LITTLE BIT...
EEE!
EEE!
HELMET.
HELMET!
YOU'RE NOT EATING MY HEAD.
I NEED IT FOR THINKING!
OKAY...
EEE!
I'M READY FOR YOU.
EEE!
OH...

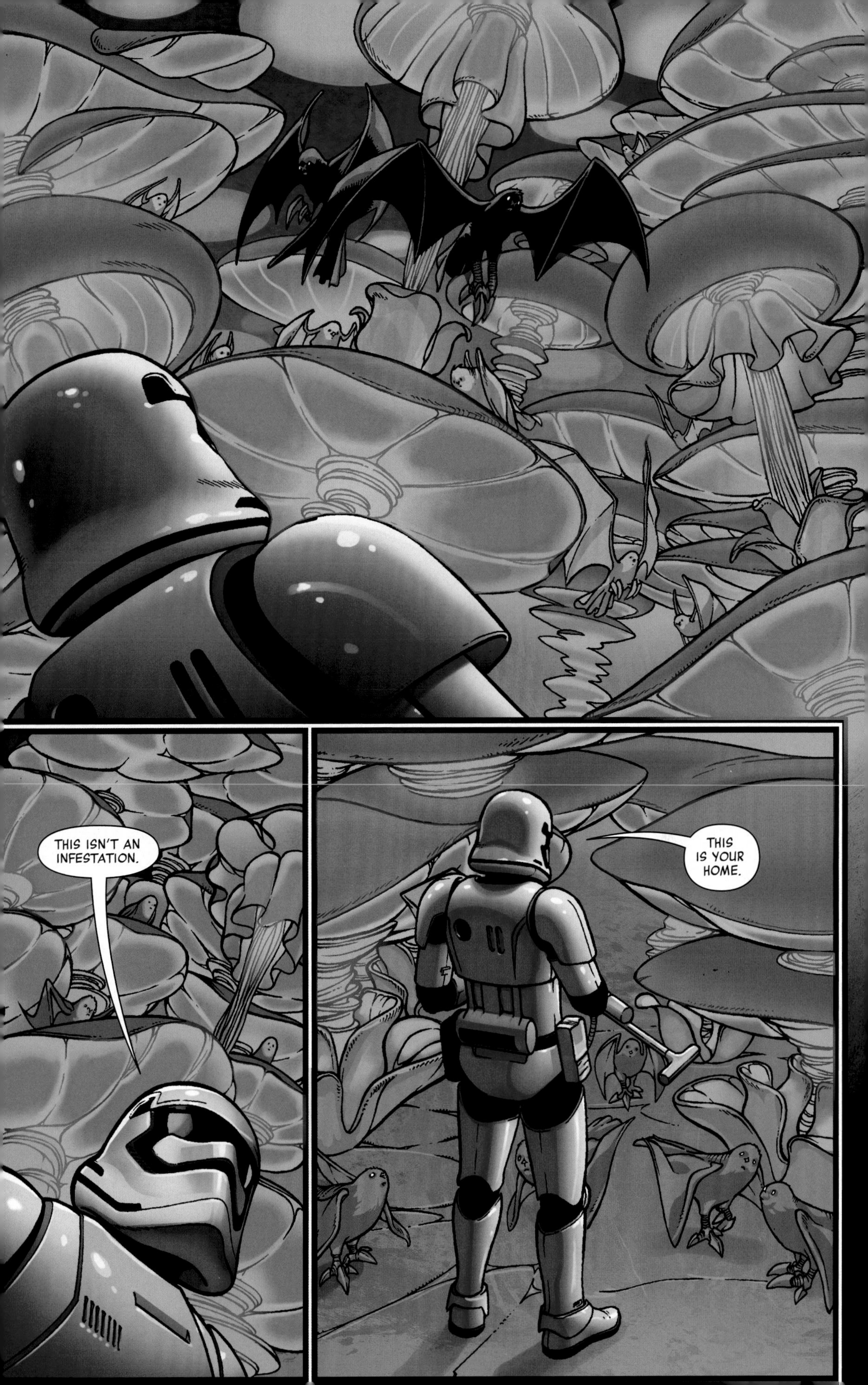
THIS ISN'T AN INFESTATION.
THIS IS YOUR HOME.

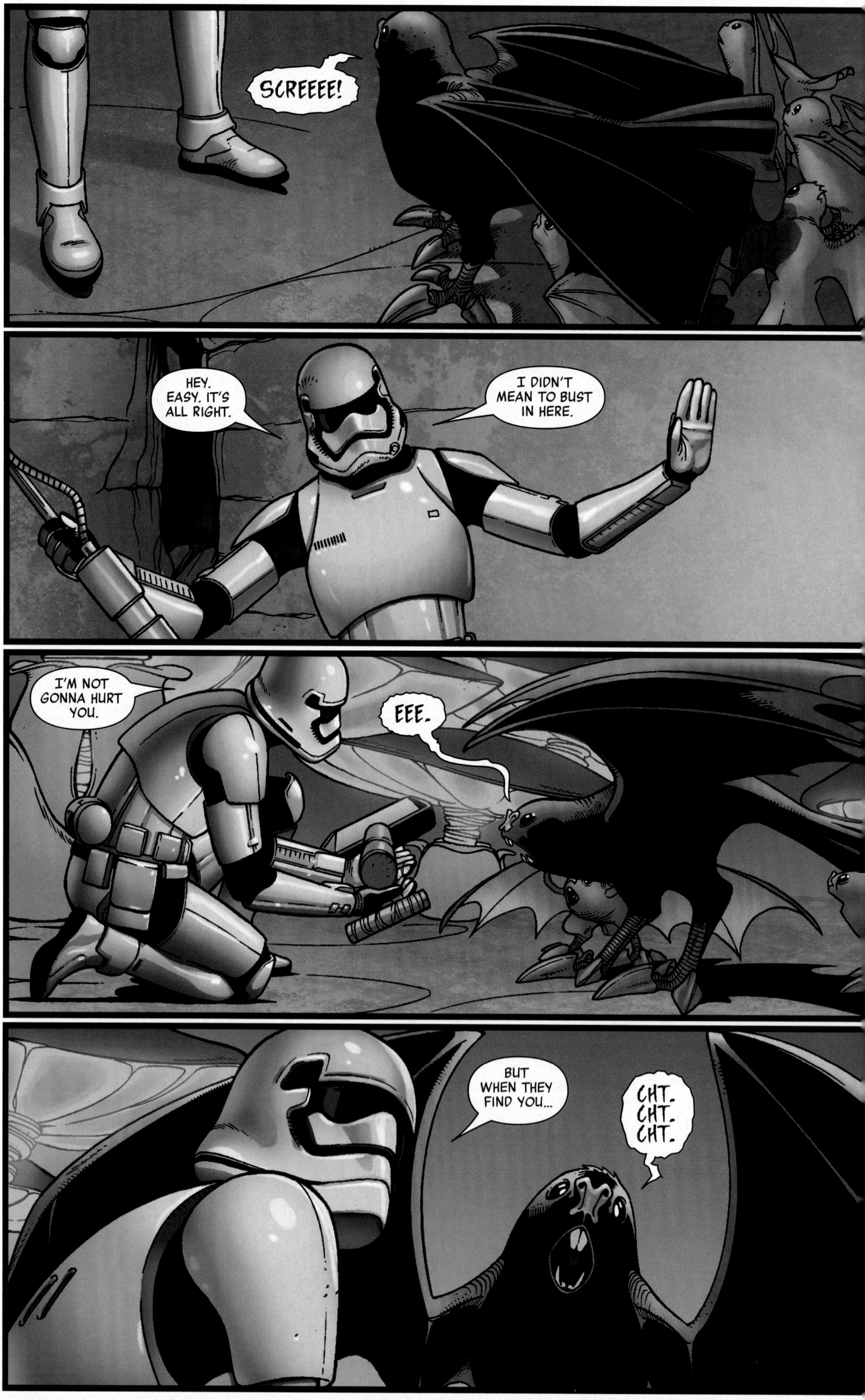
SCREEEE!
HEY. EASY. IT'S ALL RIGHT.
I DIDN'T MEAN TO BUST IN HERE.
I'M NOT GONNA HURT YOU.
EEE.
BUT WHEN THEY FIND YOU...
CHT. CHT. CHT.

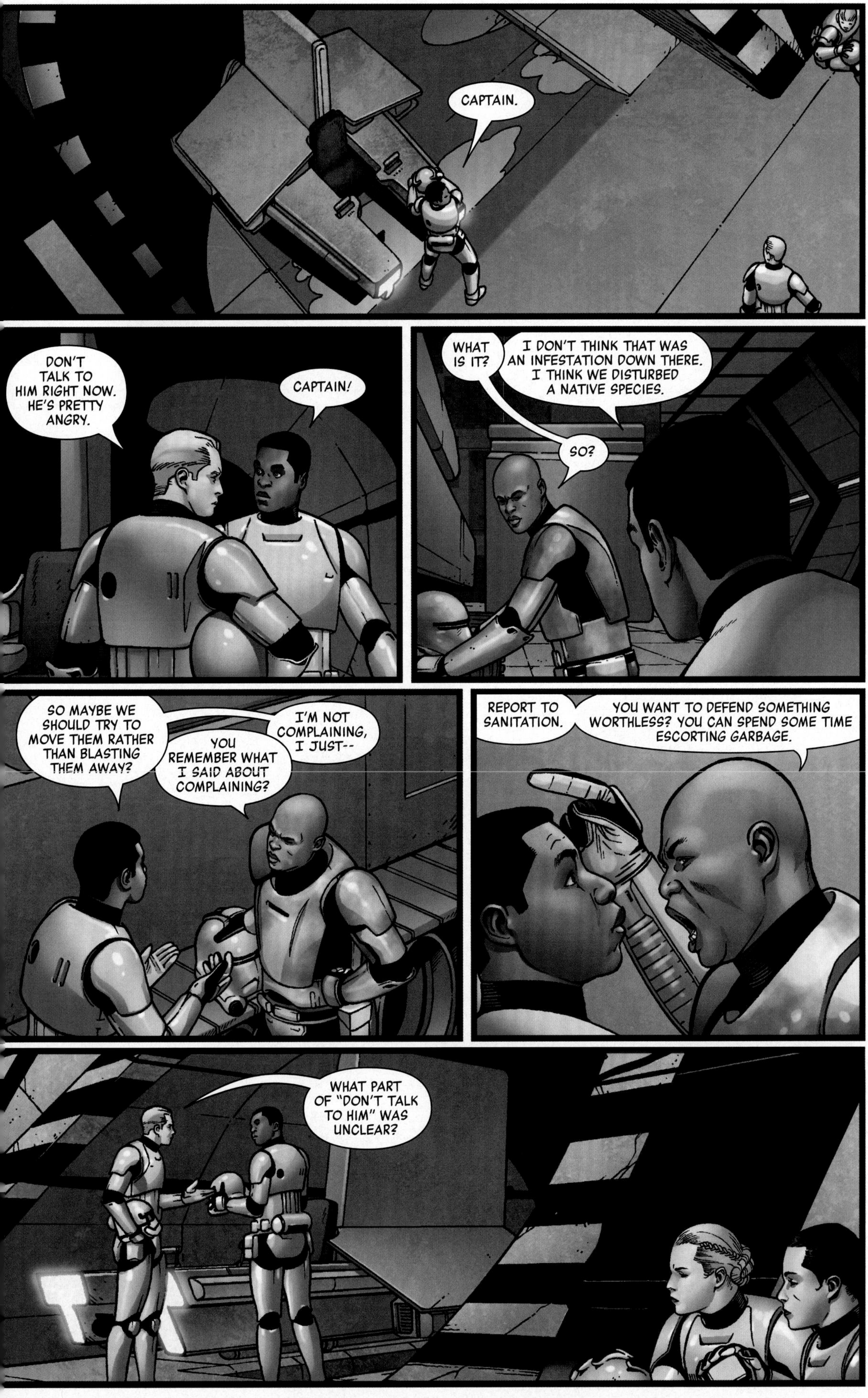
CAPTAIN.
DON'T TALK TO HIM RIGHT NOW. HE'S PRETTY ANGRY.
CAPTAIN!
WHAT IS IT?
I DON'T THINK THAT WAS AN INFESTATION DOWN THERE. I THINK WE DISTURBED A NATIVE SPECIES.
SO?
SO MAYBE WE SHOULD TRY TO MOVE THEM RATHER THAN BLASTING THEM AWAY?
YOU REMEMBER WHAT I SAID ABOUT COMPLAINING?
I'M NOT COMPLAINING, I JUST--
REPORT TO SANITATION.
YOU WANT TO DEFEND SOMETHING WORTHLESS? YOU CAN SPEND SOME TIME ESCORTING GARBAGE.
WHAT PART OF "DON'T TALK TO HIM" WAS UNCLEAR?

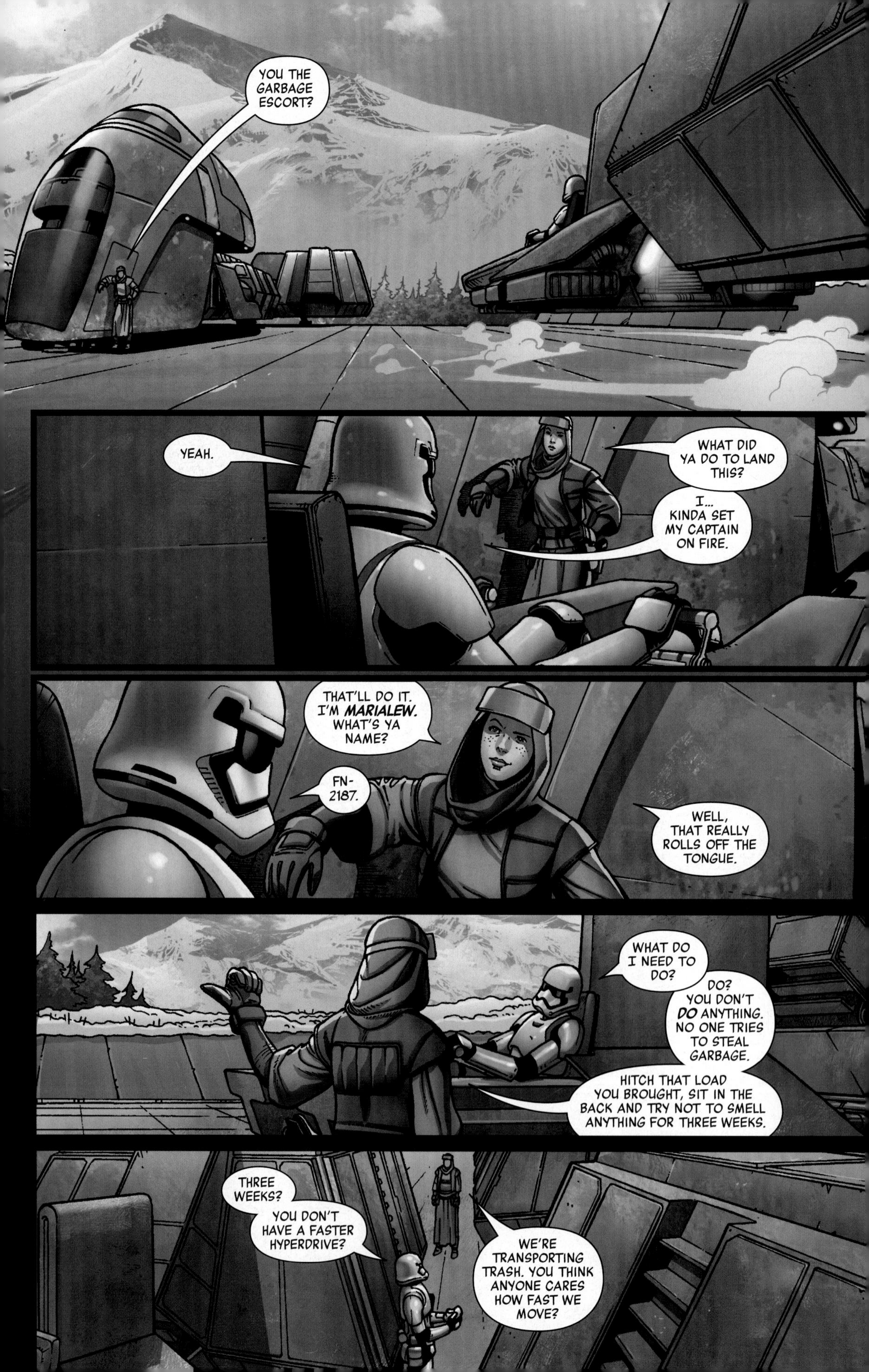
YOU THE GARBAGE ESCORT?
YEAH.
WHAT DID YA DO TO LAND THIS?
I... KINDA SET MY CAPTAIN ON FIRE.
THAT'LL DO IT. I'M ***MARIALEW.*** WHAT'S YA NAME?
FN-2187.
WELL, THAT REALLY ROLLS OFF THE TONGUE.
WHAT DO I NEED TO DO?
DO? YOU DON'T ***DO*** ANYTHING. NO ONE TRIES TO STEAL GARBAGE.
HITCH THAT LOAD YOU BROUGHT, SIT IN THE BACK AND TRY NOT TO SMELL ANYTHING FOR THREE WEEKS.
THREE WEEKS?
YOU DON'T HAVE A FASTER HYPERDRIVE?
WE'RE TRANSPORTING TRASH. YOU THINK ANYONE CARES HOW FAST WE MOVE?

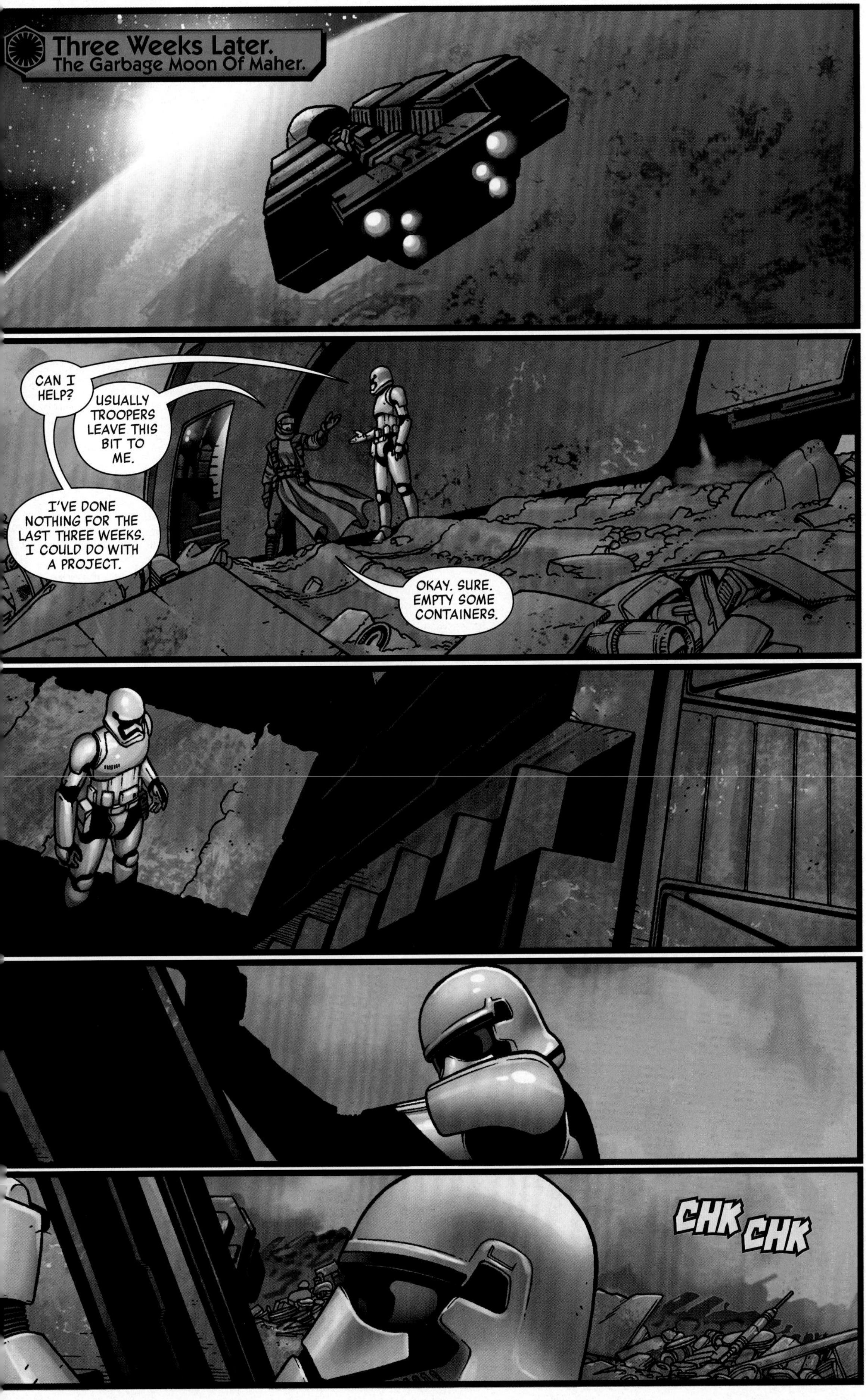
Three Weeks Later.
The Garbage Moon Of Maher.
CAN I HELP?
USUALLY TROOPERS LEAVE THIS BIT TO ME.
I'VE DONE NOTHING FOR THE LAST THREE WEEKS. I COULD DO WITH A PROJECT.
OKAY. SURE. EMPTY SOME CONTAINERS.
CHK CHK

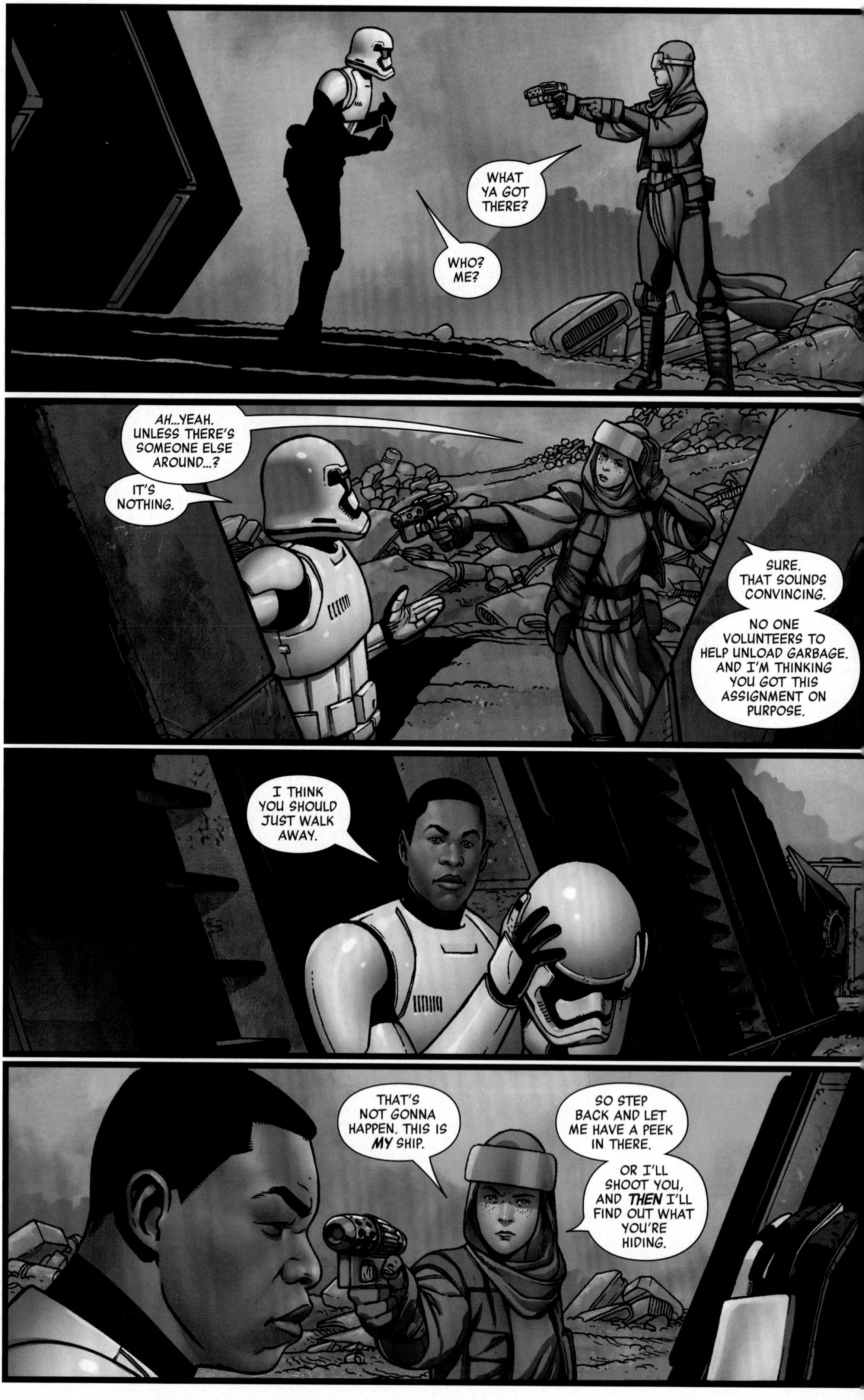
WHAT YA GOT THERE?
WHO? ME?
AH...YEAH. UNLESS THERE'S SOMEONE ELSE AROUND...?
IT'S NOTHING.
SURE. THAT SOUNDS CONVINCING.
NO ONE VOLUNTEERS TO HELP UNLOAD GARBAGE. AND I'M THINKING YOU GOT THIS ASSIGNMENT ON PURPOSE.
I THINK YOU SHOULD JUST WALK AWAY.
THAT'S NOT GONNA HAPPEN. THIS IS MY SHIP.
SO STEP BACK AND LET ME HAVE A PEEK IN THERE.
OR I'LL SHOOT YOU, AND THEN I'LL FIND OUT WHAT YOU'RE HIDING.

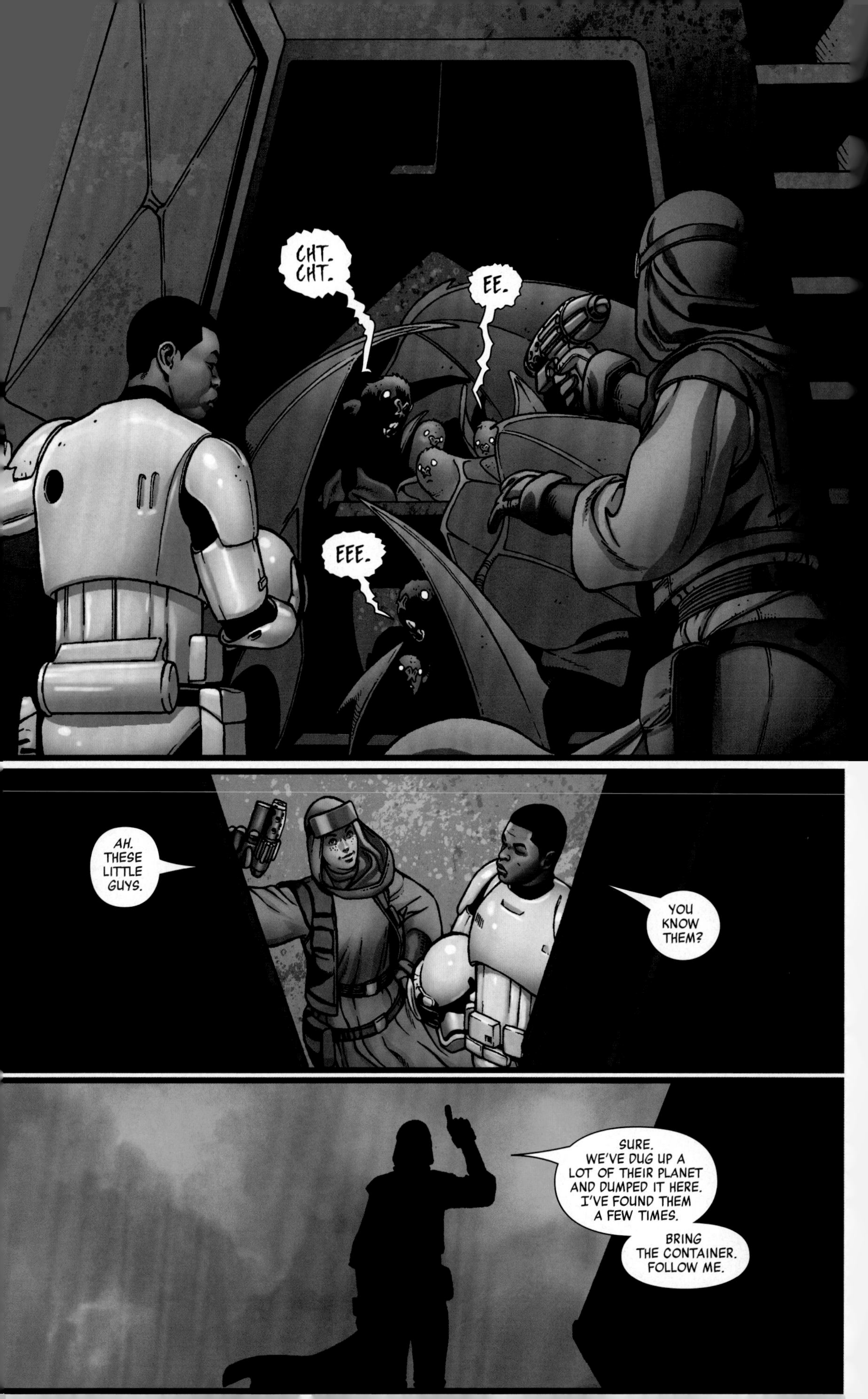
CHT. CHT.
EE.
EEE.
AH. THESE LITTLE GUYS.
YOU KNOW THEM?
SURE. WE'VE DUG UP A LOT OF THEIR PLANET AND DUMPED IT HERE. I'VE FOUND THEM A FEW TIMES.
BRING THE CONTAINER. FOLLOW ME.

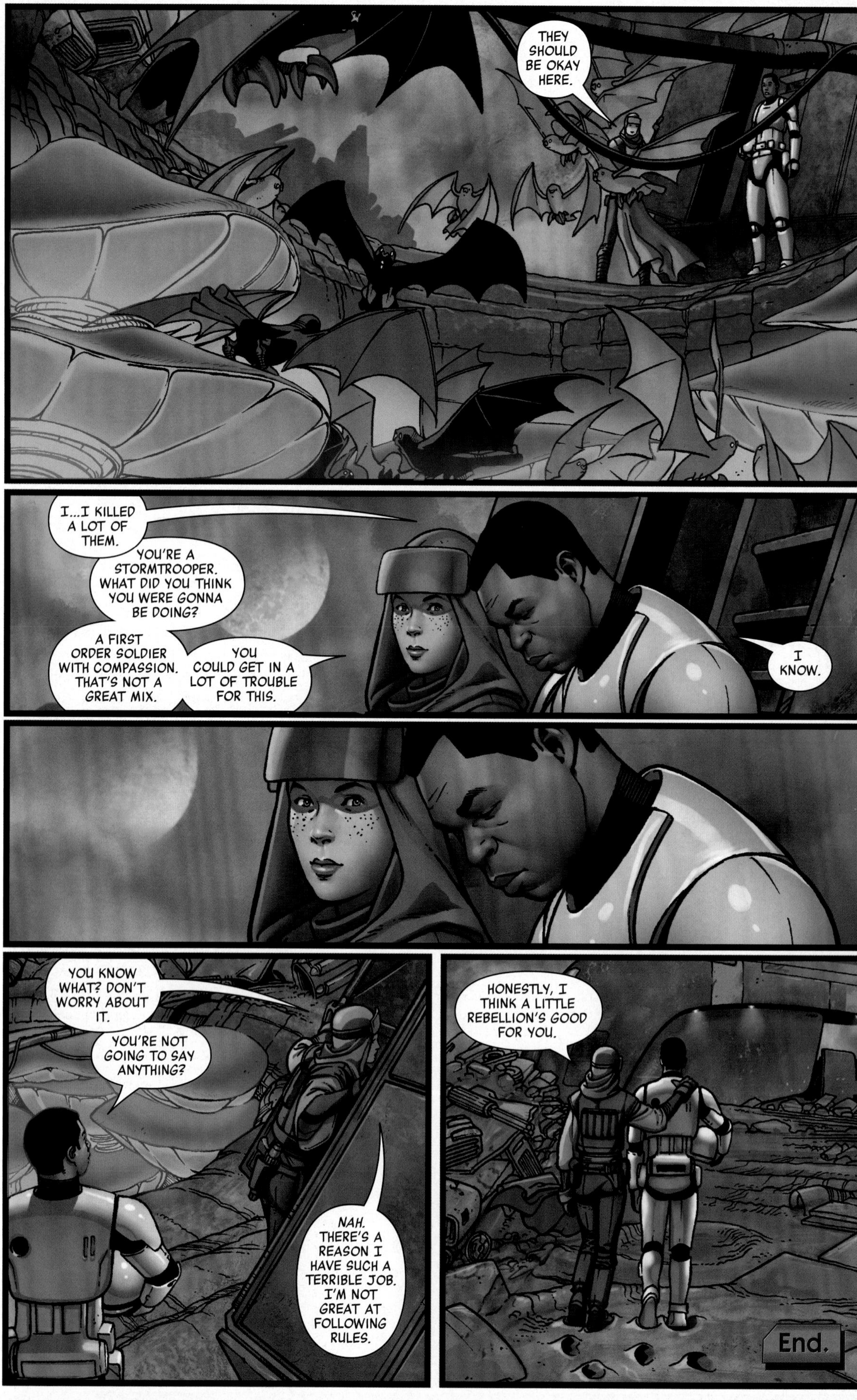
THEY SHOULD BE OKAY HERE.
I...I KILLED A LOT OF THEM.
YOU'RE A STORMTROOPER. WHAT DID YOU THINK YOU WERE GONNA BE DOING?
I KNOW.
A FIRST ORDER SOLDIER WITH COMPASSION. THAT'S NOT A GREAT MIX.
YOU COULD GET IN A LOT OF TROUBLE FOR THIS.
YOU KNOW WHAT? DON'T WORRY ABOUT IT.
YOU'RE NOT GOING TO SAY ANYTHING?
NAH. THERE'S A REASON I HAVE SUCH A TERRIBLE JOB. I'M NOT GREAT AT FOLLOWING RULES.
HONESTLY, I THINK A LITTLE REBELLION'S GOOD FOR YOU.
End.

AGE OF RESISTANCE

I'M GONNA CALL YOU FINN
The Evolution of FN-2187: From Stormtrooper to Resistance Hero
By Bryan Young

When George Lucas initially set out to make a new *Star Wars* film, he had lots of ideas. First, the art department gathered and came up with all kinds of imagery, and then he hired a writer to bring the ideas for the sequel trilogy to life. The first screenwriter to work on *The Force Awakens* was Michael Arndt, and one of the most difficult pieces of the puzzle to crack was the role of Finn. What would his place in the universe be? He told the *Entertainment Weekly* podcast about that point in the process, after both Lawrence Kasdan and J.J. Abrams had come on board to help. "We were struggling…I remember we talked about pirates and merchant marines and all this stuff, and finally Larry (Kasdan) got pissed at all of us and he's just like, "You guys, you're not thinking big. What if he's a stormtrooper that ran away?"
It was in this fit of creative exasperation from the writer of *The Empire Strikes Back* that Finn's real place in the Skywalker saga was first found.

THERE HAS BEEN AN AWAKENING

There's a desert landscape and the strike of a harsh note of John Williams music. An unfamiliar stormtrooper without a helmet rises into frame, pouring sweat and panting. This would be the world's first official introduction to Finn, from the first teaser trailer to *The Force Awakens*.

But who was he? Where had he come from?

This was FN-2187, whose number is dripping in *Star Wars* history of its own—this was the cell block Princess Leia was held in aboard the Death Star. "We didn't get a chance to go back into Finn's day-to-day life as a stormtrooper," John Boyega said in an interview at Awesome Con in 2018. "You didn't get a chance to see the years he had to stay quiet and try to submit to a movement that he doesn't truly believe in. Playing that, in the beginning, was very, very important so people felt like they could go on this journey with him and [believe] his convictions to take a stand and leave."

In *The Force Awakens*, Finn realized he's not cut out to be a stormtrooper and did what he had to to escape that life, but his primary interest was still self-preservation, even though he made some important friends along the way. But is he a hero? Finn certainly doesn't seem to think so.

LEARN YOU SOMETHING BIG

Finn's desire to not die in the war between the First Order and the Resistance comes into focus in *The Last Jedi*, where the film explores his dilemma. Rose Tico acts as an angel on one shoulder, and DJ acts as the devil on the other. Each of them tries to show him the benefits of the two paths before him. Rose's respect and admiration for Finn is something he can earn for choosing a side that would stand against evil. DJ's ambivalence about the conflict is equally attractive to Finn; this shady character has no qualms walking out in the middle of a situation to save his own hide, no matter the cost.

It's only when Finn sees the true cost of "remaining neutral" that he's finally able to pick a side.

Through *The Force Awakens* and *The Last Jedi*, Finn's only thought was to save Rey, whom he'd found a connection with, and to get away safely; the cause of the Resistance wasn't his. Though the realization that he cared for Rey came as his head was on a literal chopping block, Finn's new conviction was as real as if it had been there the whole time. His evolution from stormtrooper to Resistance fighter was not an easy one, nor was it quick, but the seeds had been there from the beginning, and it fueled his fight against Captain Phasma and the system that created him.

"You were always scum," Phasma told Finn, but he got the last word.

"Rebel scum."
And it was true.

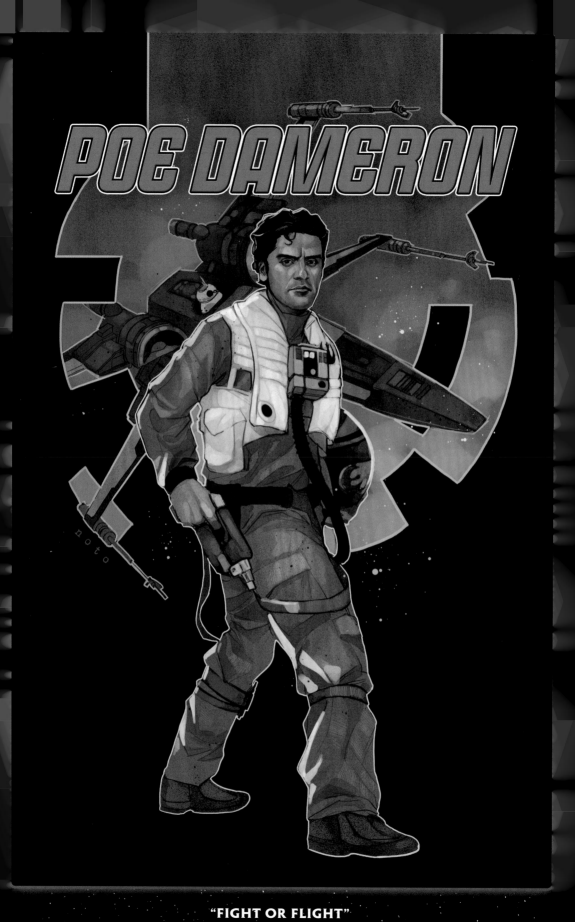

POE DAMERON

"FIGHT OR FLIGHT"

Poe Dameron was born to fly among the stars: There's no one better behind the yoke of an X-wing starfighter, and the young pilot is doing his best to help the New Republic maintain peace in the galaxy after the fall of the evil Empire. But does Poe's destiny truly lie with the Republic?

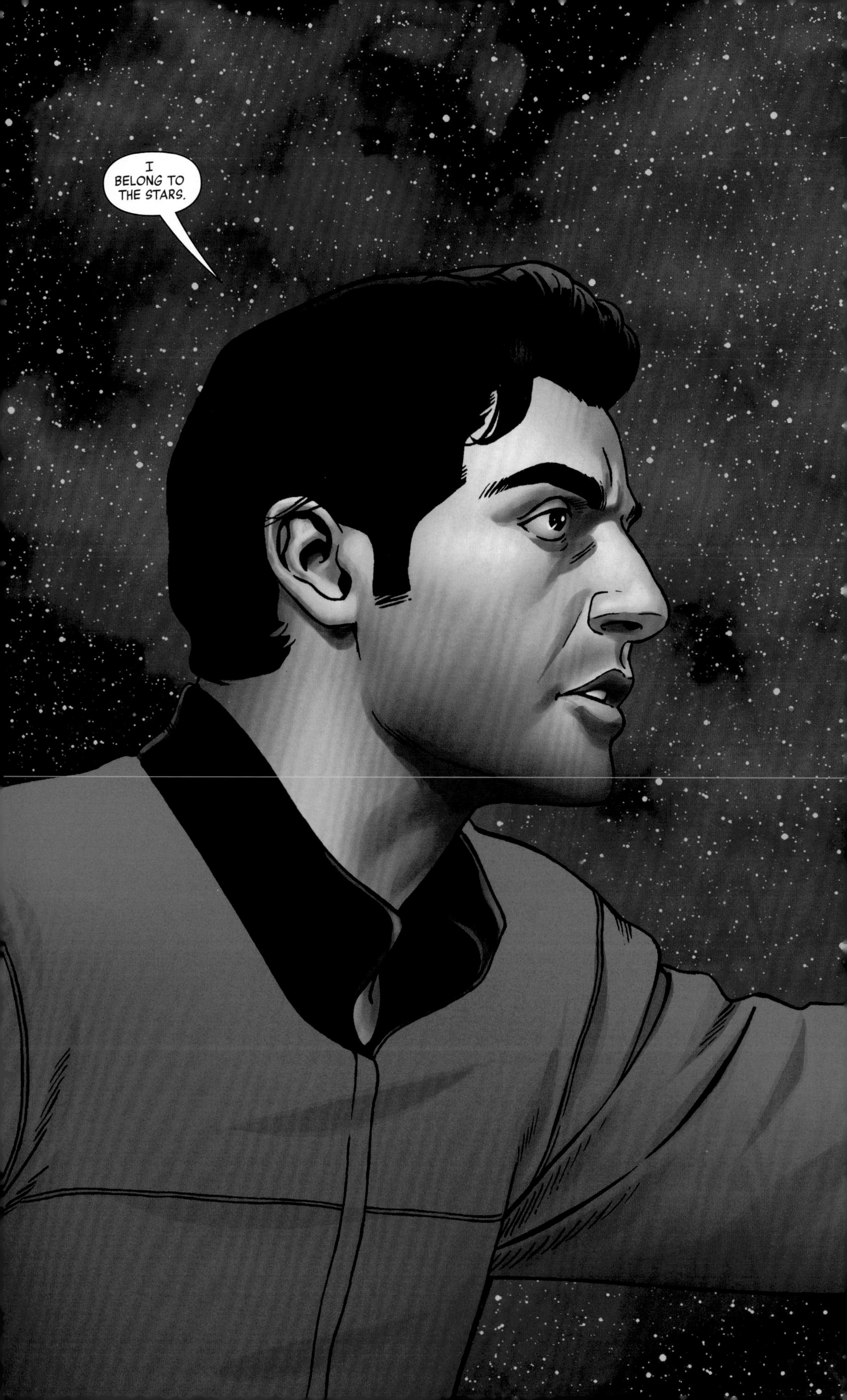
I BELONG TO THE STARS.

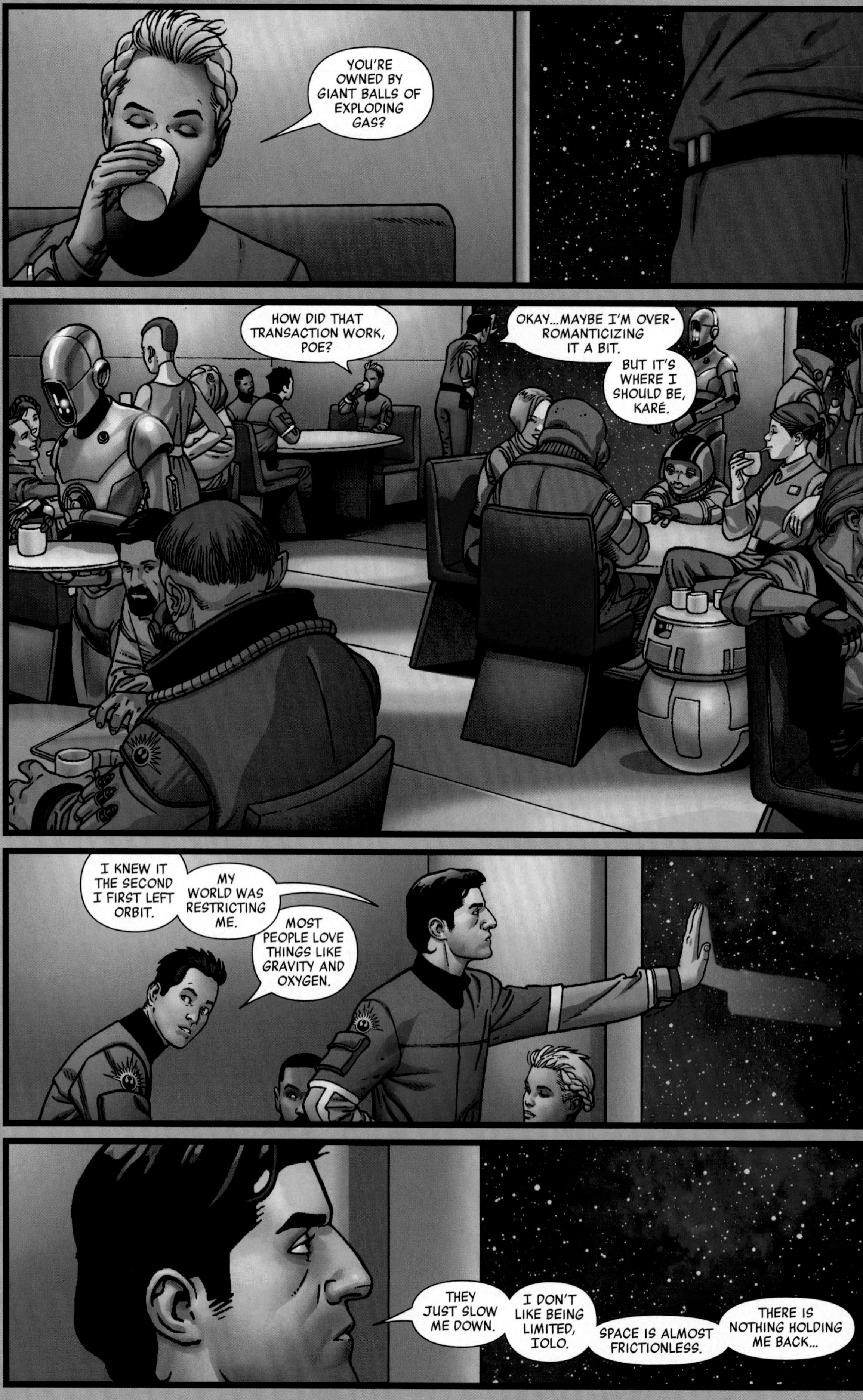
YOU'RE OWNED BY GIANT BALLS OF EXPLODING GAS?
HOW DID THAT TRANSACTION WORK, POE?
OKAY...MAYBE I'M OVER-ROMANTICIZING IT A BIT.
BUT IT'S WHERE I SHOULD BE, KARÉ.
I KNEW IT THE SECOND I FIRST LEFT ORBIT.
MY WORLD WAS RESTRICTING ME.
MOST PEOPLE LOVE THINGS LIKE GRAVITY AND OXYGEN.
THEY JUST SLOW ME DOWN.
I DON'T LIKE BEING LIMITED, IOLO.
SPACE IS ALMOST FRICTIONLESS.
THERE IS NOTHING HOLDING ME BACK...

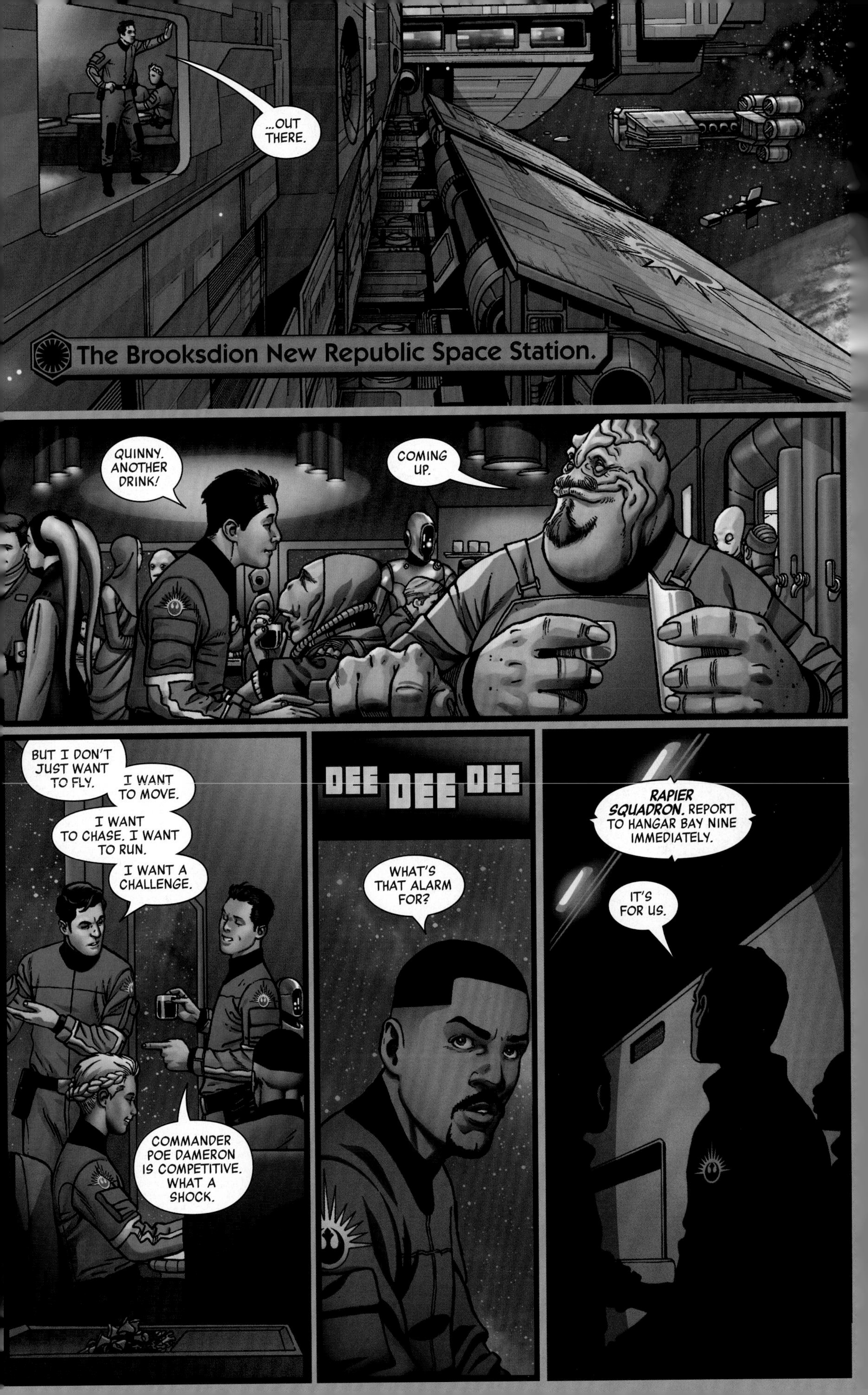
...OUT THERE.
The Brooksdion New Republic Space Station.
QUINNY. ANOTHER DRINK!
COMING UP.
BUT I DON'T JUST WANT TO FLY.
I WANT TO MOVE.
I WANT TO CHASE. I WANT TO RUN.
I WANT A CHALLENGE.
COMMANDER POE DAMERON IS COMPETITIVE. WHAT A SHOCK.
DEE DEE DEE
WHAT'S THAT ALARM FOR?
RAPIER SQUADRON. REPORT TO HANGAR BAY NINE IMMEDIATELY.
IT'S FOR US.

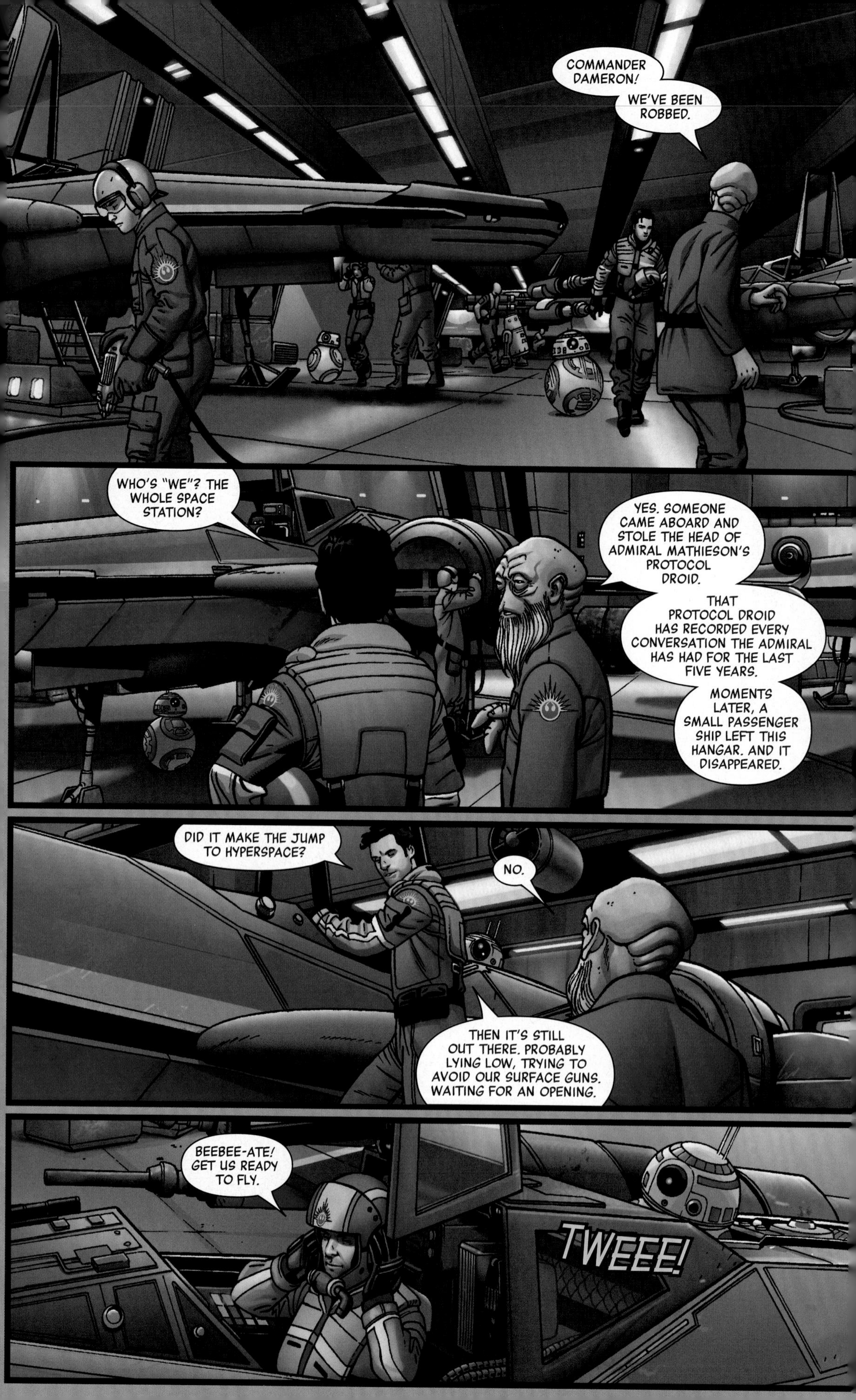
COMMANDER DAMERON!
WE'VE BEEN ROBBED.
WHO'S "WE"? THE WHOLE SPACE STATION?
YES. SOMEONE CAME ABOARD AND STOLE THE HEAD OF ADMIRAL MATHIESON'S PROTOCOL DROID.
THAT PROTOCOL DROID HAS RECORDED EVERY CONVERSATION THE ADMIRAL HAS HAD FOR THE LAST FIVE YEARS.
MOMENTS LATER, A SMALL PASSENGER SHIP LEFT THIS HANGAR. AND IT DISAPPEARED.
DID IT MAKE THE JUMP TO HYPERSPACE?
NO.
THEN IT'S STILL OUT THERE. PROBABLY LYING LOW, TRYING TO AVOID OUR SURFACE GUNS. WAITING FOR AN OPENING.
BEEBEE-ATE! GET US READY TO FLY.
TWEEE!

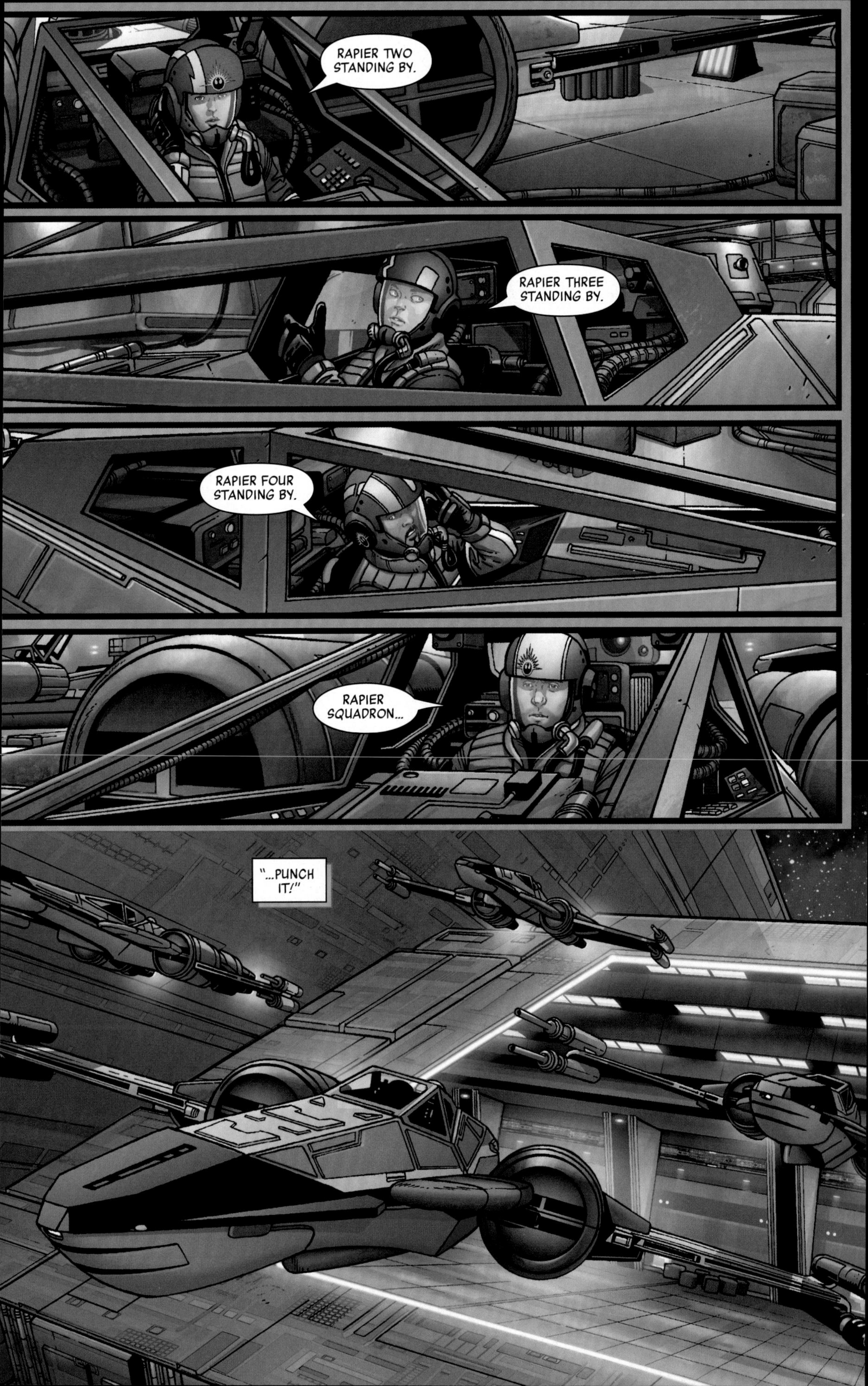
RAPIER TWO STANDING BY.
RAPIER THREE STANDING BY.
RAPIER FOUR STANDING BY.
RAPIER SQUADRON...
"...PUNCH IT!"

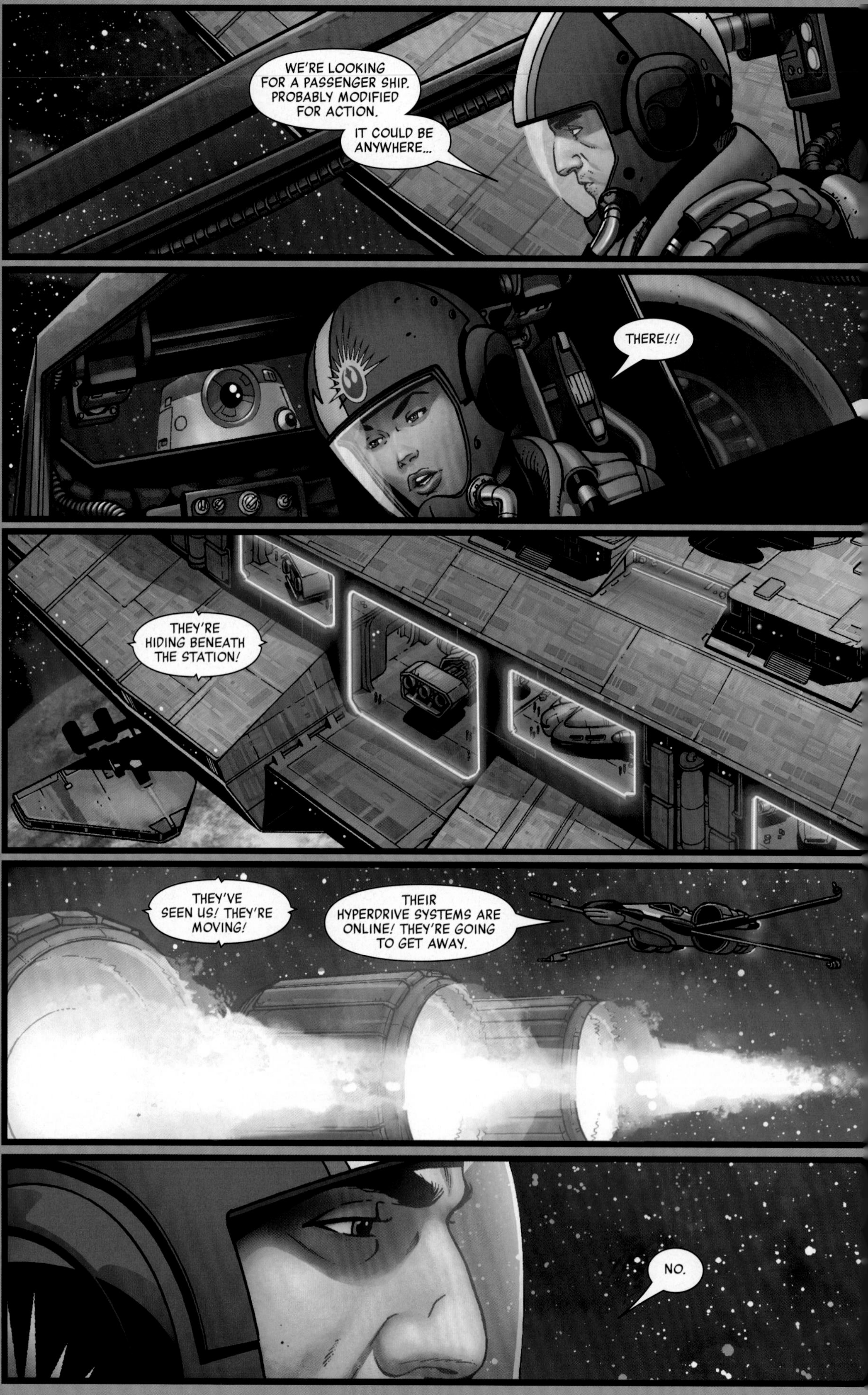
WE'RE LOOKING FOR A PASSENGER SHIP. PROBABLY MODIFIED FOR ACTION.
IT COULD BE ANYWHERE...
THERE!!!
THEY'RE HIDING BENEATH THE STATION!
THEY'VE SEEN US! THEY'RE MOVING!
THEIR HYPERDRIVE SYSTEMS ARE ONLINE! THEY'RE GOING TO GET AWAY.
NO.

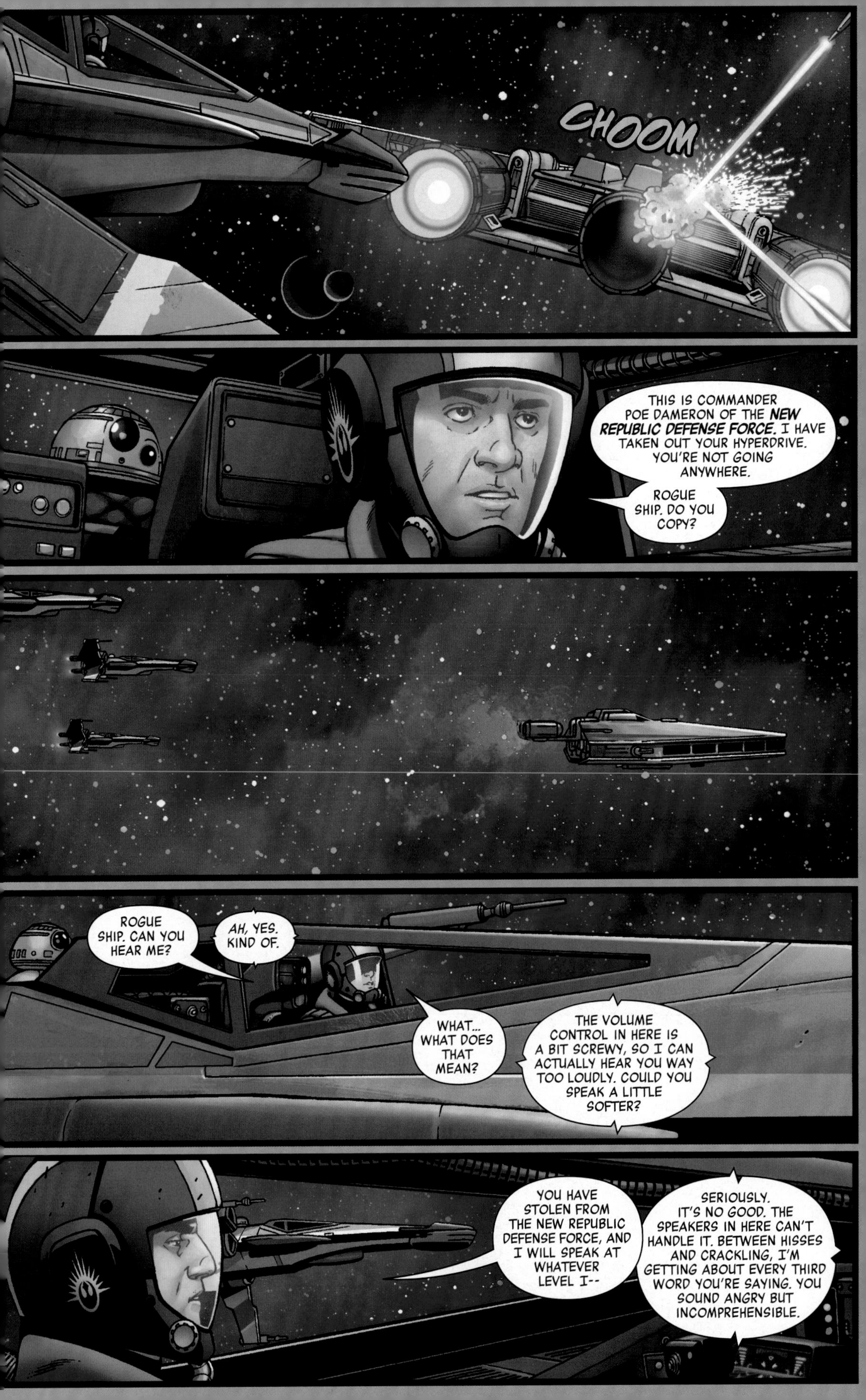
CHOOM
THIS IS COMMANDER POE DAMERON OF THE NEW REPUBLIC DEFENSE FORCE. I HAVE TAKEN OUT YOUR HYPERDRIVE. YOU'RE NOT GOING ANYWHERE.
ROGUE SHIP. DO YOU COPY?
ROGUE SHIP. CAN YOU HEAR ME?
AH, YES. KIND OF.
WHAT... WHAT DOES THAT MEAN?
THE VOLUME CONTROL IN HERE IS A BIT SCREWY, SO I CAN ACTUALLY HEAR YOU WAY TOO LOUDLY. COULD YOU SPEAK A LITTLE SOFTER?
YOU HAVE STOLEN FROM THE NEW REPUBLIC DEFENSE FORCE, AND I WILL SPEAK AT WHATEVER LEVEL I--
SERIOUSLY. IT'S NO GOOD. THE SPEAKERS IN HERE CAN'T HANDLE IT. BETWEEN HISSES AND CRACKLING, I'M GETTING ABOUT EVERY THIRD WORD YOU'RE SAYING. YOU SOUND ANGRY BUT INCOMPREHENSIBLE.

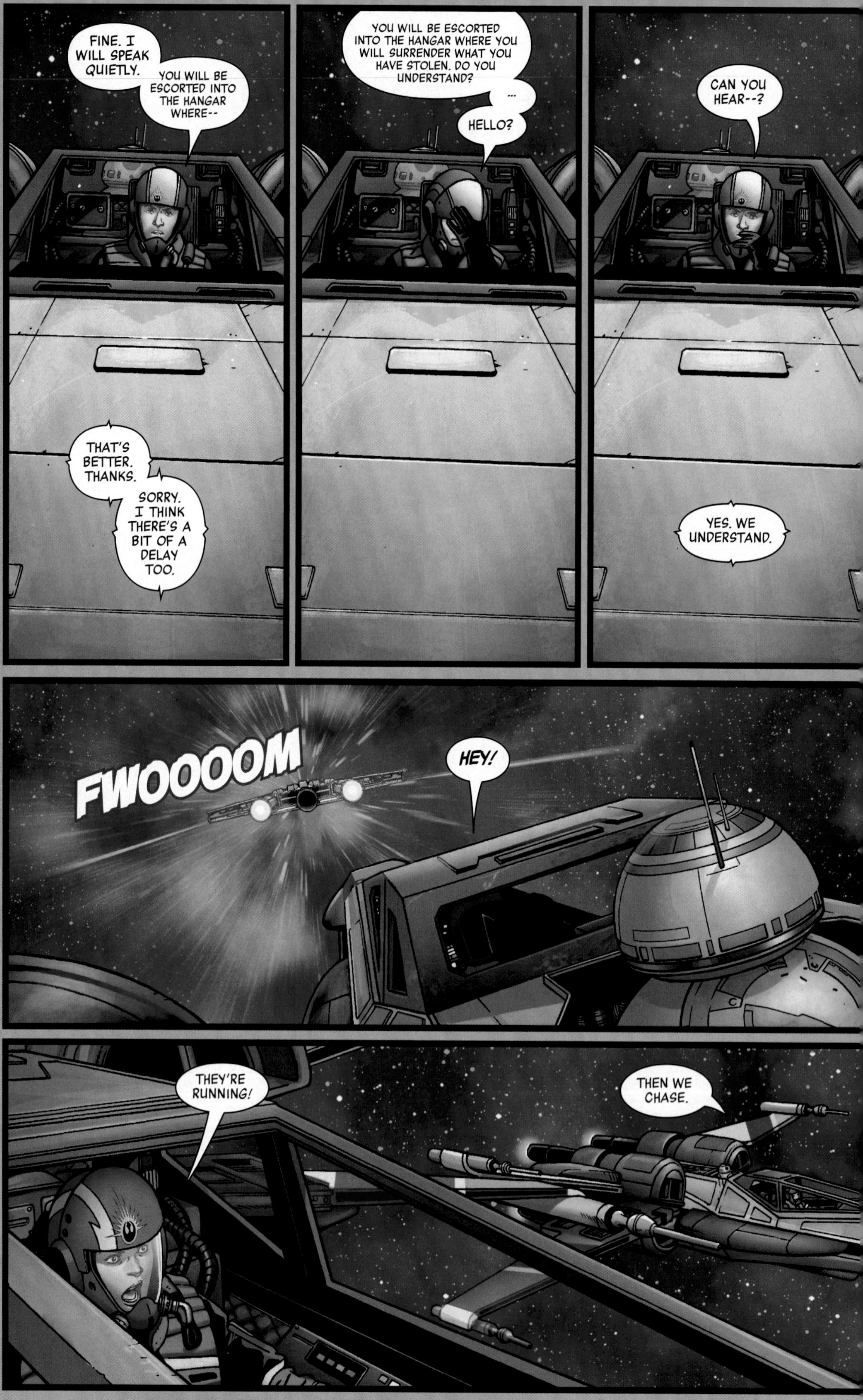
FINE. I WILL SPEAK QUIETLY.
YOU WILL BE ESCORTED INTO THE HANGAR WHERE--
THAT'S BETTER. THANKS.
SORRY. I THINK THERE'S A BIT OF A DELAY TOO.
YOU WILL BE ESCORTED INTO THE HANGAR WHERE YOU WILL SURRENDER WHAT YOU HAVE STOLEN. DO YOU UNDERSTAND?
...
HELLO?
CAN YOU HEAR--?
YES. WE UNDERSTAND.
FWOOOOM
HEY!
THEY'RE RUNNING!
THEN WE CHASE.

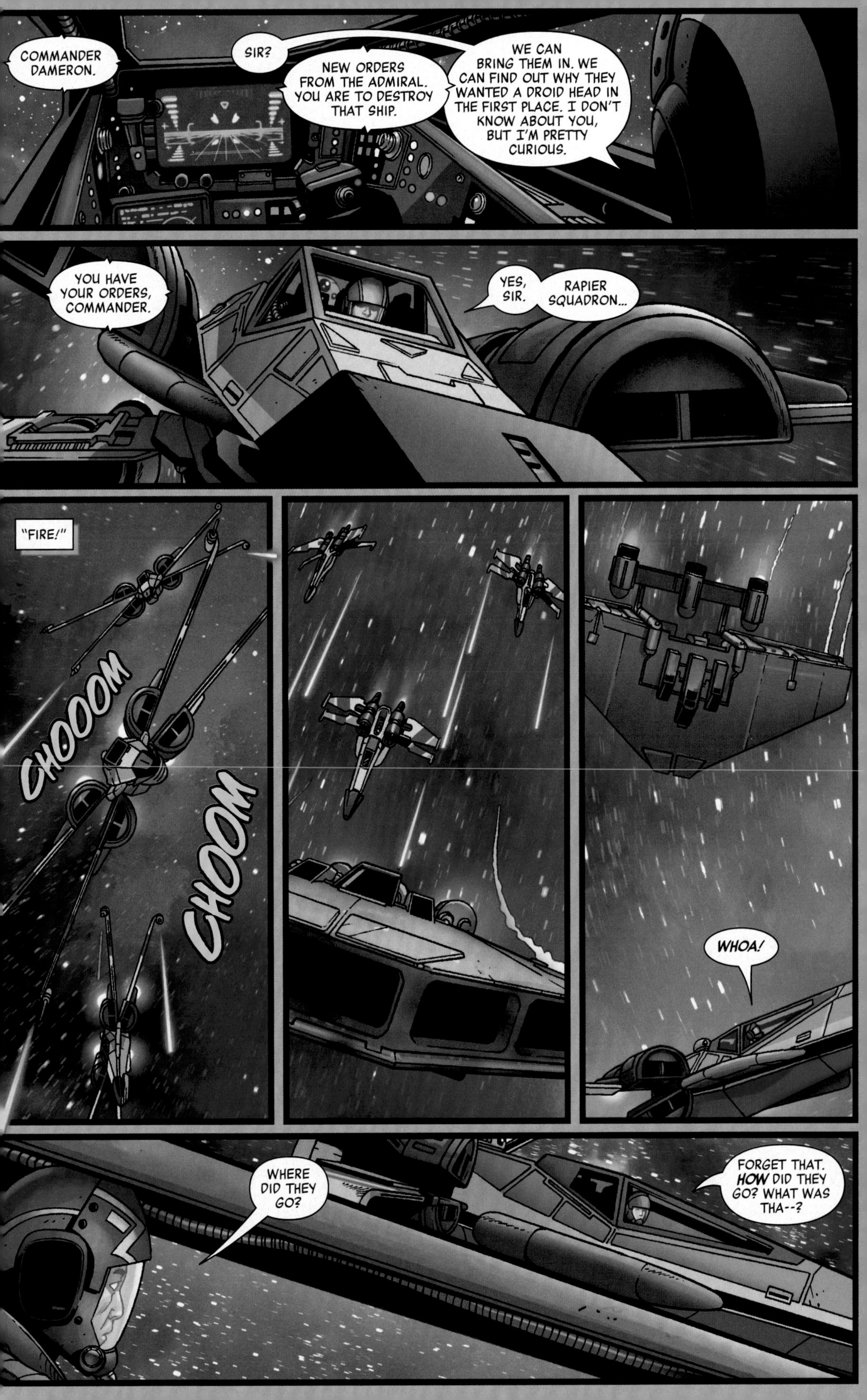
COMMANDER DAMERON.
SIR?
NEW ORDERS FROM THE ADMIRAL. YOU ARE TO DESTROY THAT SHIP.
WE CAN BRING THEM IN. WE CAN FIND OUT WHY THEY WANTED A DROID HEAD IN THE FIRST PLACE. I DON'T KNOW ABOUT YOU, BUT I'M PRETTY CURIOUS.
YOU HAVE YOUR ORDERS, COMMANDER.
YES, SIR.
RAPIER SQUADRON...
"FIRE!"
CHOOOM
CHOOOM
WHOA!
WHERE DID THEY GO?
FORGET THAT. HOW DID THEY GO? WHAT WAS THA--?

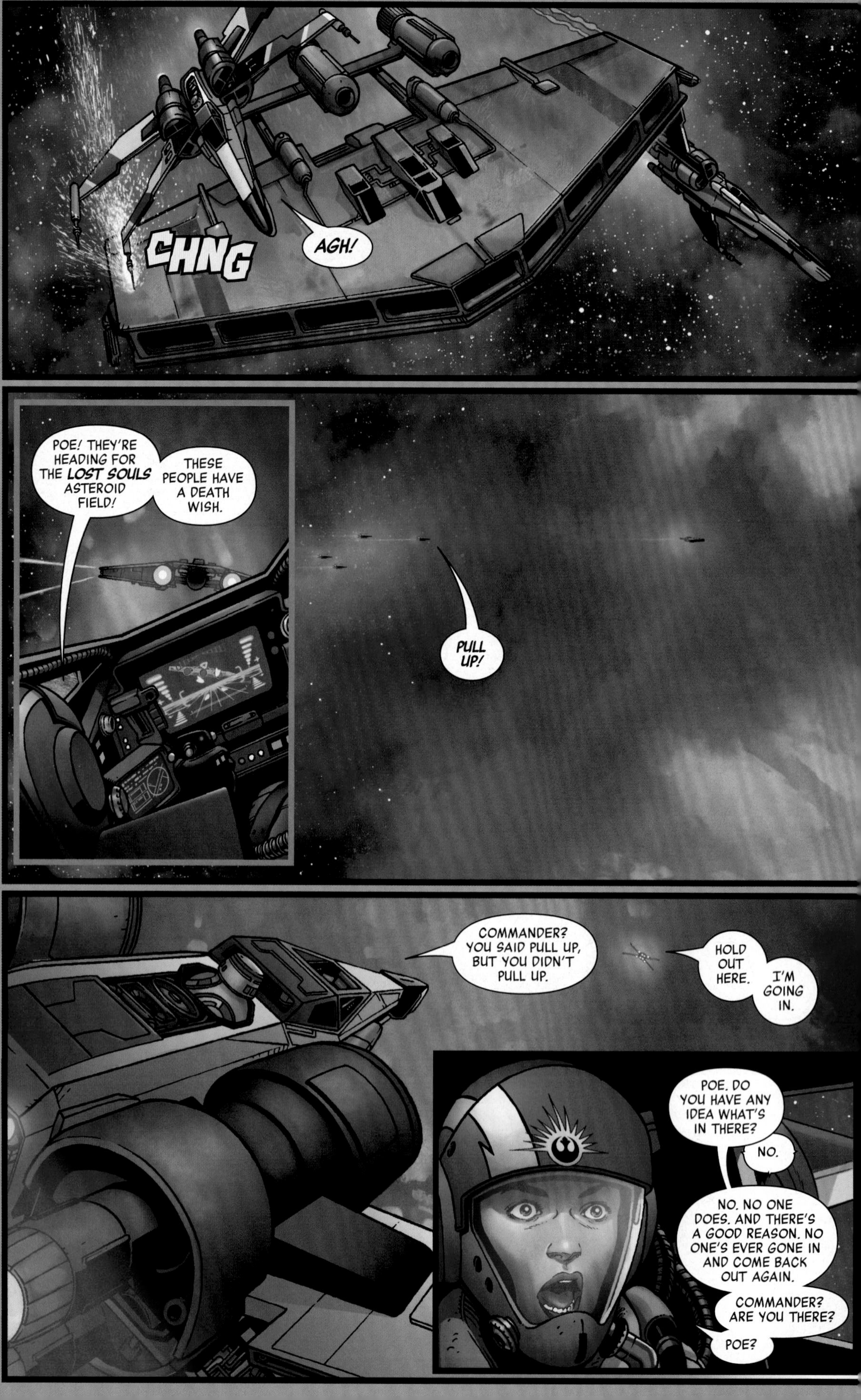
CHNG
AGH!
POE! THEY'RE HEADING FOR THE LOST SOULS ASTEROID FIELD!
THESE PEOPLE HAVE A DEATH WISH.
PULL UP!
COMMANDER? YOU SAID PULL UP, BUT YOU DIDN'T PULL UP.
HOLD OUT HERE.
I'M GOING IN.
POE. DO YOU HAVE ANY IDEA WHAT'S IN THERE?
NO.
NO. NO ONE DOES. AND THERE'S A GOOD REASON. NO ONE'S EVER GONE IN AND COME BACK OUT AGAIN.
COMMANDER? ARE YOU THERE?
POE?

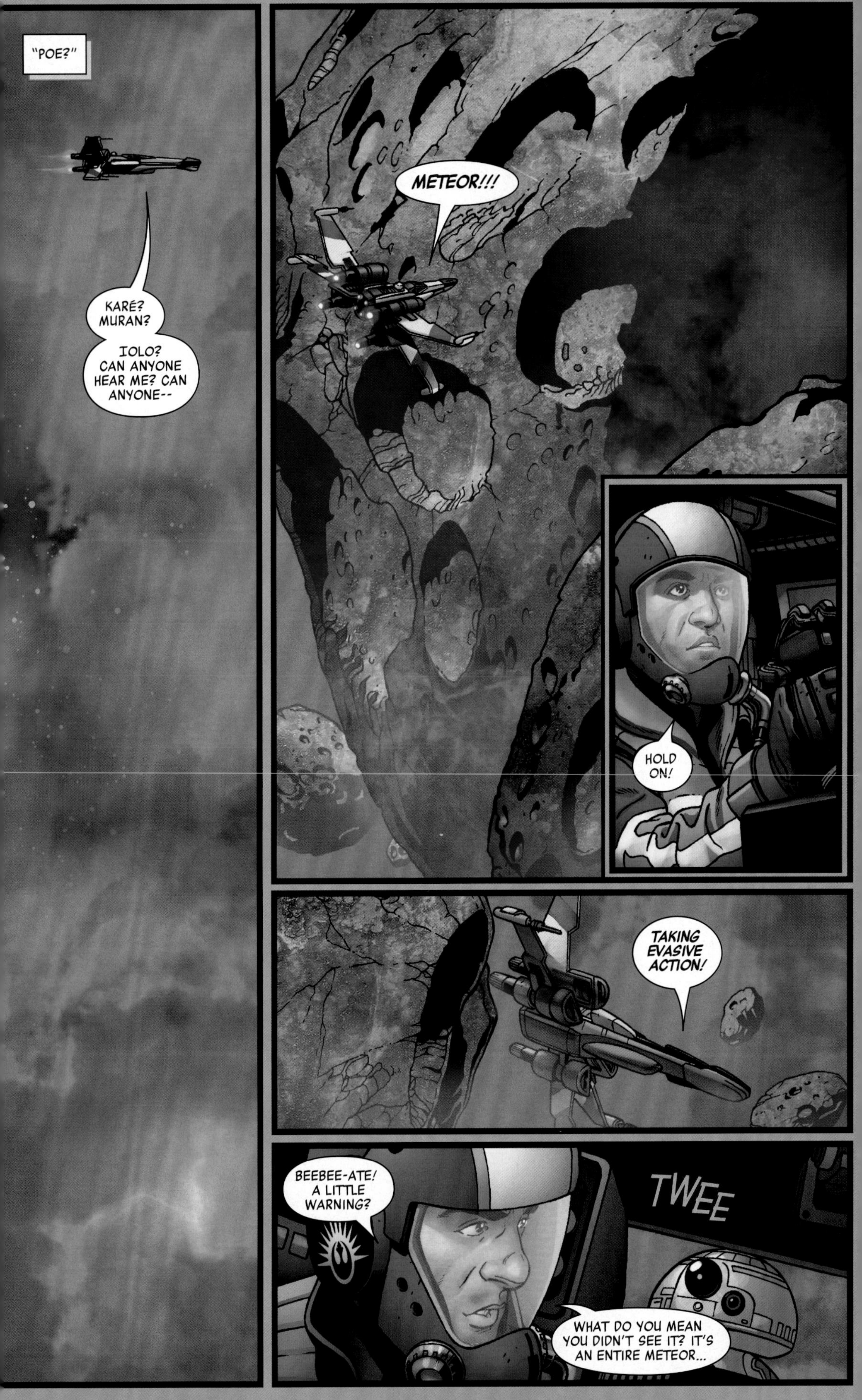
"POE?"
KARÉ? MURAN?
IOLO? CAN ANYONE HEAR ME? CAN ANYONE--
METEOR!!!
HOLD ON!
TAKING EVASIVE ACTION!
BEEBEE-ATE! A LITTLE WARNING?
TWEE
WHAT DO YOU MEAN YOU DIDN'T SEE IT? IT'S AN ENTIRE METEOR...

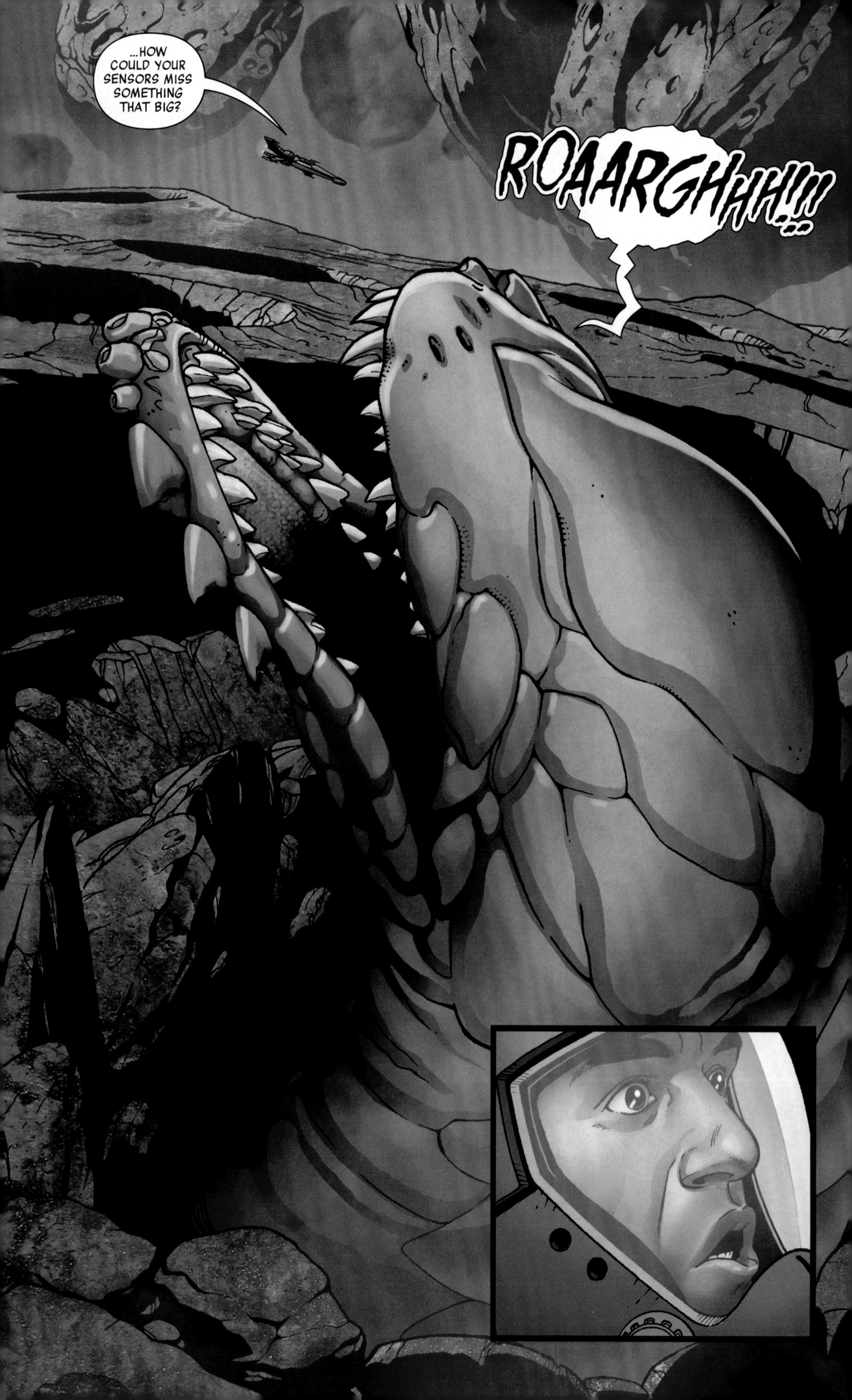
...HOW COULD YOUR SENSORS MISS SOMETHING THAT BIG?
ROAARGHHH!!!

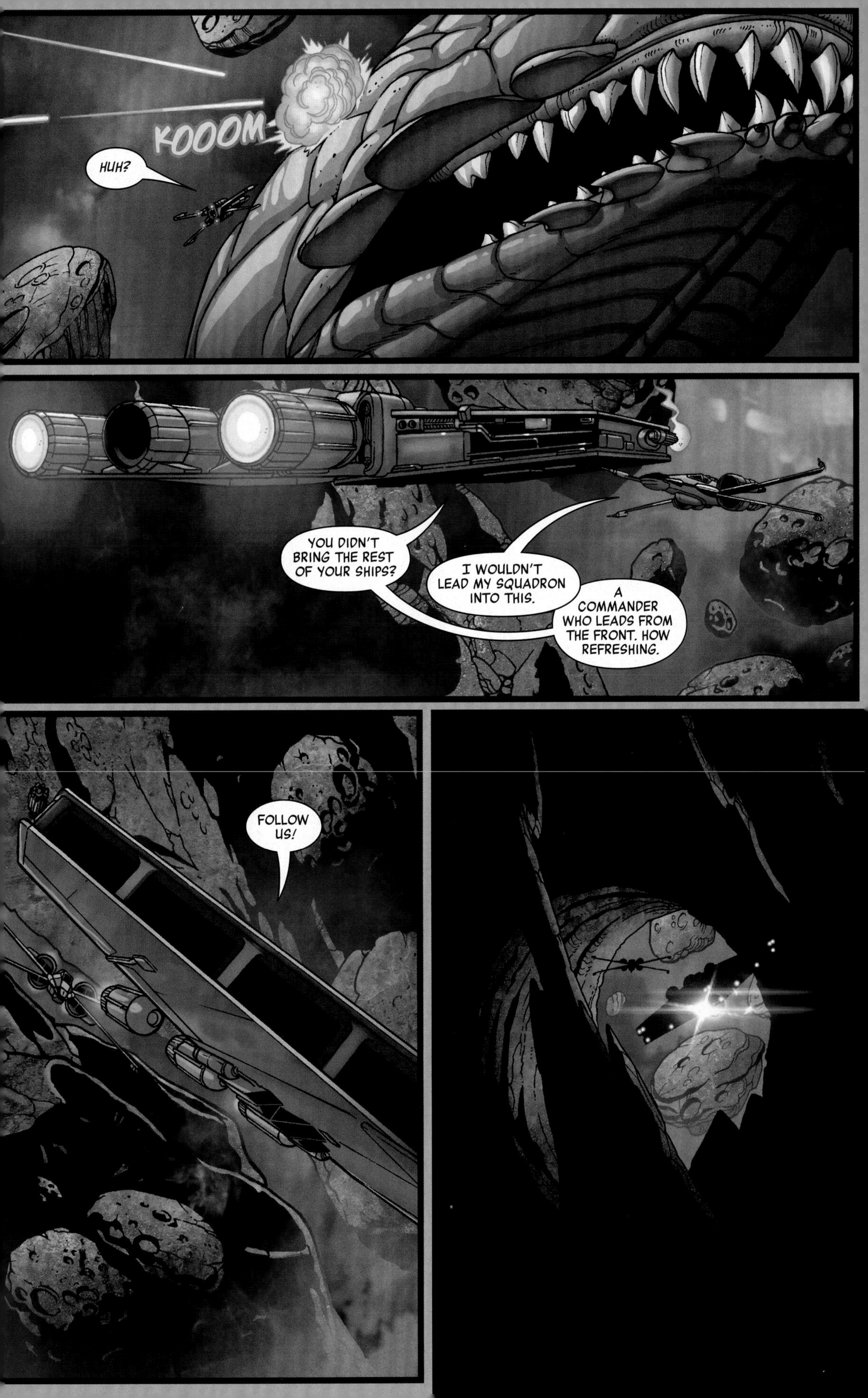
KOOOM
HUH?
YOU DIDN'T BRING THE REST OF YOUR SHIPS?
I WOULDN'T LEAD MY SQUADRON INTO THIS.
A COMMANDER WHO LEADS FROM THE FRONT. HOW REFRESHING.
FOLLOW US!

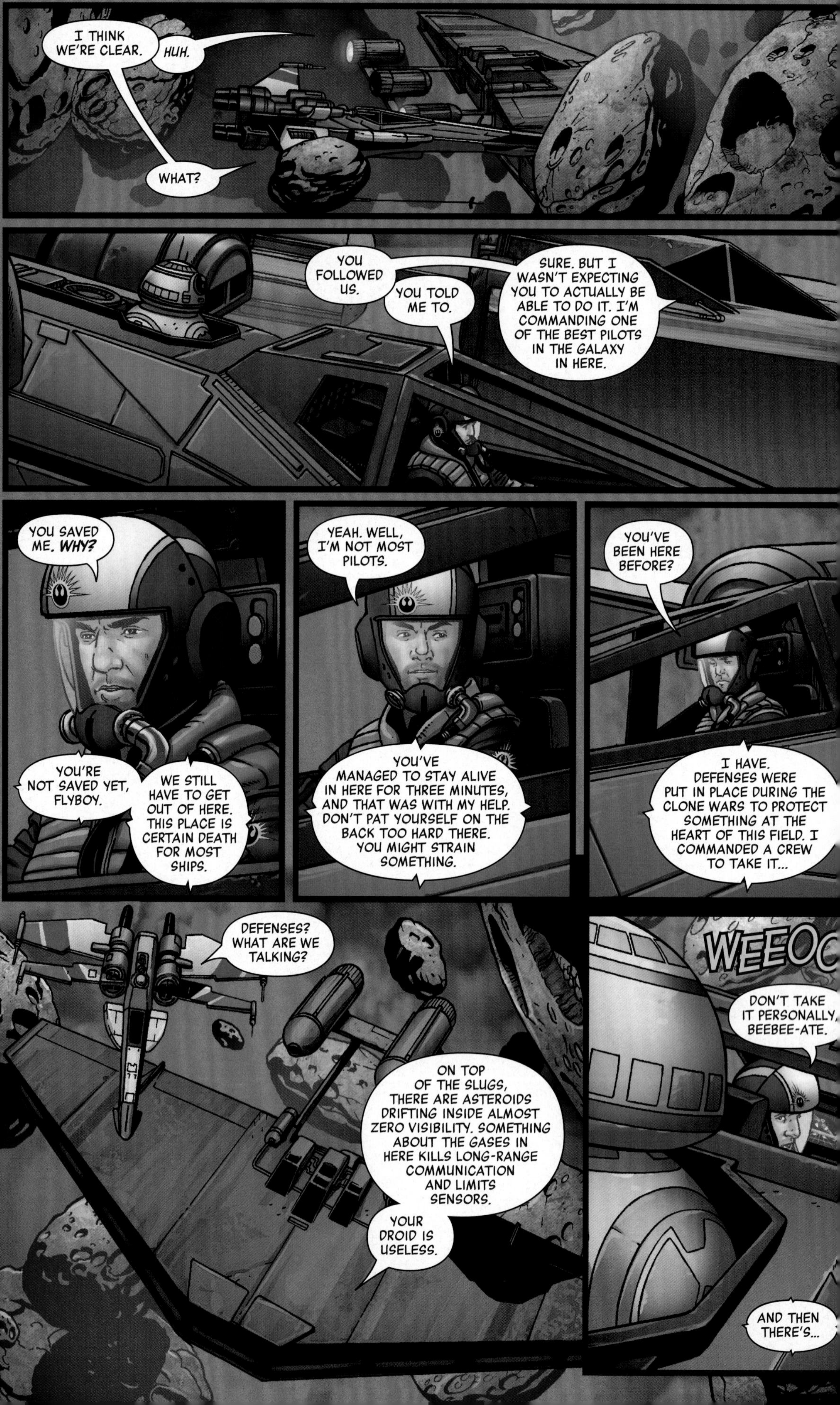
I THINK WE'RE CLEAR.
HUH.
WHAT?
YOU FOLLOWED US.
YOU TOLD ME TO.
SURE. BUT I WASN'T EXPECTING YOU TO ACTUALLY BE ABLE TO DO IT. I'M COMMANDING ONE OF THE BEST PILOTS IN THE GALAXY IN HERE.
YOU SAVED ME. WHY?
YOU'RE NOT SAVED YET, FLYBOY.
WE STILL HAVE TO GET OUT OF HERE. THIS PLACE IS CERTAIN DEATH FOR MOST SHIPS.
YEAH. WELL, I'M NOT MOST PILOTS.
YOU'VE MANAGED TO STAY ALIVE IN HERE FOR THREE MINUTES, AND THAT WAS WITH MY HELP. DON'T PAT YOURSELF ON THE BACK TOO HARD THERE. YOU MIGHT STRAIN SOMETHING.
YOU'VE BEEN HERE BEFORE?
I HAVE. DEFENSES WERE PUT IN PLACE DURING THE CLONE WARS TO PROTECT SOMETHING AT THE HEART OF THIS FIELD. I COMMANDED A CREW TO TAKE IT...
DEFENSES? WHAT ARE WE TALKING?
ON TOP OF THE SLUGS, THERE ARE ASTEROIDS DRIFTING INSIDE ALMOST ZERO VISIBILITY. SOMETHING ABOUT THE GASES IN HERE KILLS LONG-RANGE COMMUNICATION AND LIMITS SENSORS.
YOUR DROID IS USELESS.
WEEOO
DON'T TAKE IT PERSONALLY, BEEBEE-ATE.
AND THEN THERE'S...

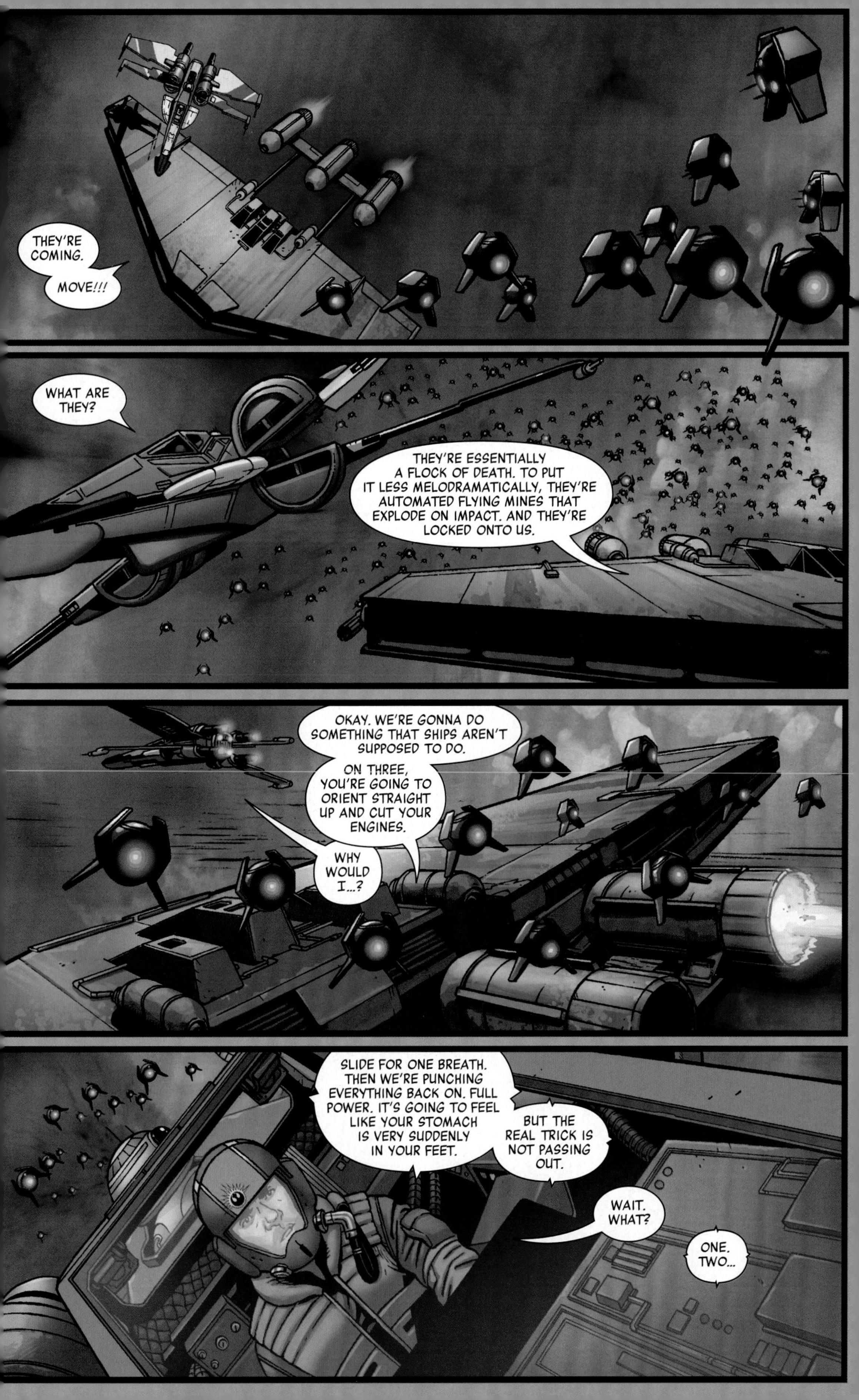
THEY'RE COMING.
MOVE!!!
WHAT ARE THEY?
THEY'RE ESSENTIALLY A FLOCK OF DEATH. TO PUT IT LESS MELODRAMATICALLY, THEY'RE AUTOMATED FLYING MINES THAT EXPLODE ON IMPACT. AND THEY'RE LOCKED ONTO US.
OKAY. WE'RE GONNA DO SOMETHING THAT SHIPS AREN'T SUPPOSED TO DO.
ON THREE, YOU'RE GOING TO ORIENT STRAIGHT UP AND CUT YOUR ENGINES.
WHY WOULD I...?
SLIDE FOR ONE BREATH. THEN WE'RE PUNCHING EVERYTHING BACK ON. FULL POWER. IT'S GOING TO FEEL LIKE YOUR STOMACH IS VERY SUDDENLY IN YOUR FEET.
BUT THE REAL TRICK IS NOT PASSING OUT.
WAIT. WHAT?
ONE. TWO...

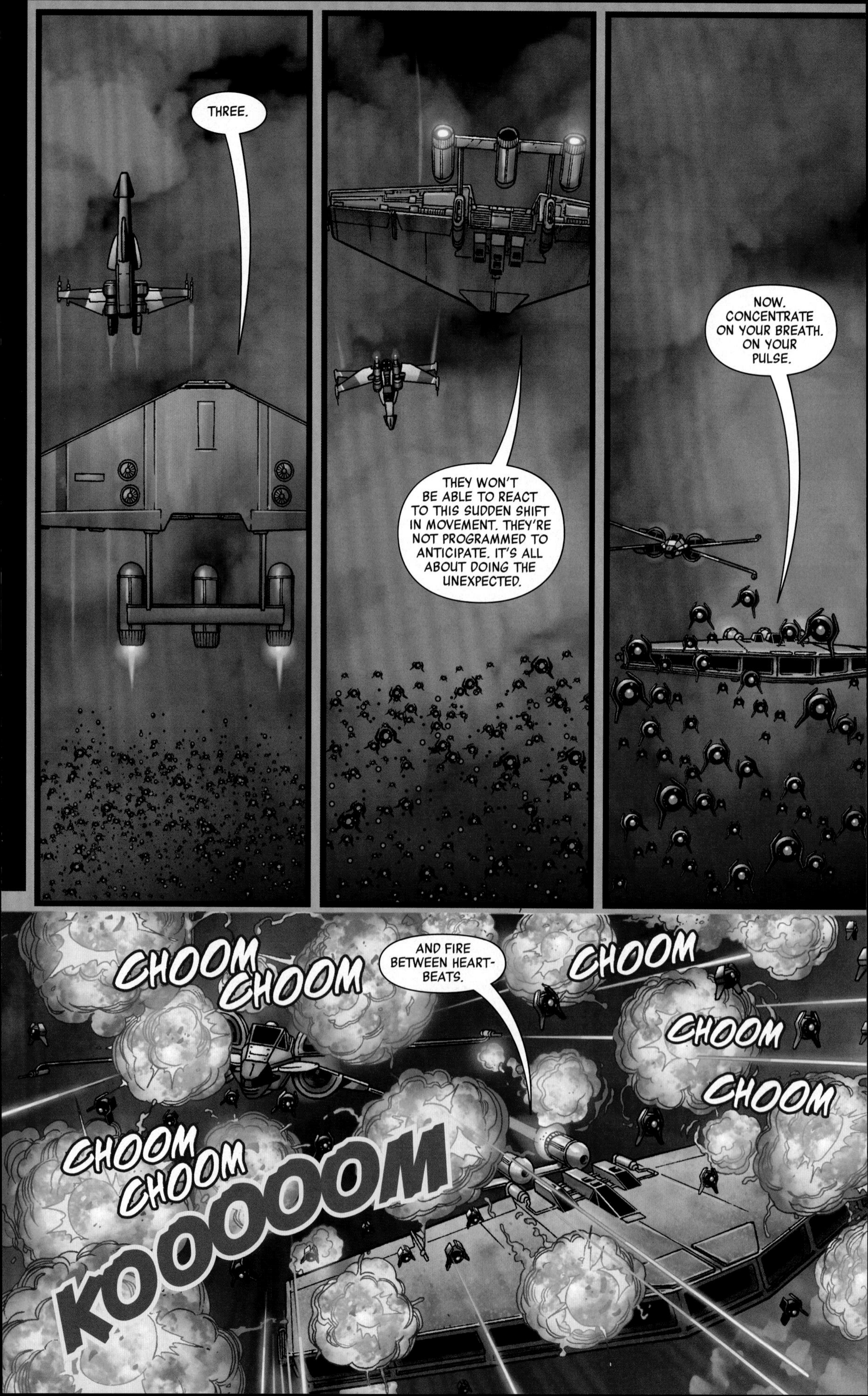
THREE.
THEY WON'T BE ABLE TO REACT TO THIS SUDDEN SHIFT IN MOVEMENT. THEY'RE NOT PROGRAMMED TO ANTICIPATE. IT'S ALL ABOUT DOING THE UNEXPECTED.
NOW. CONCENTRATE ON YOUR BREATH. ON YOUR PULSE.
CHOOM CHOOM
AND FIRE BETWEEN HEART-BEATS.
CHOOM
CHOOM
CHOOM
CHOOM CHOOM
KOOOOOM

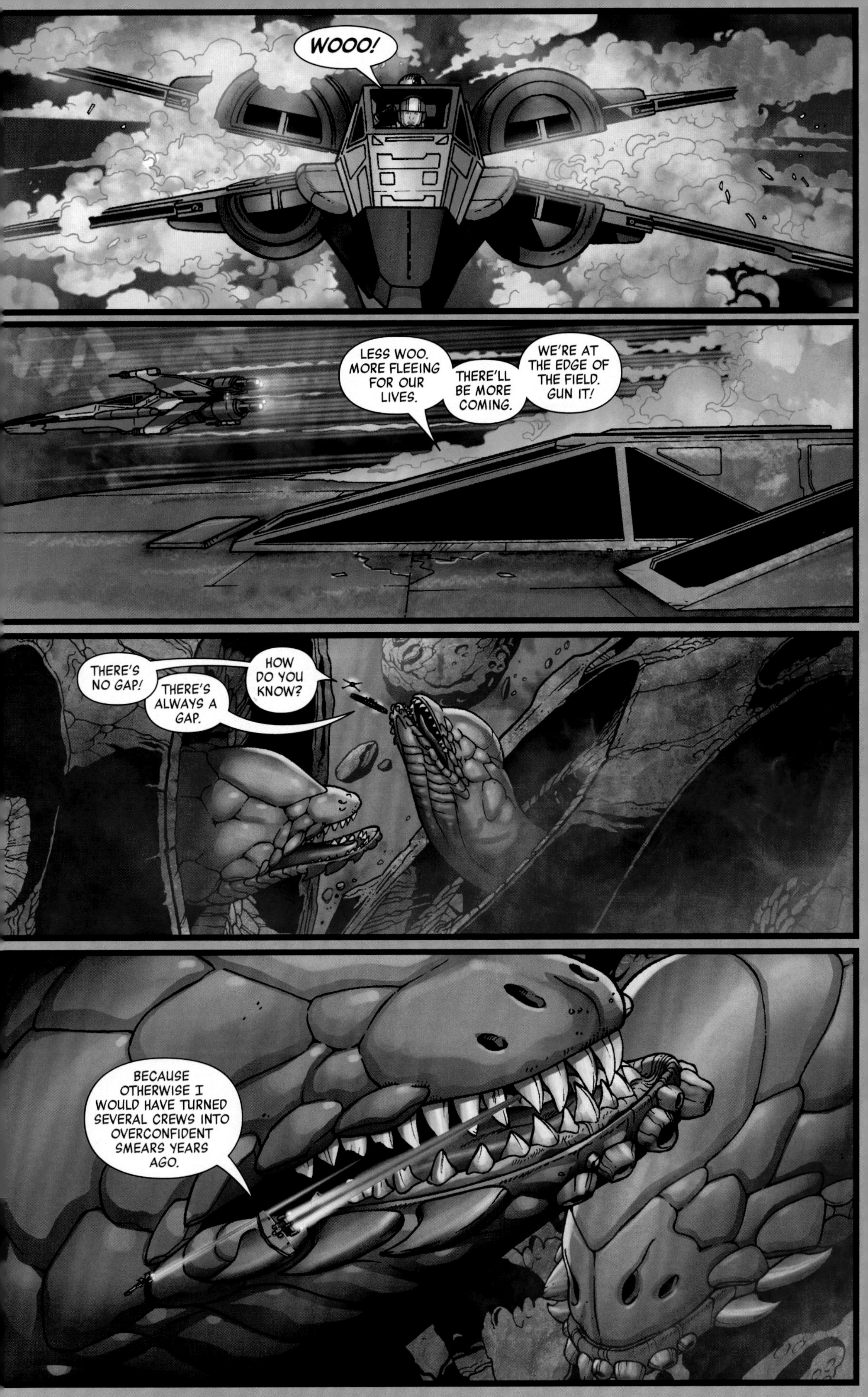
WOOO!
LESS WOO. MORE FLEEING FOR OUR LIVES.
THERE'LL BE MORE COMING.
WE'RE AT THE EDGE OF THE FIELD. GUN IT!
THERE'S NO GAP!
HOW DO YOU KNOW?
THERE'S ALWAYS A GAP.
BECAUSE OTHERWISE I WOULD HAVE TURNED SEVERAL CREWS INTO OVERCONFIDENT SMEARS YEARS AGO.

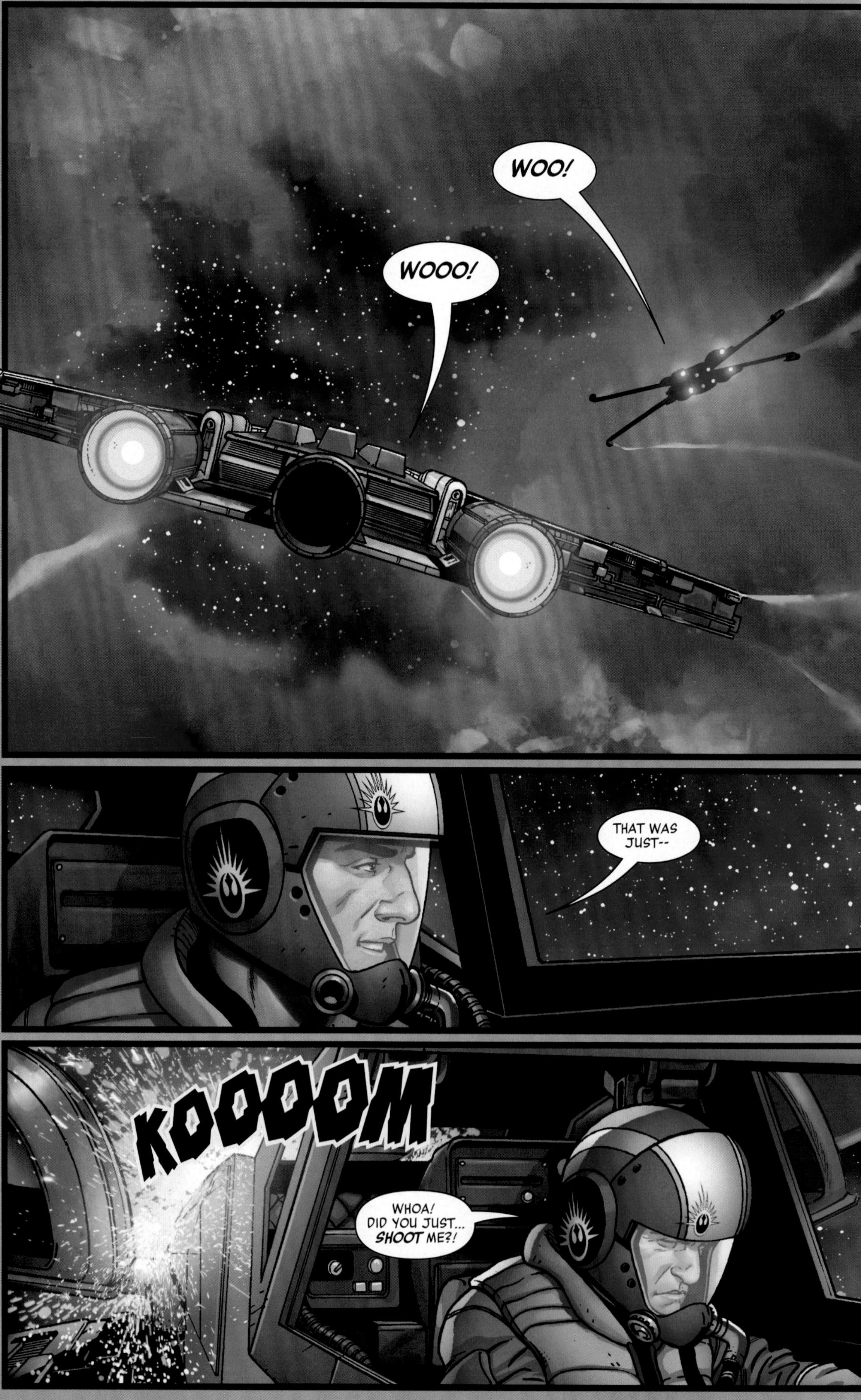
WOO!
WOOO!
THAT WAS JUST--
KOOOOM
WHOA! DID YOU JUST... SHOOT ME?!

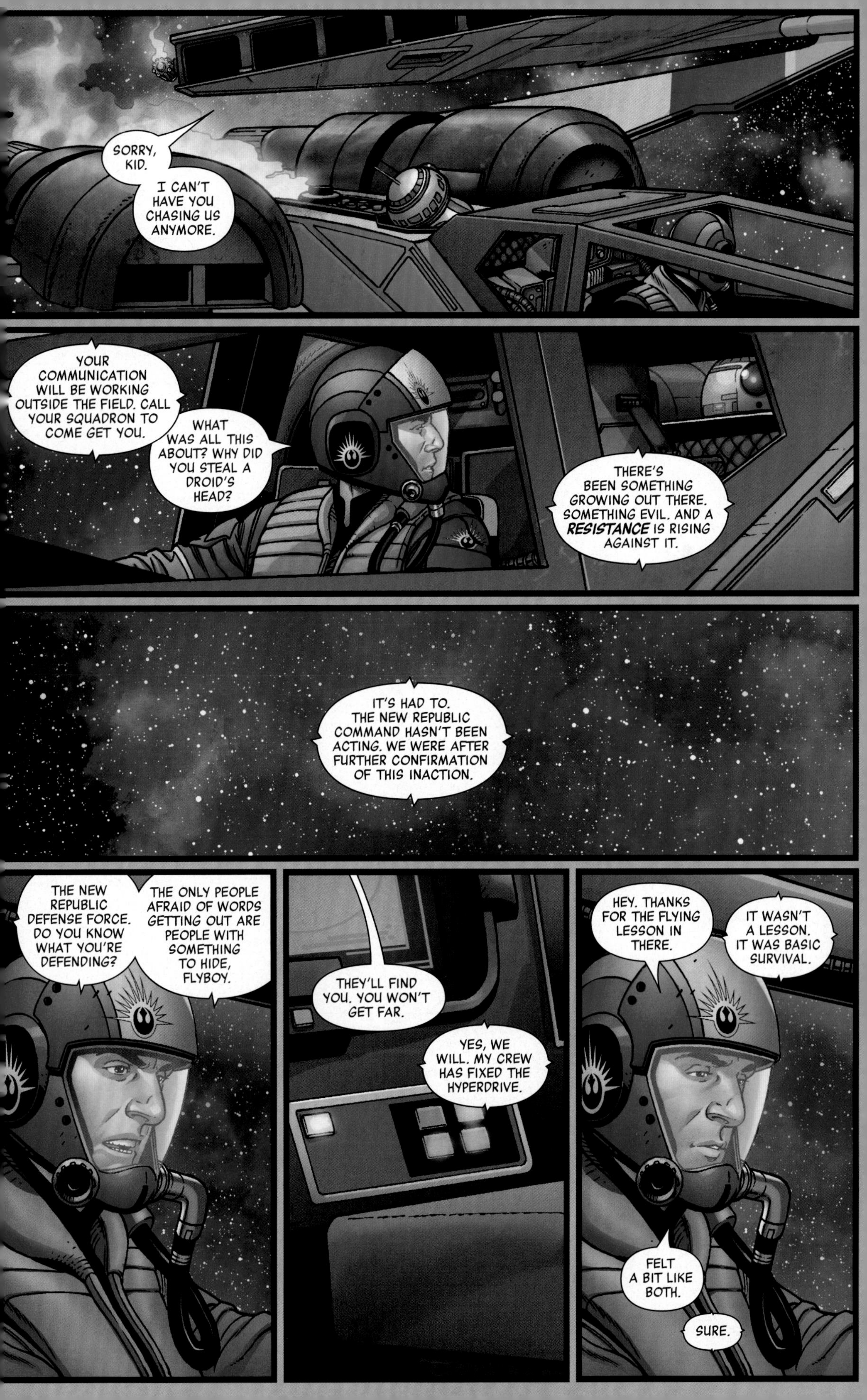
SORRY, KID.
I CAN'T HAVE YOU CHASING US ANYMORE.
YOUR COMMUNICATION WILL BE WORKING OUTSIDE THE FIELD. CALL YOUR SQUADRON TO COME GET YOU.
WHAT WAS ALL THIS ABOUT? WHY DID YOU STEAL A DROID'S HEAD?
THERE'S BEEN SOMETHING GROWING OUT THERE. SOMETHING EVIL. AND A *RESISTANCE* IS RISING AGAINST IT.
IT'S HAD TO. THE NEW REPUBLIC COMMAND HASN'T BEEN ACTING. WE WERE AFTER FURTHER CONFIRMATION OF THIS INACTION.
THE NEW REPUBLIC DEFENSE FORCE. DO YOU KNOW WHAT YOU'RE DEFENDING?
THE ONLY PEOPLE AFRAID OF WORDS GETTING OUT ARE PEOPLE WITH SOMETHING TO HIDE, FLYBOY.
THEY'LL FIND YOU. YOU WON'T GET FAR.
YES, WE WILL. MY CREW HAS FIXED THE HYPERDRIVE.
HEY. THANKS FOR THE FLYING LESSON IN THERE.
IT WASN'T A LESSON. IT WAS BASIC SURVIVAL.
FELT A BIT LIKE BOTH.
SURE.

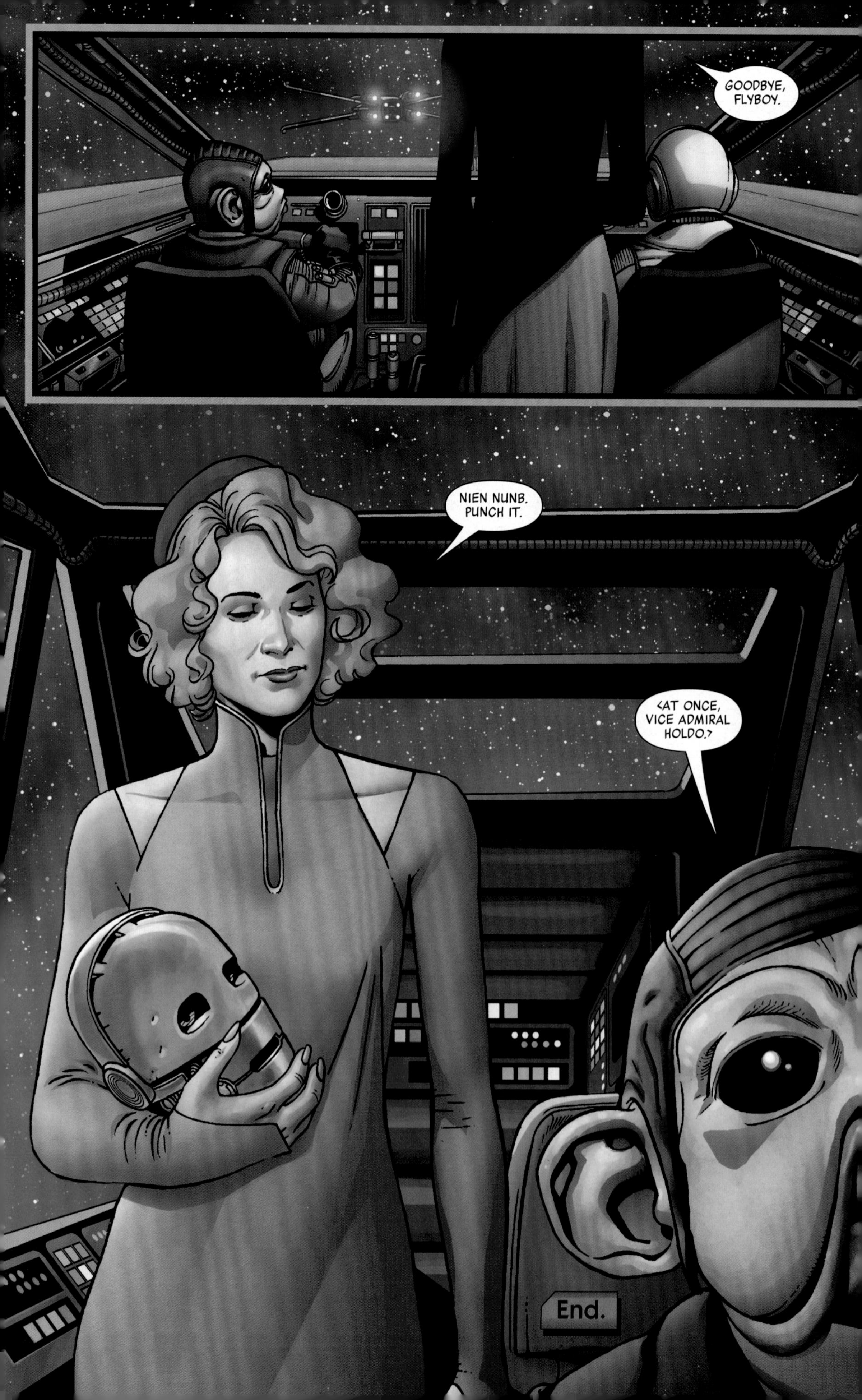
GOODBYE, FLYBOY.
NIEN NUNB. PUNCH IT.
<AT ONCE, VICE ADMIRAL HOLDO.>
End.

AGE OF RESISTANCE

AGE OF RESISTANCE -
Poe Dameron: Flyboy, Hero, Leader
By Bria LaVorgna

Poe Dameron is a hero, and he knows it.

The thing about Poe Dameron is that it's impossible not to notice him, whether he's standing in the landing field of a Resistance base or he's in the cockpit of a starfighter. Sometimes it's because he's being slapped across the face by General Organa and sometimes it's because he's taking out nine TIE fighters over the waters of Takodana without breaking a sweat. The son of A-wing pilot Shara Bey and rebel commando Kes Dameron, Poe seems like he was always destined to end up where he is: the leader of Black Squadron and the best pilot in Leia Organa's not-so-secret Resistance. Not bad for a character who was initially supposed to die early on in *The Force Awakens*.

In some ways, Poe has had the weight of the Resistance on his shoulders both inside and outside the *Star Wars* universe. Of this new generation of heroes, he's the one we've spent the most time with as we've watched his journey from being a mere pilot in the New Republic Defense Fleet to earning

back his commander rank patch in the wake of the Battle of Crait. We've seen the bond he shares with his fellow pilots, how much he loves BB-8, the respect between him and General Organa and even how younger members of the Resistance, like Kazuda Xiono, so clearly look up to him. Perhaps he takes crazy risks and comes up with plans that rely just as much on luck as they do on skill because of the weight of those expectations. Or perhaps it just comes with the flyboy gig. Maybe it's both.

Much of Poe's natural charisma and charm can be placed squarely at the feet of Oscar Isaac. Director J.J. Abrams made it a point to get the actor on board for the character he described as "wonderful, daring, sardonic, brave, loyal," even back when Poe was supposed to be short-lived. "This is a hero that you need to believe is also a human being," Abrams said of Isaac's performance in an interview with *GQ*. "And he gave the role a nuance that I think made it one of the strongest in [*The Force Awakens*]." Poe's quip to Kylo Ren on Jakku ("Who talks first? You talk first? I talk first?") showed

audiences exactly that, because it takes someone incredibly brave to mouth off to an evil Force-user in a mask.

Poe's inherent humanity is what makes him a great character. He's not someone who struggles with right and wrong or good and evil. Instead, his struggle is more with his tendency to need to be the person who pulls off some last-minute, thrilling heroics in service to the greater good. Because Leia's right: You can't solve everything by jumping in an X-wing to blow things up. When last we saw him in the final pages of the POE DAMERON comic, Poe was coming to terms with that. "I don't think it's about heroes. I used to," Poe tells Snap Wexley. "It's not about saving the galaxy. It's about saving *your* galaxy. You choose right over wrong. When it's dark, you try to bring some light. You end your journey knowing you made things brighter."

Poe Dameron will always be a hero, and right now, he's on the path to be the Resistance leader Leia always thought he could be too.

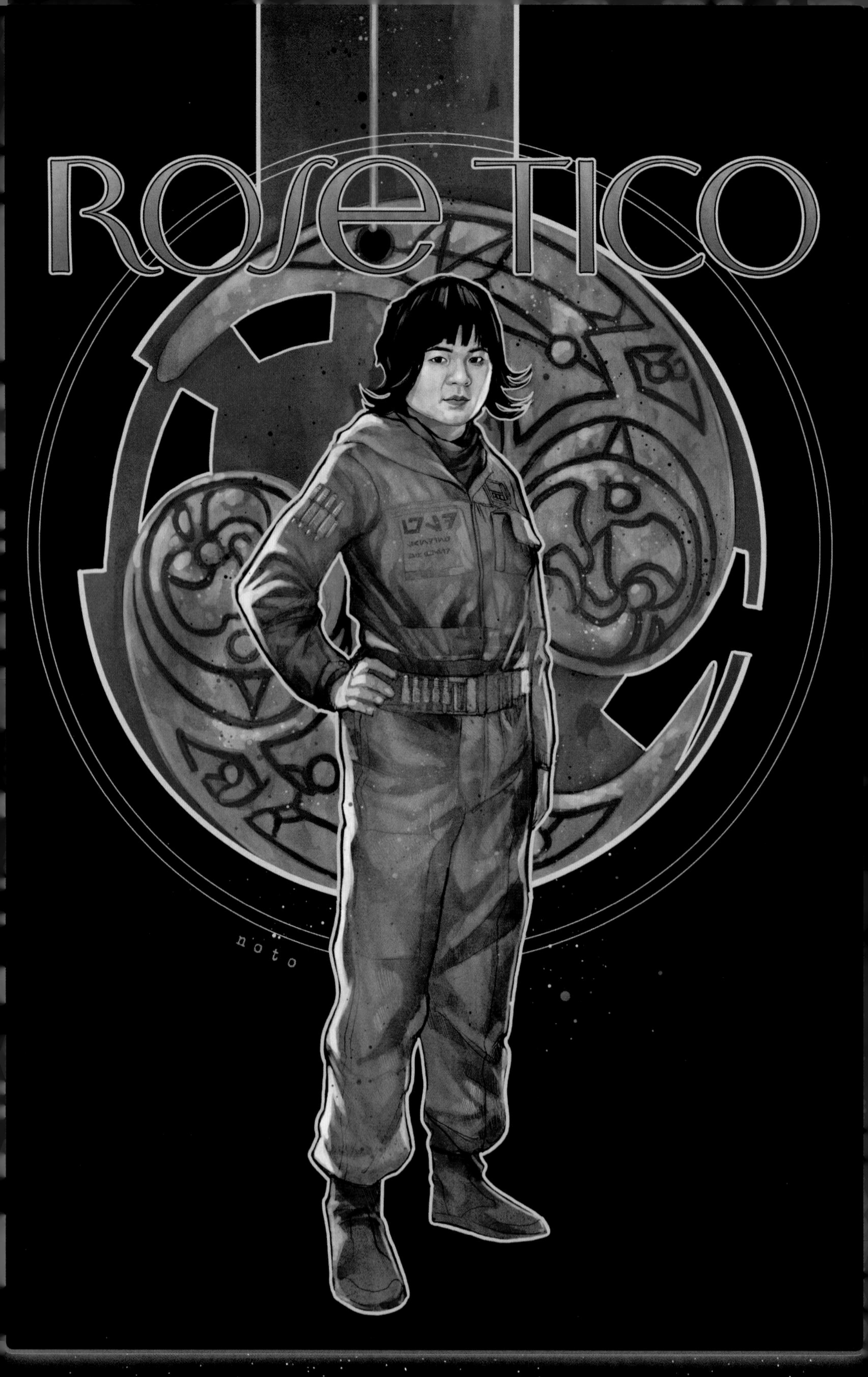
ROSE TICO
noto

"MY HERO"

Young sisters Rose and Paige Tico are inseparable, and growing up in an era of hope and peace—the time of the glorious New Republic—means that their futures are as bright and boundless as the stars of the galaxy. But a war is coming...

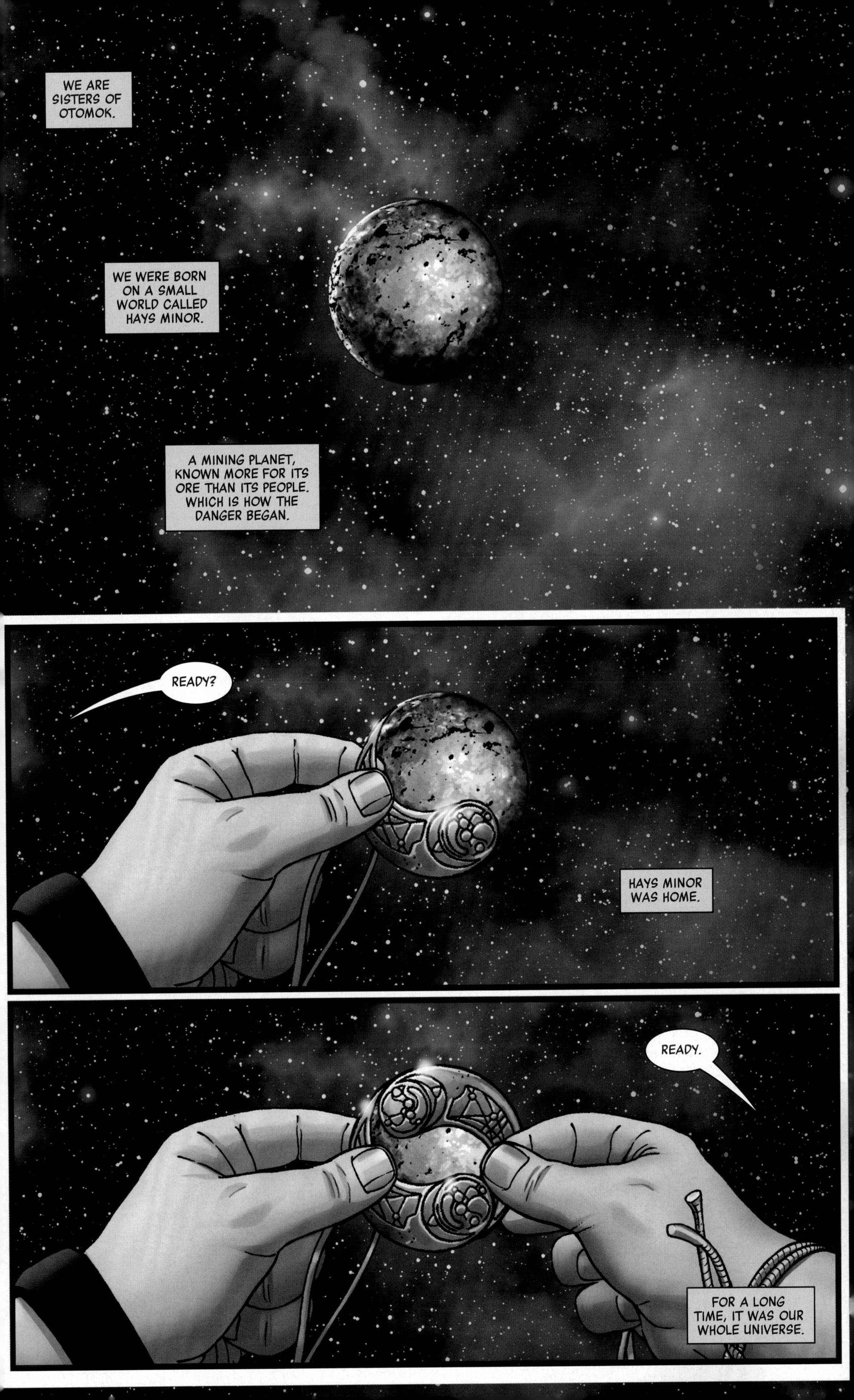
WE ARE SISTERS OF OTOMOK.
WE WERE BORN ON A SMALL WORLD CALLED HAYS MINOR.
A MINING PLANET, KNOWN MORE FOR ITS ORE THAN ITS PEOPLE. WHICH IS HOW THE DANGER BEGAN.
READY?
HAYS MINOR WAS HOME.
READY.
FOR A LONG TIME, IT WAS OUR WHOLE UNIVERSE.

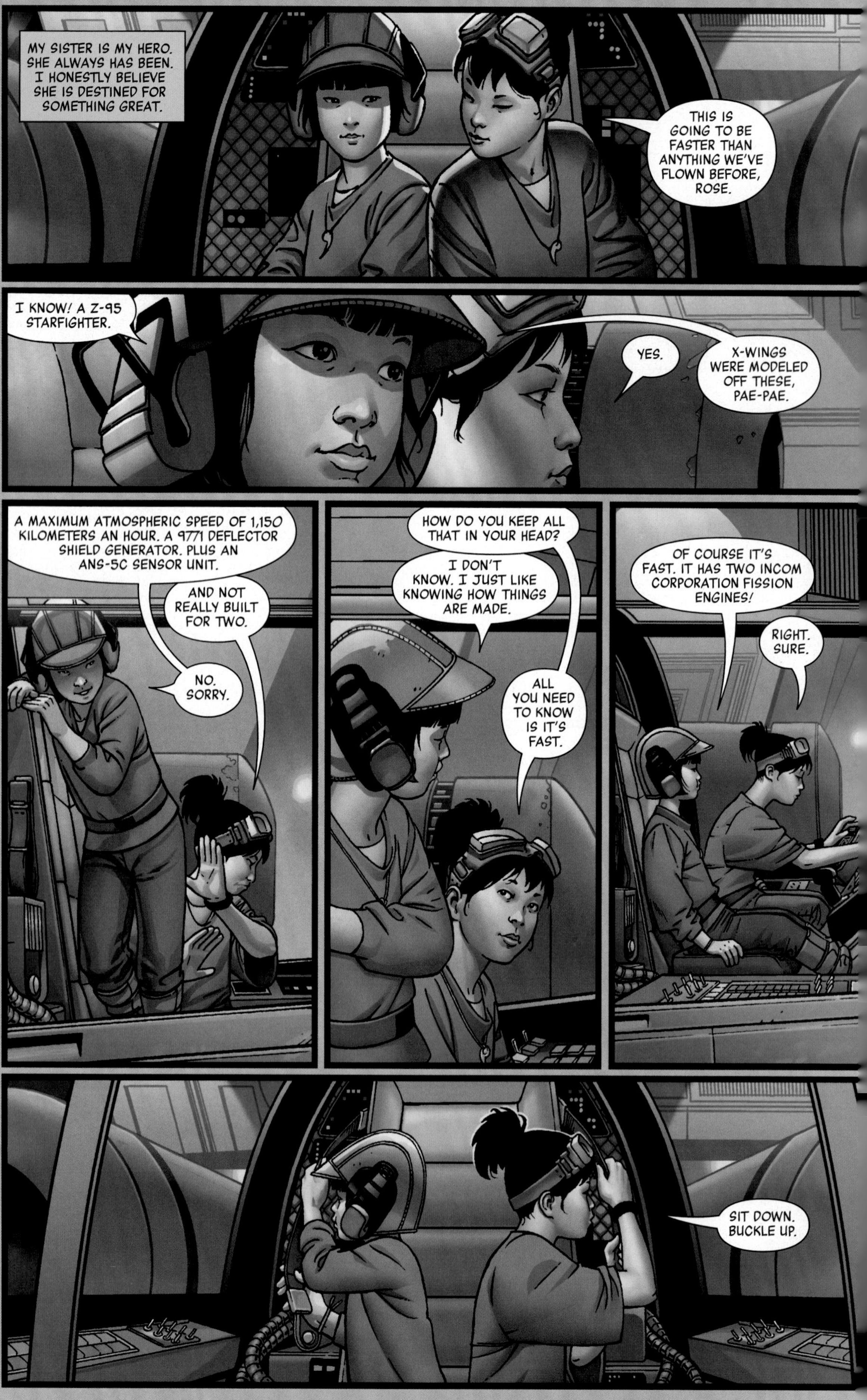
MY SISTER IS MY HERO. SHE ALWAYS HAS BEEN. I HONESTLY BELIEVE SHE IS DESTINED FOR SOMETHING GREAT.
THIS IS GOING TO BE FASTER THAN ANYTHING WE'VE FLOWN BEFORE, ROSE.
I KNOW! A Z-95 STARFIGHTER.
YES.
X-WINGS WERE MODELED OFF THESE, PAE-PAE.
A MAXIMUM ATMOSPHERIC SPEED OF 1,150 KILOMETERS AN HOUR. A 9771 DEFLECTOR SHIELD GENERATOR. PLUS AN ANS-5C SENSOR UNIT.
AND NOT REALLY BUILT FOR TWO.
NO. SORRY.
HOW DO YOU KEEP ALL THAT IN YOUR HEAD?
I DON'T KNOW. I JUST LIKE KNOWING HOW THINGS ARE MADE.
ALL YOU NEED TO KNOW IS IT'S FAST.
OF COURSE IT'S FAST. IT HAS TWO INCOM CORPORATION FISSION ENGINES!
RIGHT. SURE.
SIT DOWN. BUCKLE UP.

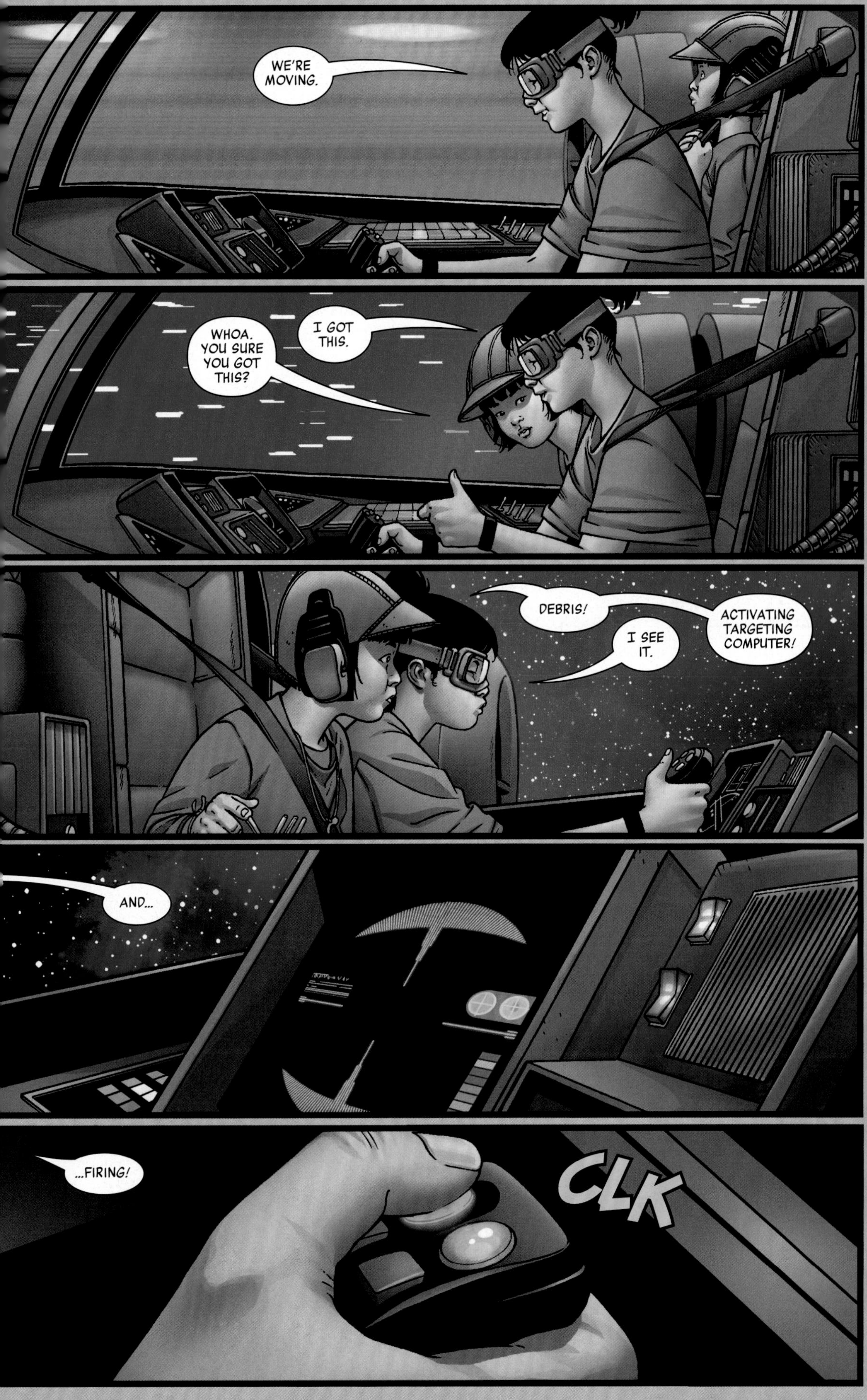
WE'RE MOVING.
WHOA. YOU SURE YOU GOT THIS?
I GOT THIS.
DEBRIS!
I SEE IT.
ACTIVATING TARGETING COMPUTER!
AND...
...FIRING!
CLK

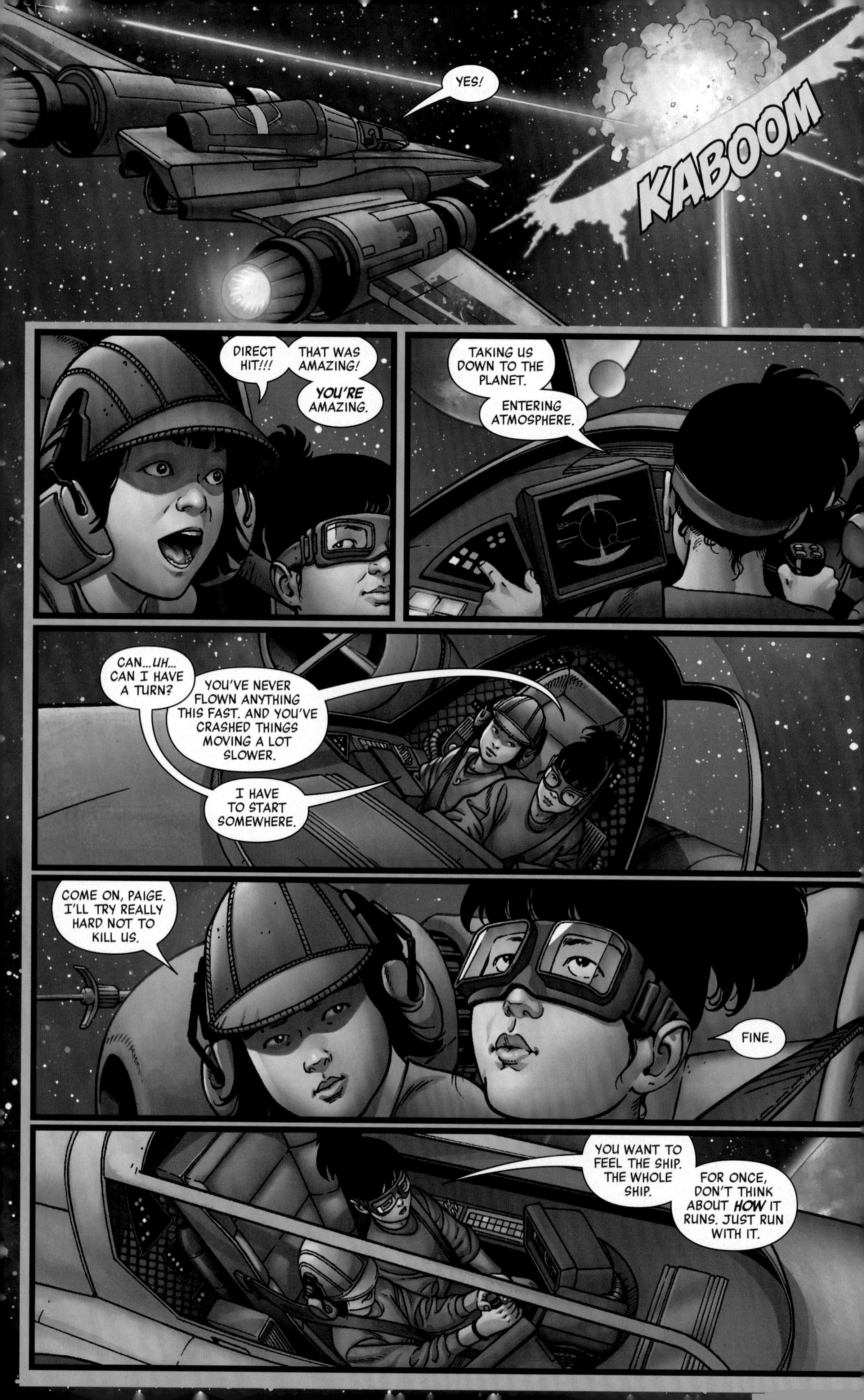
YES!
KABOOM
DIRECT HIT!!!
THAT WAS AMAZING!
YOU'RE AMAZING.
TAKING US DOWN TO THE PLANET.
ENTERING ATMOSPHERE.
CAN...UH... CAN I HAVE A TURN?
YOU'VE NEVER FLOWN ANYTHING THIS FAST. AND YOU'VE CRASHED THINGS MOVING A LOT SLOWER.
I HAVE TO START SOMEWHERE.
COME ON, PAIGE. I'LL TRY REALLY HARD NOT TO KILL US.
FINE.
YOU WANT TO FEEL THE SHIP. THE WHOLE SHIP.
FOR ONCE, DON'T THINK ABOUT HOW IT RUNS. JUST RUN WITH IT.

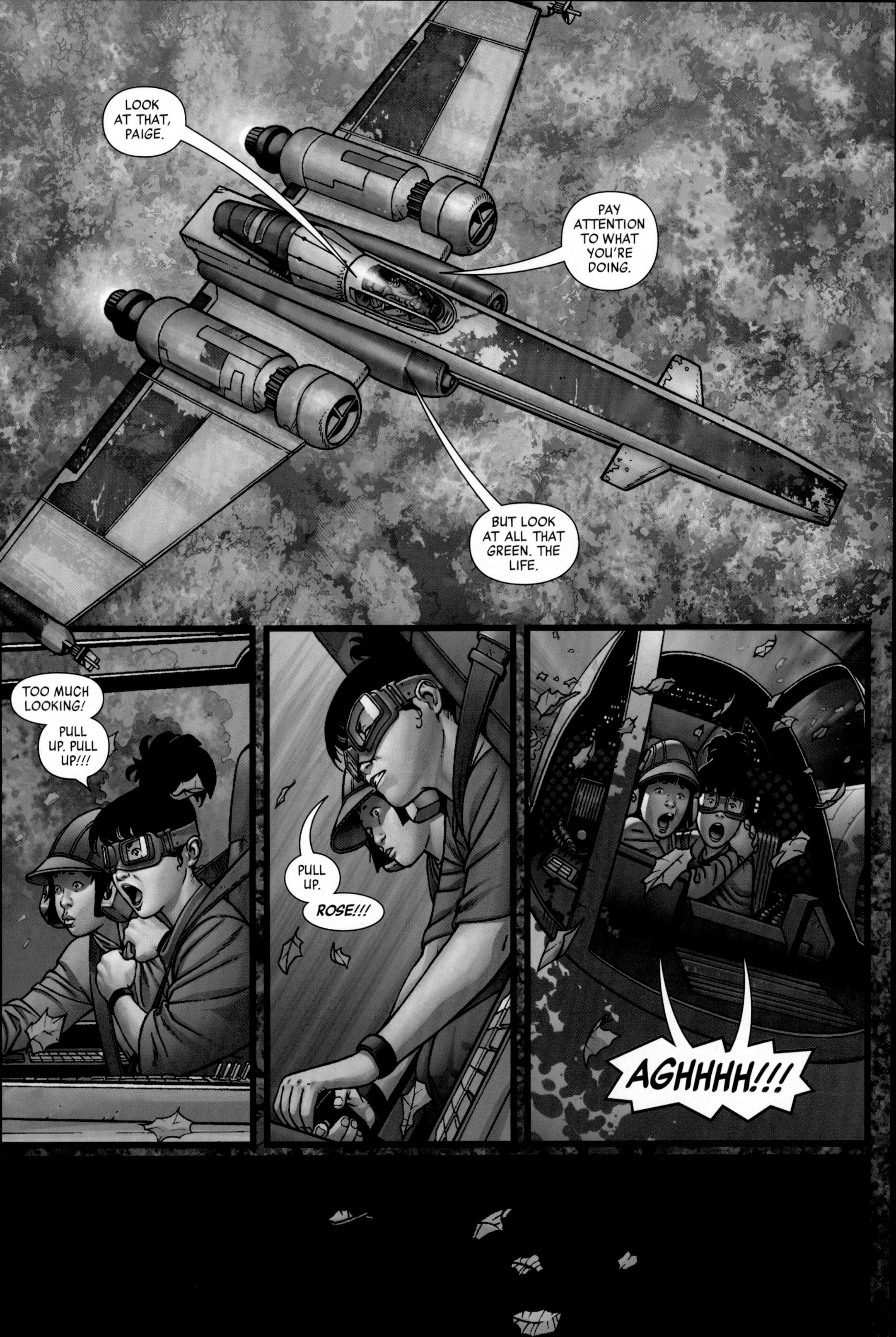

LOOK AT THAT, PAIGE.
PAY ATTENTION TO WHAT YOU'RE DOING.
BUT LOOK AT ALL THAT GREEN. THE LIFE.
TOO MUCH LOOKING!
PULL UP. PULL UP!!!
PULL UP.
ROSE!!!
AGHHHH!!!

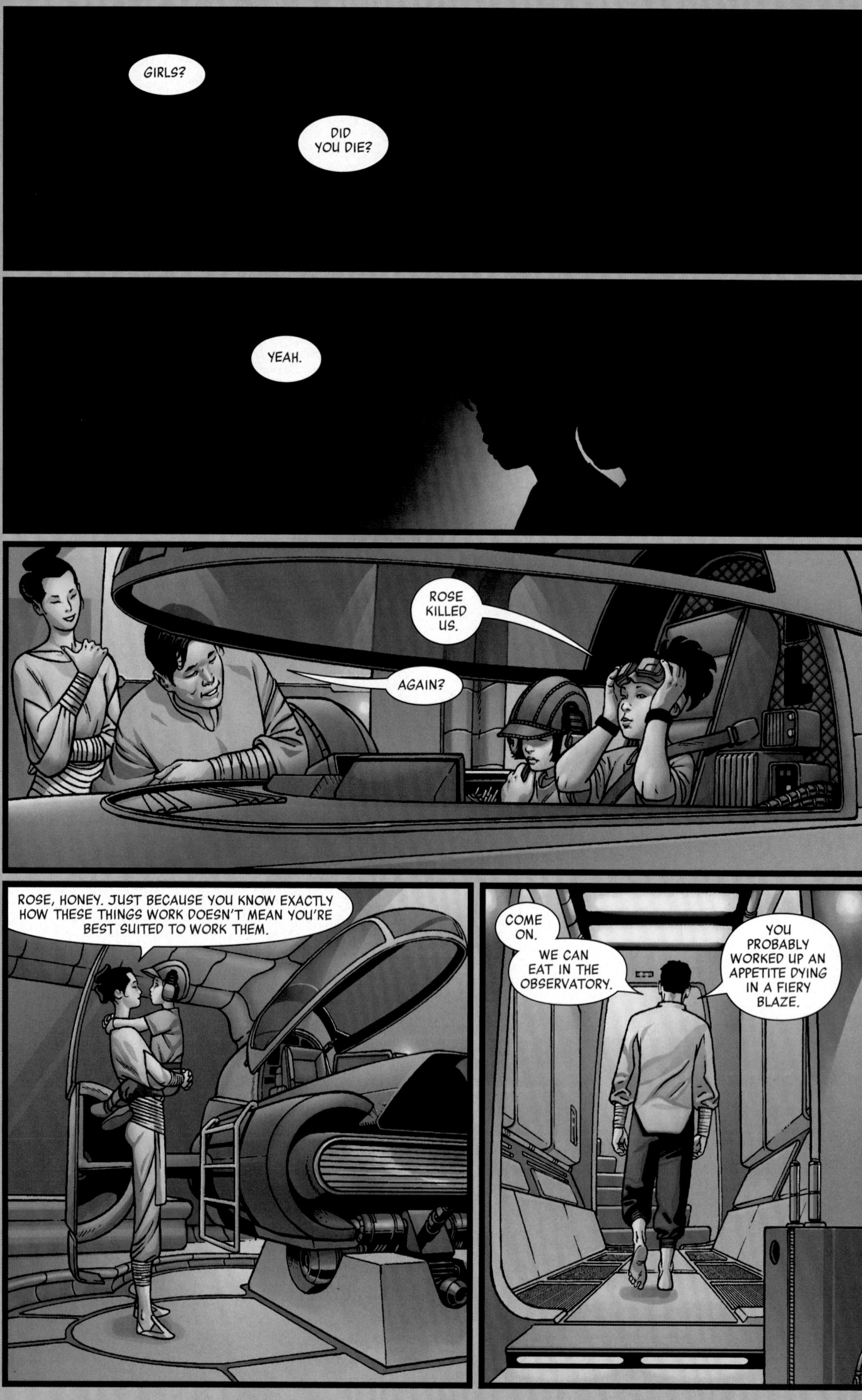

GIRLS?
DID YOU DIE?
YEAH.
ROSE KILLED US.
AGAIN?
ROSE, HONEY. JUST BECAUSE YOU KNOW EXACTLY HOW THESE THINGS WORK DOESN'T MEAN YOU'RE BEST SUITED TO WORK THEM.
COME ON.
WE CAN EAT IN THE OBSERVATORY.
YOU PROBABLY WORKED UP AN APPETITE DYING IN A FIERY BLAZE.

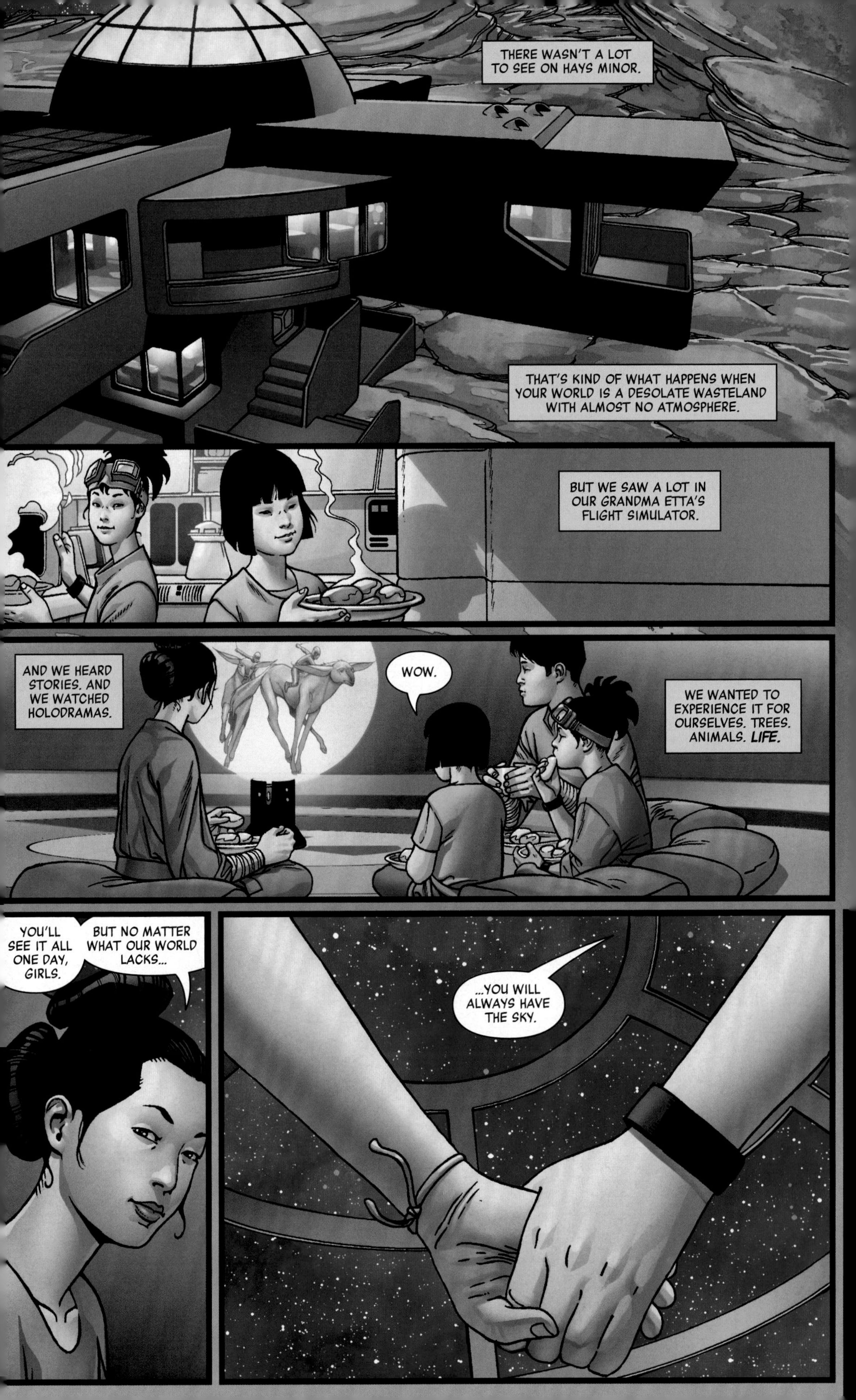
THERE WASN'T A LOT TO SEE ON HAYS MINOR.
THAT'S KIND OF WHAT HAPPENS WHEN YOUR WORLD IS A DESOLATE WASTELAND WITH ALMOST NO ATMOSPHERE.
BUT WE SAW A LOT IN OUR GRANDMA ETTA'S FLIGHT SIMULATOR.
AND WE HEARD STORIES. AND WE WATCHED HOLODRAMAS.
WOW.
WE WANTED TO EXPERIENCE IT FOR OURSELVES. TREES. ANIMALS. LIFE.
YOU'LL SEE IT ALL ONE DAY, GIRLS.
BUT NO MATTER WHAT OUR WORLD LACKS...
...YOU WILL ALWAYS HAVE THE SKY.

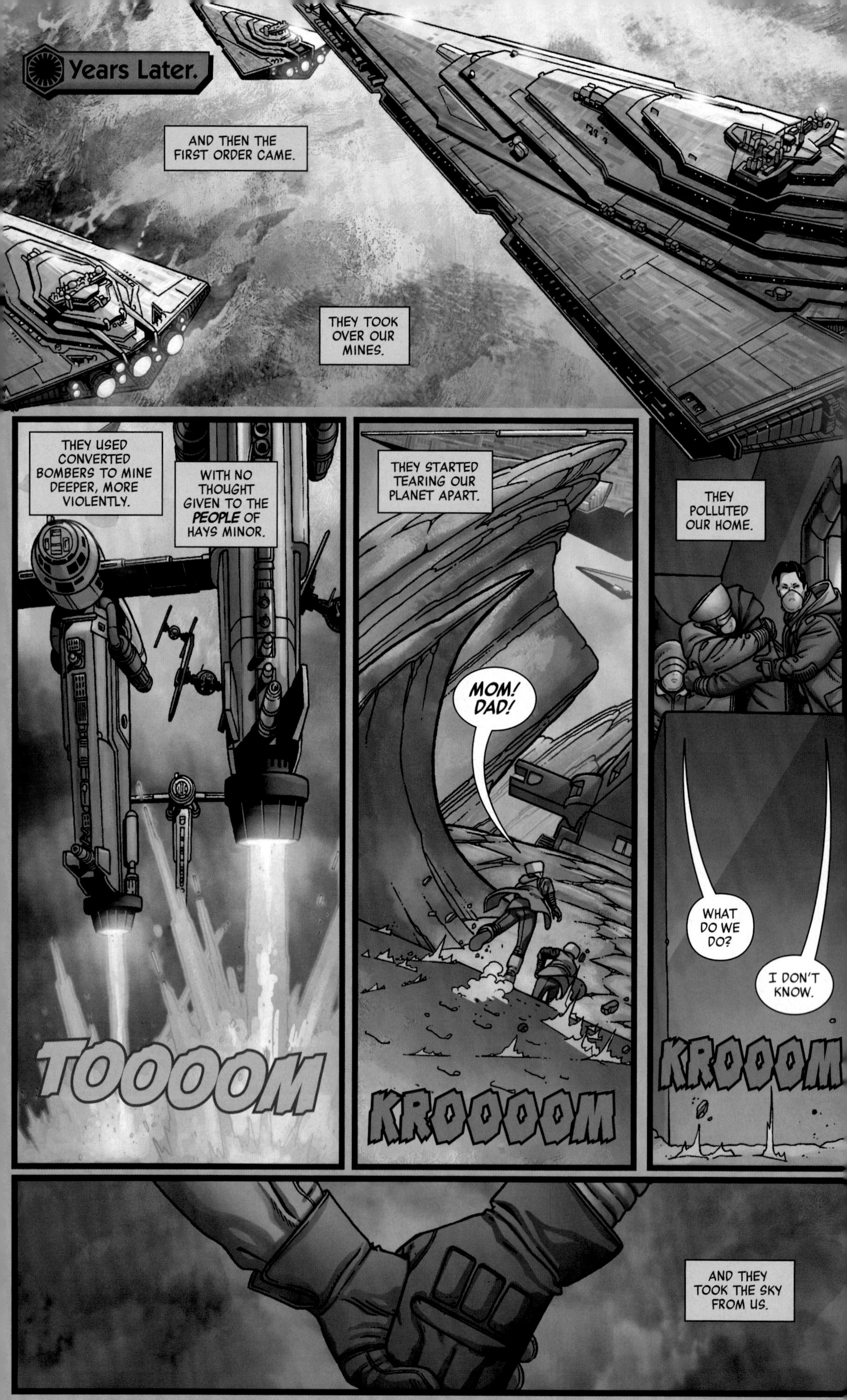
Years Later.
AND THEN THE FIRST ORDER CAME.
THEY TOOK OVER OUR MINES.
THEY USED CONVERTED BOMBERS TO MINE DEEPER, MORE VIOLENTLY.
WITH NO THOUGHT GIVEN TO THE *PEOPLE* OF HAYS MINOR.
TOOOOM
THEY STARTED TEARING OUR PLANET APART.
MOM! DAD!
KROOOOM
THEY POLLUTED OUR HOME.
WHAT DO WE DO?
I DON'T KNOW.
KROOOM
AND THEY TOOK THE SKY FROM US.

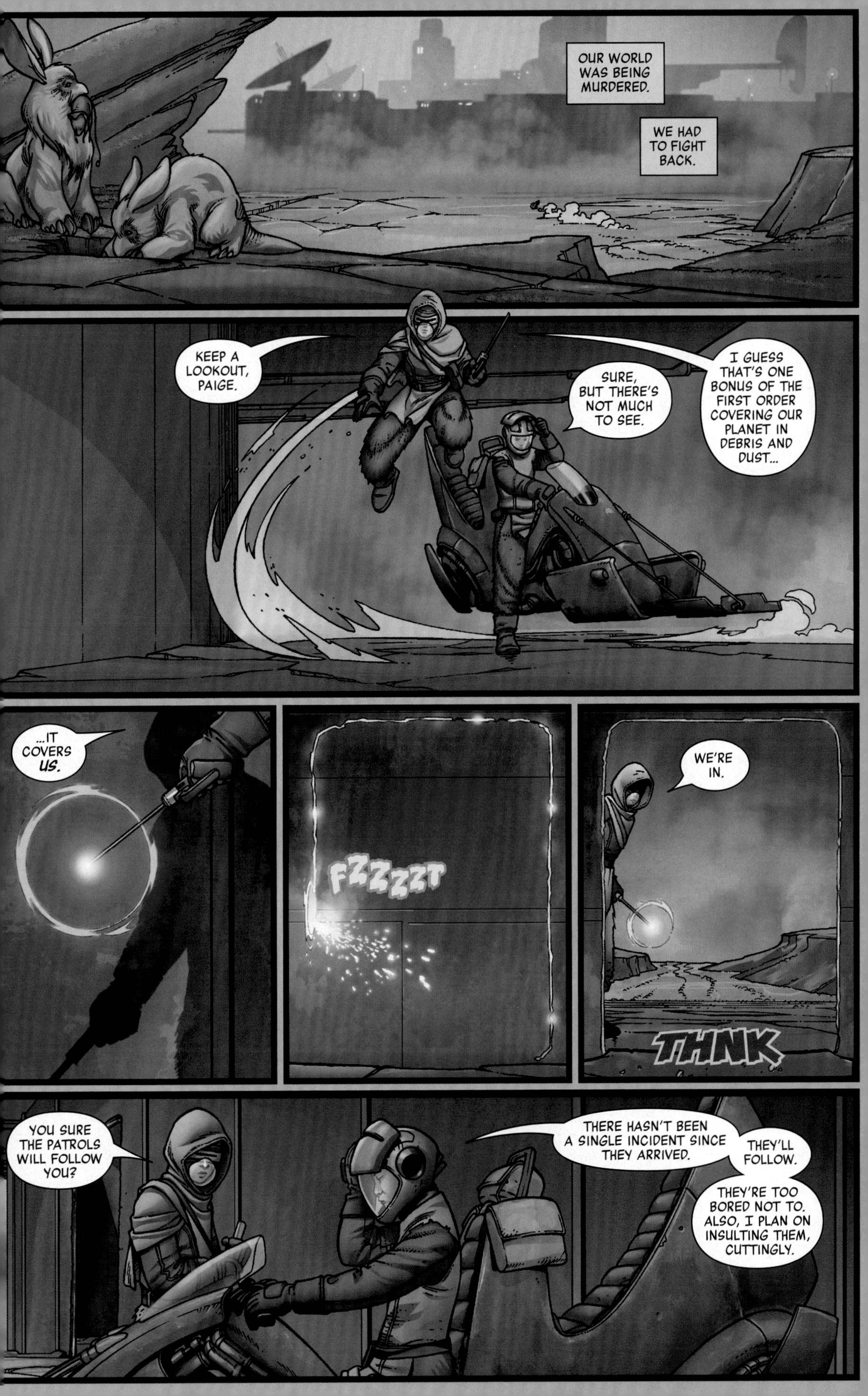
OUR WORLD WAS BEING MURDERED.
WE HAD TO FIGHT BACK.
KEEP A LOOKOUT, PAIGE.
SURE, BUT THERE'S NOT MUCH TO SEE.
I GUESS THAT'S ONE BONUS OF THE FIRST ORDER COVERING OUR PLANET IN DEBRIS AND DUST...
...IT COVERS US.
FZZZZT
WE'RE IN.
THNK
YOU SURE THE PATROLS WILL FOLLOW YOU?
THERE HASN'T BEEN A SINGLE INCIDENT SINCE THEY ARRIVED.
THEY'LL FOLLOW.
THEY'RE TOO BORED NOT TO. ALSO, I PLAN ON INSULTING THEM, CUTTINGLY.

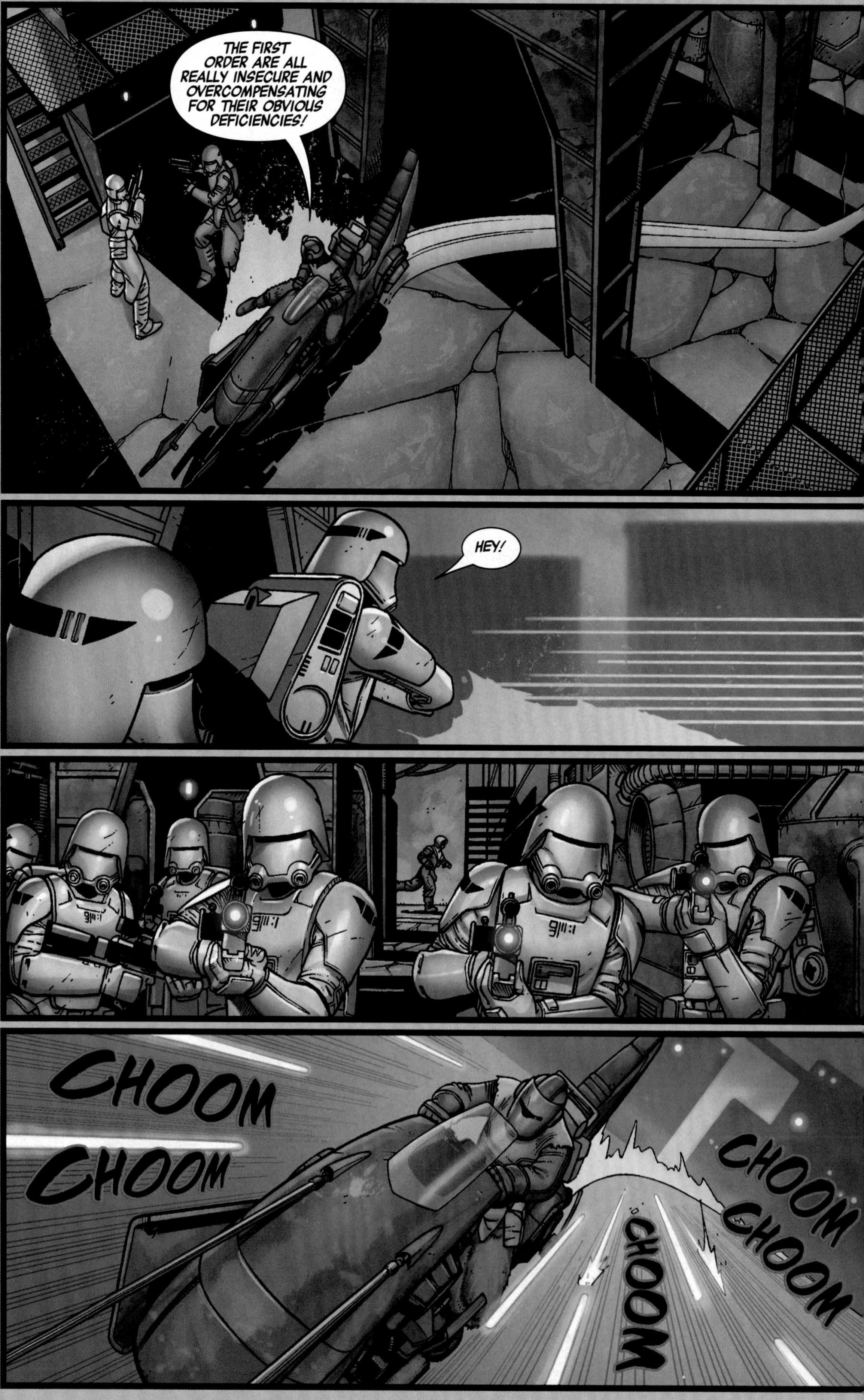
THE FIRST ORDER ARE ALL REALLY INSECURE AND OVERCOMPENSATING FOR THEIR OBVIOUS DEFICIENCIES!
HEY!
CHOOM
CHOOM
CHOOM
CHOOM
CHOOM
CHOOM

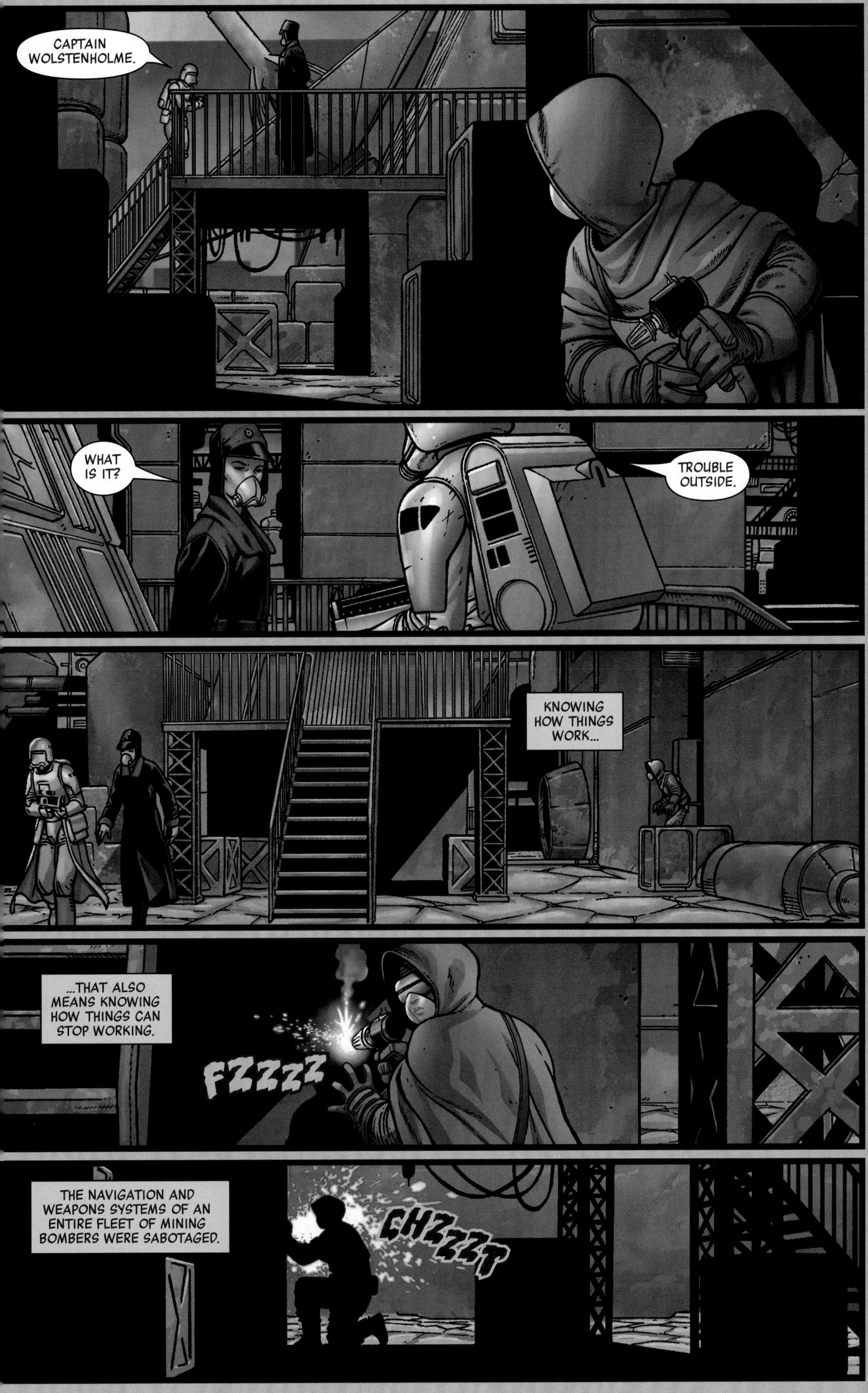
CAPTAIN WOLSTENHOLME.
WHAT IS IT?
TROUBLE OUTSIDE.
KNOWING HOW THINGS WORK...
...THAT ALSO MEANS KNOWING HOW THINGS CAN STOP WORKING.
FZZZZ
THE NAVIGATION AND WEAPONS SYSTEMS OF AN ENTIRE FLEET OF MINING BOMBERS WERE SABOTAGED.
CHZZZT

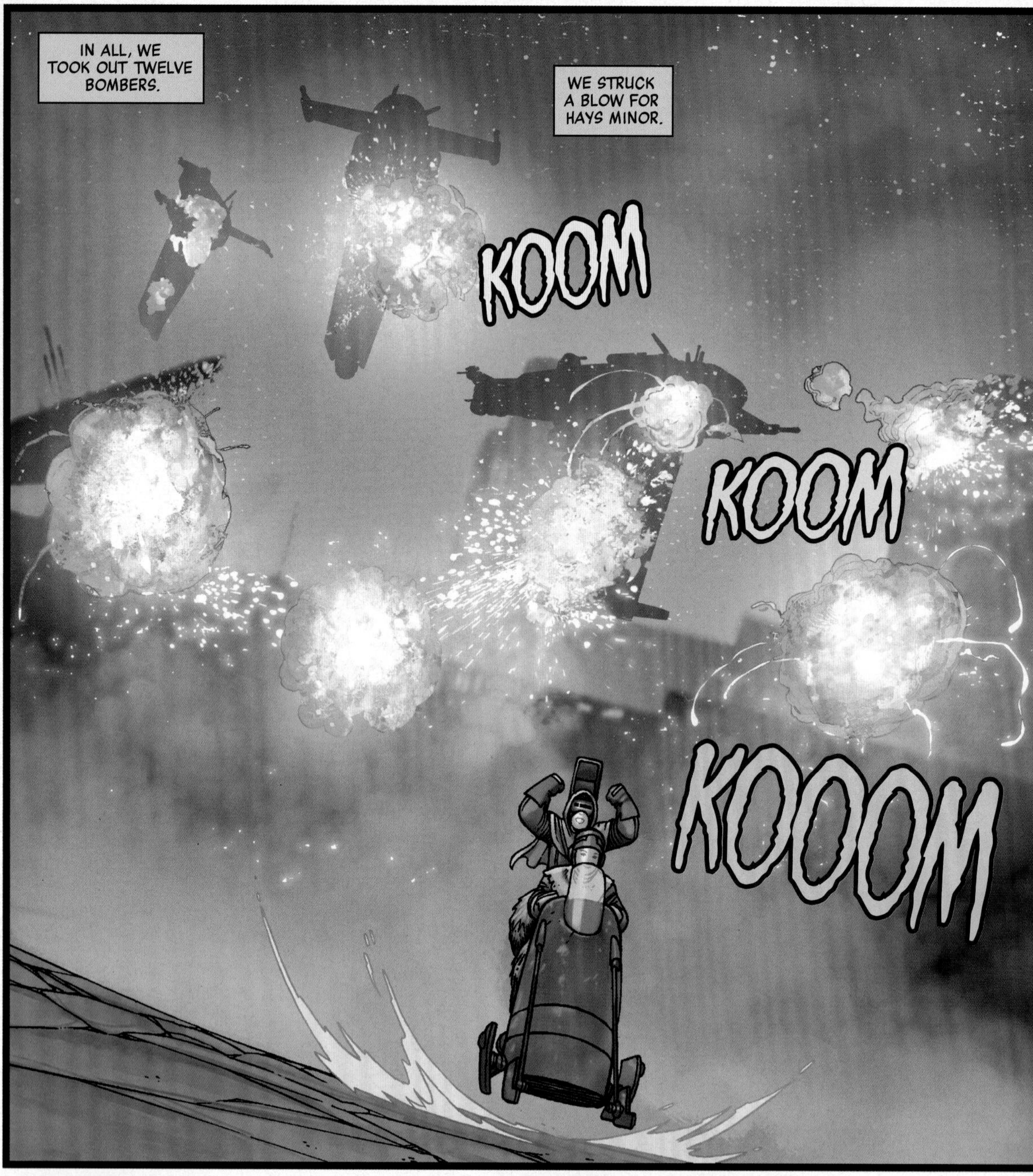
IN ALL, WE TOOK OUT TWELVE BOMBERS.
WE STRUCK A BLOW FOR HAYS MINOR.
KOOM
KOOM
KOOOM

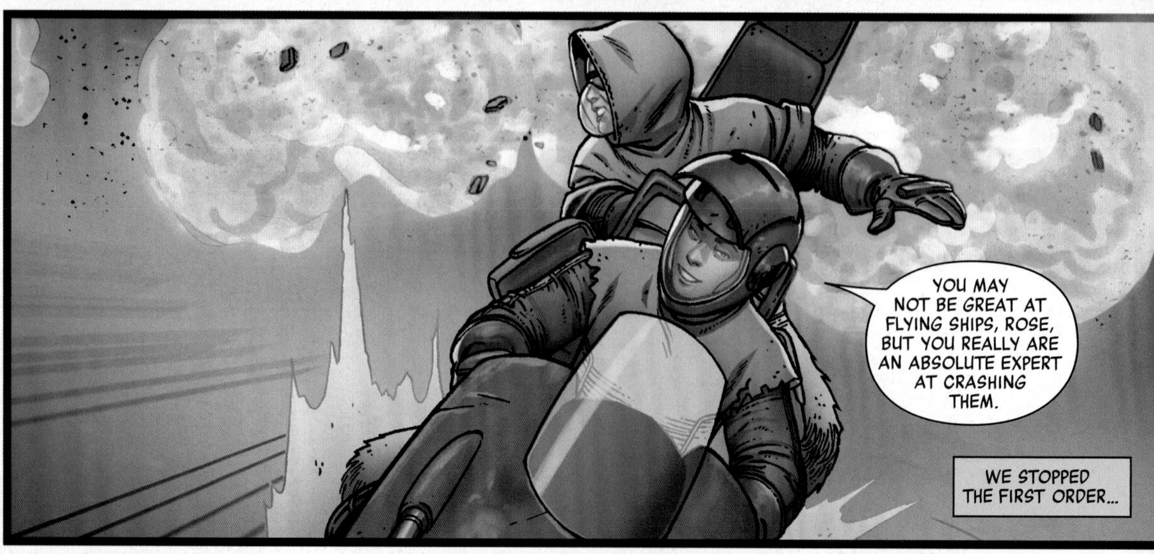
YOU MAY NOT BE GREAT AT FLYING SHIPS, ROSE, BUT YOU REALLY ARE AN ABSOLUTE EXPERT AT CRASHING THEM.
WE STOPPED THE FIRST ORDER...

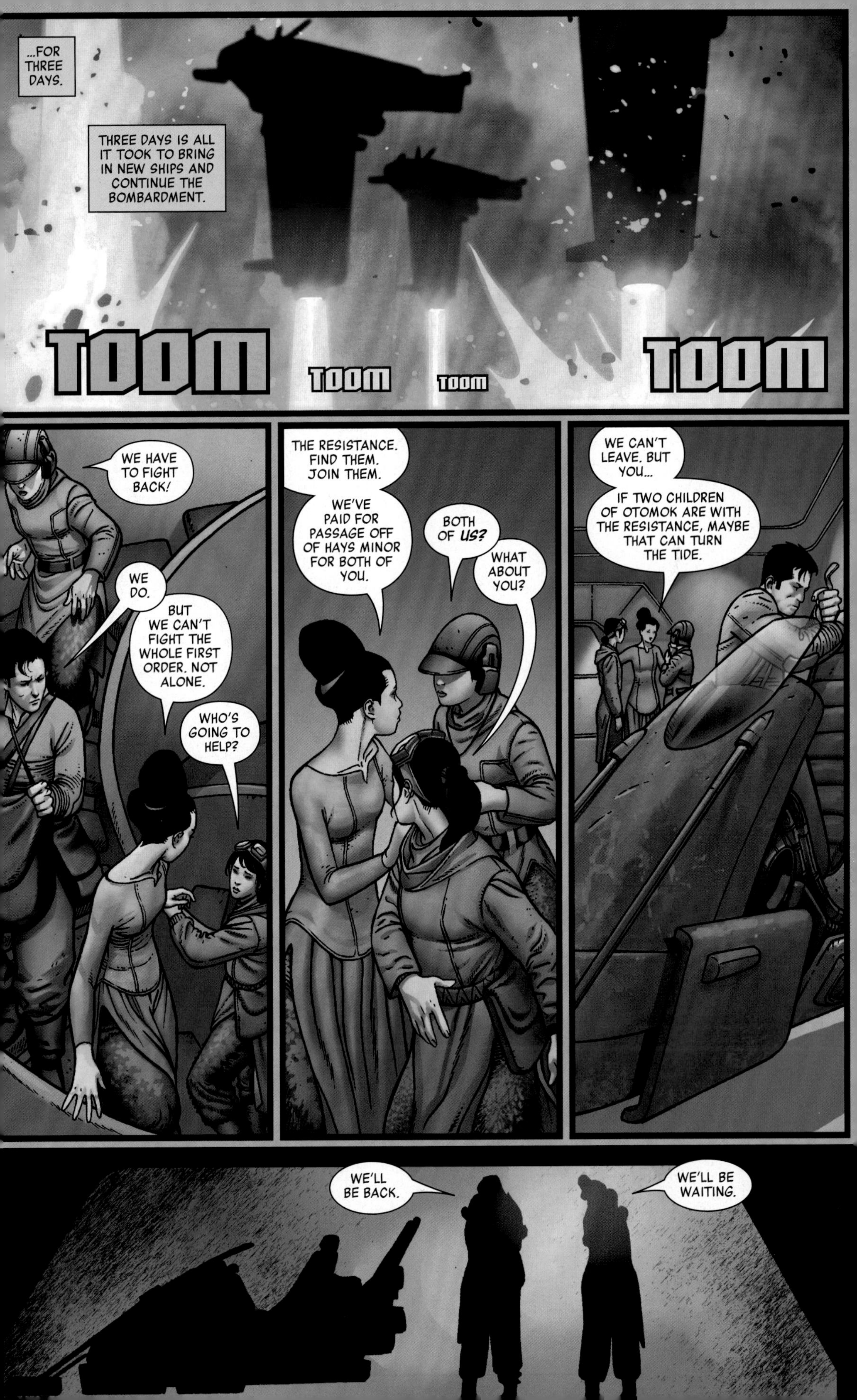
...FOR THREE DAYS.
THREE DAYS IS ALL IT TOOK TO BRING IN NEW SHIPS AND CONTINUE THE BOMBARDMENT.
TOOM
TOOM
TOOM
TOOM
WE HAVE TO FIGHT BACK!
WE DO.
BUT WE CAN'T FIGHT THE WHOLE FIRST ORDER. NOT ALONE.
WHO'S GOING TO HELP?
THE RESISTANCE. FIND THEM. JOIN THEM.
WE'VE PAID FOR PASSAGE OFF OF HAYS MINOR FOR BOTH OF YOU.
BOTH OF US?
WHAT ABOUT YOU?
WE CAN'T LEAVE. BUT YOU...
IF TWO CHILDREN OF OTOMOK ARE WITH THE RESISTANCE, MAYBE THAT CAN TURN THE TIDE.
WE'LL BE BACK.
WE'LL BE WAITING.

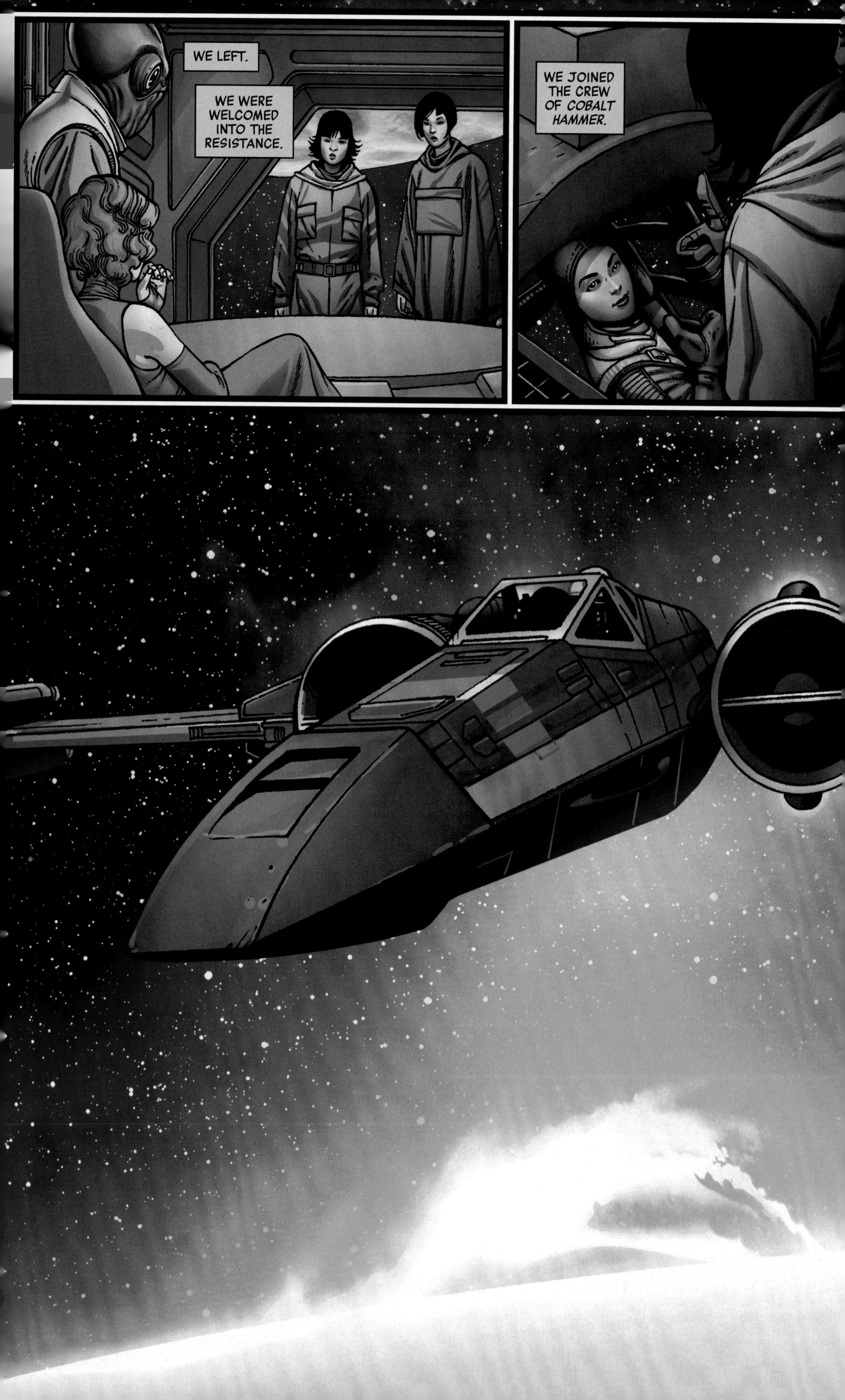
WE LEFT.
WE WERE WELCOMED INTO THE RESISTANCE.
WE JOINED THE CREW OF *COBALT HAMMER*.

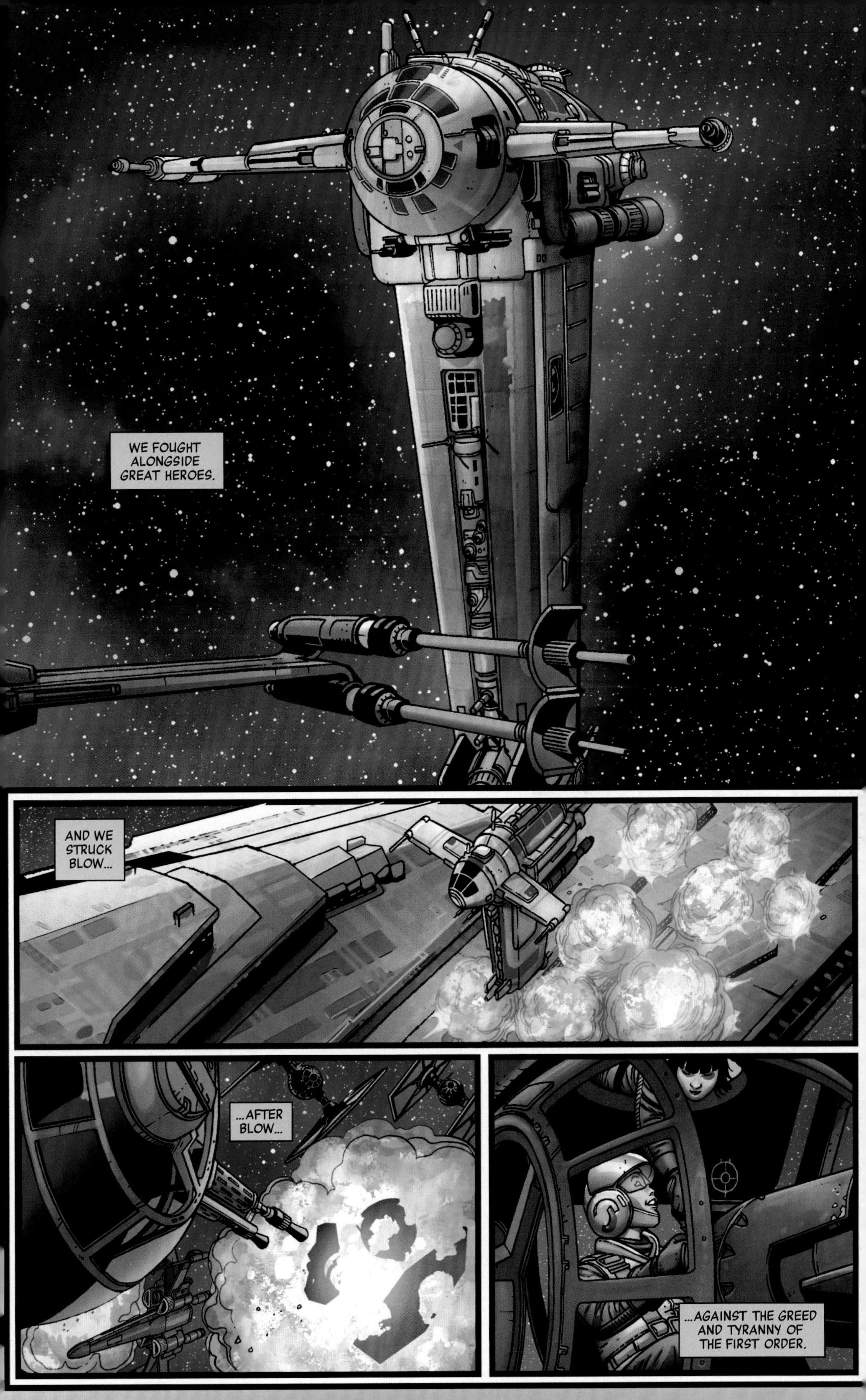
WE FOUGHT ALONGSIDE GREAT HEROES.
AND WE STRUCK BLOW...
...AFTER BLOW...
...AGAINST THE GREED AND TYRANNY OF THE FIRST ORDER.

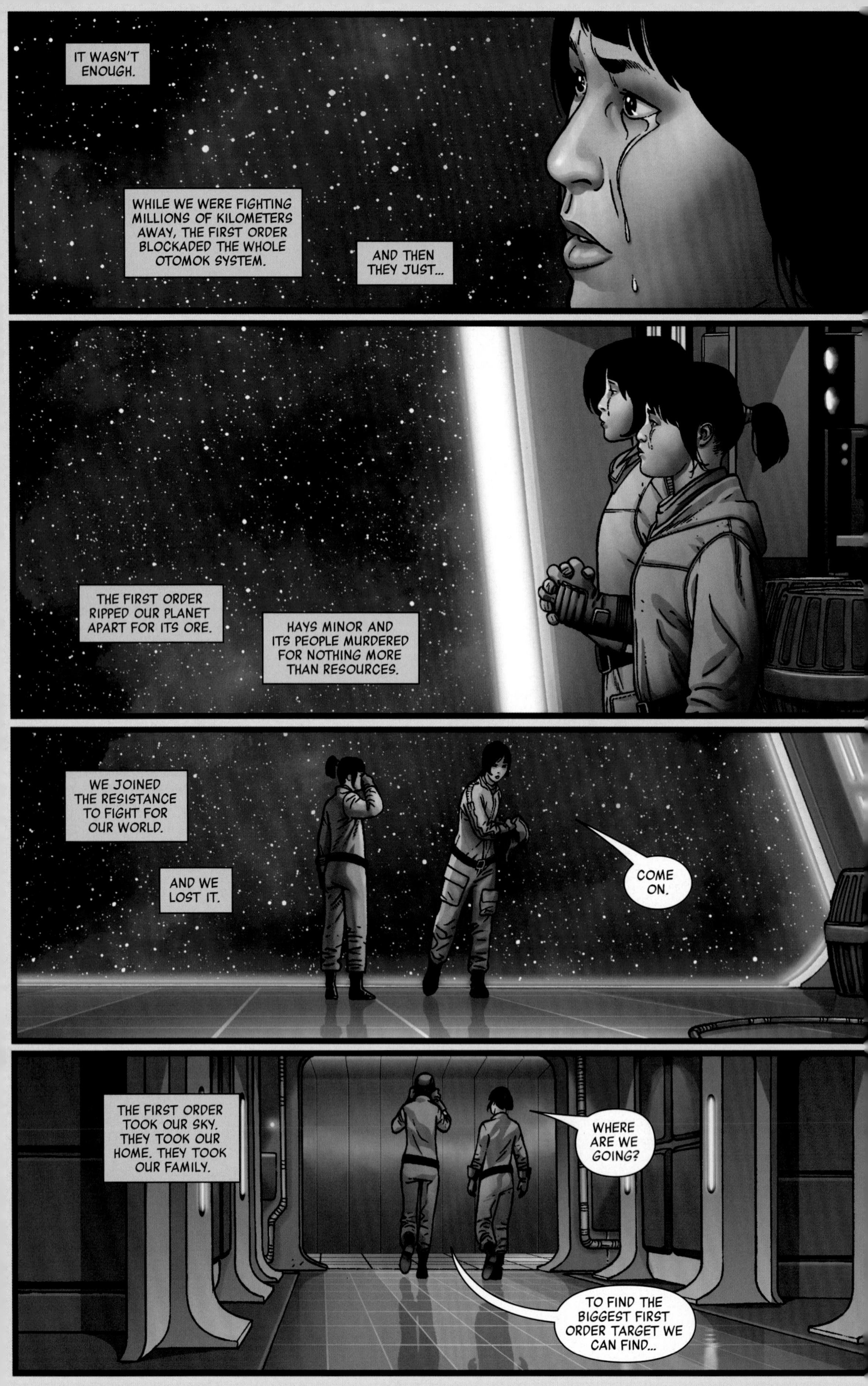
IT WASN'T ENOUGH.
WHILE WE WERE FIGHTING MILLIONS OF KILOMETERS AWAY, THE FIRST ORDER BLOCKADED THE WHOLE OTOMOK SYSTEM.
AND THEN THEY JUST...
THE FIRST ORDER RIPPED OUR PLANET APART FOR ITS ORE.
HAYS MINOR AND ITS PEOPLE MURDERED FOR NOTHING MORE THAN RESOURCES.
WE JOINED THE RESISTANCE TO FIGHT FOR OUR WORLD.
AND WE LOST IT.
COME ON.
THE FIRST ORDER TOOK OUR SKY. THEY TOOK OUR HOME. THEY TOOK OUR FAMILY.
WHERE ARE WE GOING?
TO FIND THE BIGGEST FIRST ORDER TARGET WE CAN FIND...

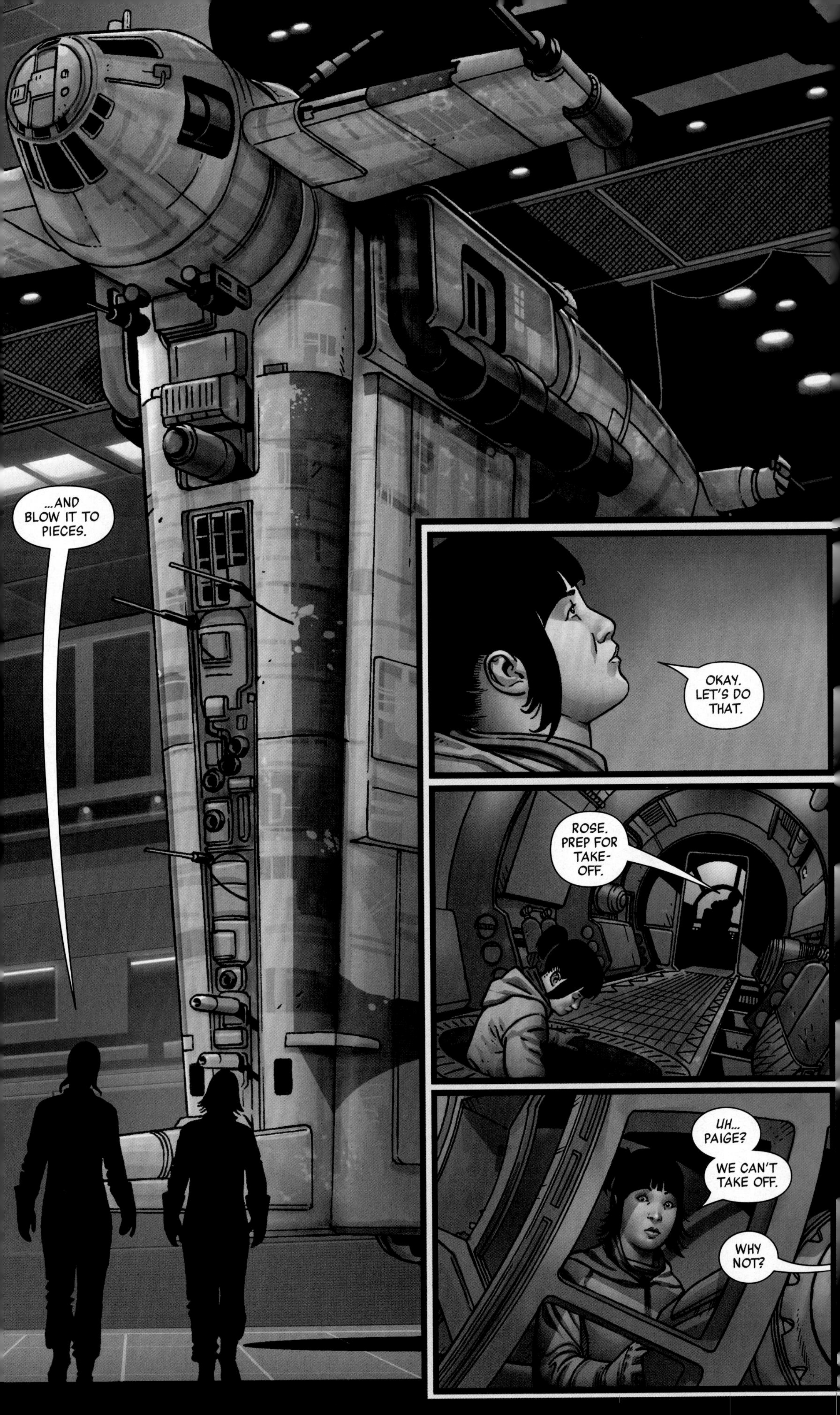
...AND BLOW IT TO PIECES.
OKAY. LET'S DO THAT.
ROSE. PREP FOR TAKE-OFF.
UH... PAIGE?
WE CAN'T TAKE OFF.
WHY NOT?

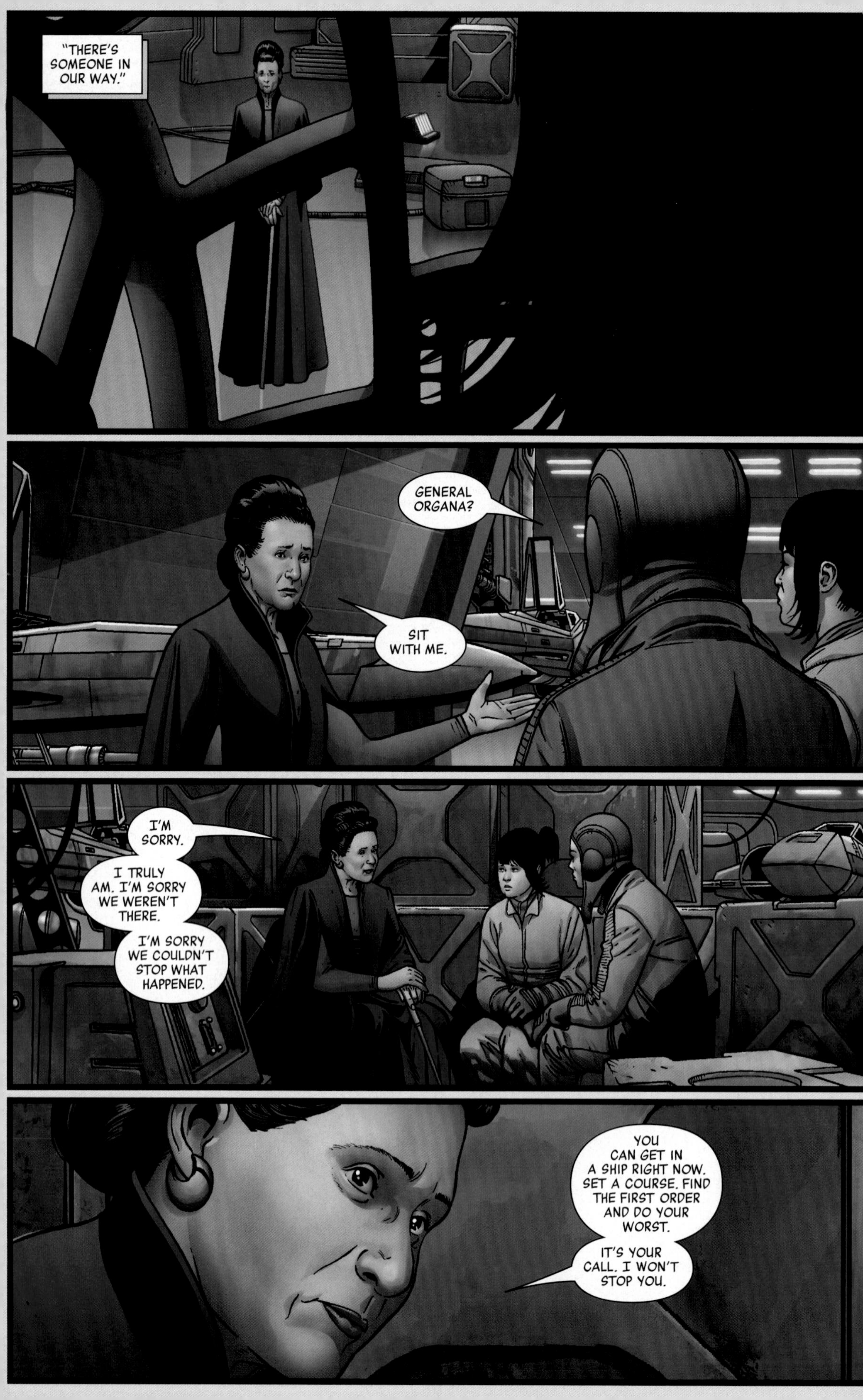
"THERE'S SOMEONE IN OUR WAY."
GENERAL ORGANA?
SIT WITH ME.
I'M SORRY.
I TRULY AM. I'M SORRY WE WEREN'T THERE.
I'M SORRY WE COULDN'T STOP WHAT HAPPENED.
YOU CAN GET IN A SHIP RIGHT NOW. SET A COURSE. FIND THE FIRST ORDER AND DO YOUR WORST.
IT'S YOUR CALL. I WON'T STOP YOU.

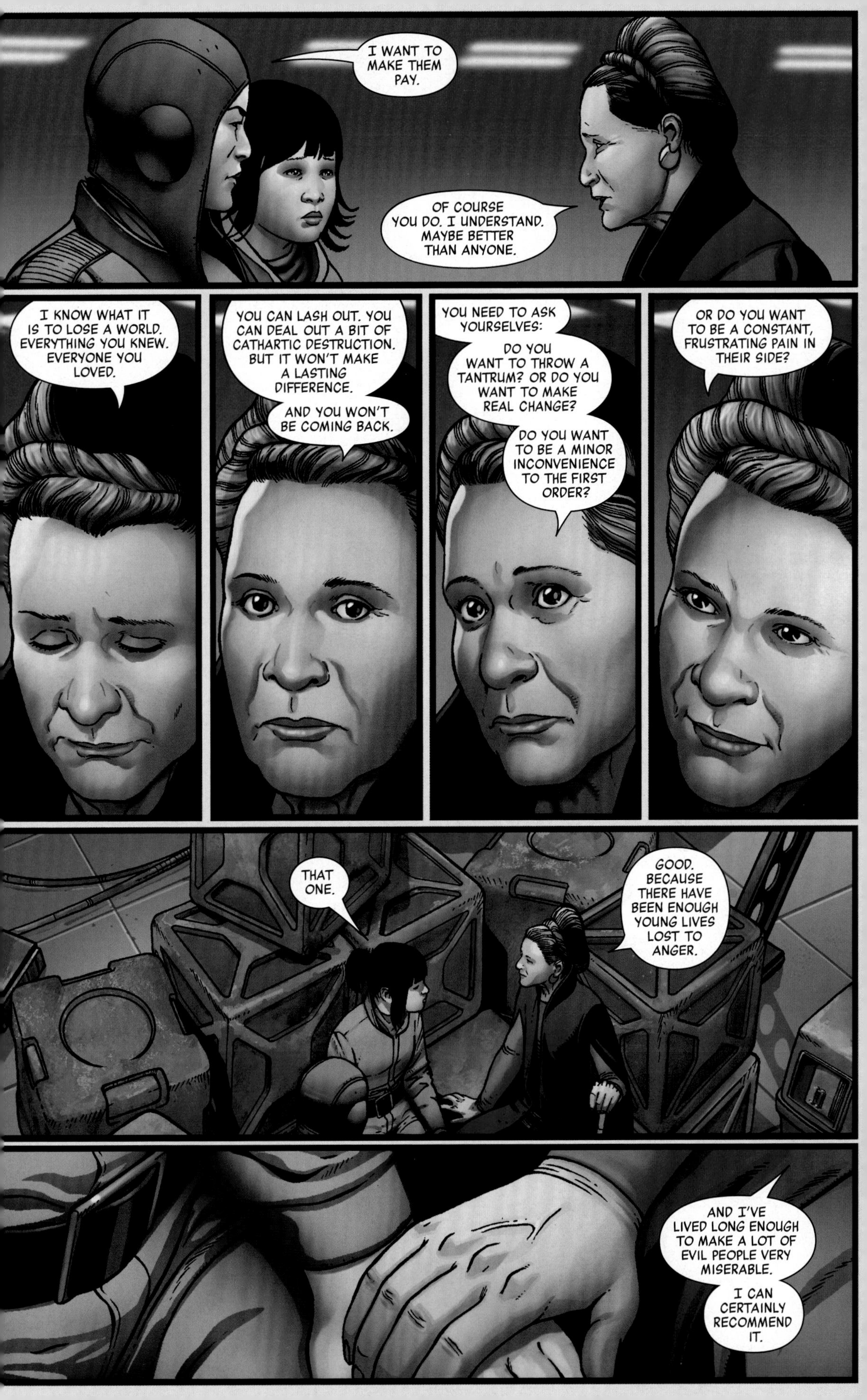
I WANT TO MAKE THEM PAY.
OF COURSE YOU DO. I UNDERSTAND. MAYBE BETTER THAN ANYONE.
I KNOW WHAT IT IS TO LOSE A WORLD. EVERYTHING YOU KNEW. EVERYONE YOU LOVED.
YOU CAN LASH OUT. YOU CAN DEAL OUT A BIT OF CATHARTIC DESTRUCTION. BUT IT WON'T MAKE A LASTING DIFFERENCE.
AND YOU WON'T BE COMING BACK.
YOU NEED TO ASK YOURSELVES:
DO YOU WANT TO THROW A TANTRUM? OR DO YOU WANT TO MAKE REAL CHANGE?
DO YOU WANT TO BE A MINOR INCONVENIENCE TO THE FIRST ORDER?
OR DO YOU WANT TO BE A CONSTANT, FRUSTRATING PAIN IN THEIR SIDE?
THAT ONE.
GOOD. BECAUSE THERE HAVE BEEN ENOUGH YOUNG LIVES LOST TO ANGER.
AND I'VE LIVED LONG ENOUGH TO MAKE A LOT OF EVIL PEOPLE VERY MISERABLE.
I CAN CERTAINLY RECOMMEND IT.

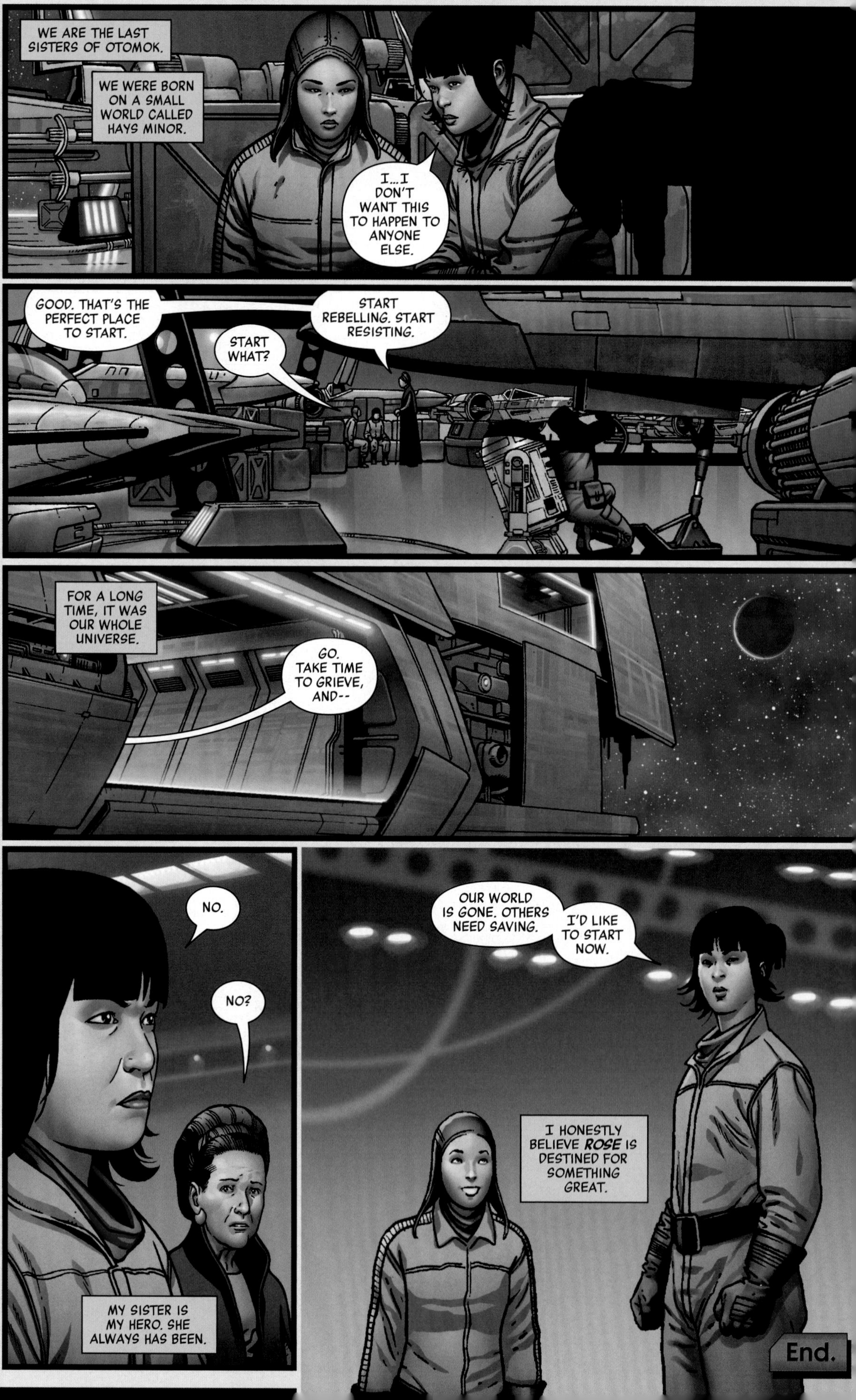
WE ARE THE LAST SISTERS OF OTOMOK.
WE WERE BORN ON A SMALL WORLD CALLED HAYS MINOR.
I...I DON'T WANT THIS TO HAPPEN TO ANYONE ELSE.
GOOD. THAT'S THE PERFECT PLACE TO START.
START WHAT?
START REBELLING. START RESISTING.
FOR A LONG TIME, IT WAS OUR WHOLE UNIVERSE.
GO. TAKE TIME TO GRIEVE, AND--
NO.
NO?
MY SISTER IS MY HERO. SHE ALWAYS HAS BEEN.
OUR WORLD IS GONE. OTHERS NEED SAVING.
I'D LIKE TO START NOW.
I HONESTLY BELIEVE ROSE IS DESTINED FOR SOMETHING GREAT.
End.

AGE OF RESISTANCE
Rose Tico: A Resistance Hero Worth Fighting For
By Bria LaVorgna

"Are you okay?" a random stranger in the crowd gathered around the *Star Wars* Show stage asked me at *Star Wars* Celebration Orlando in 2017. "Do you, like, know her or something?"

The "her" in question was Kelly Marie Tran. I didn't, of course. At that point, most *Star Wars* fans could barely even say that we knew who Tran was until director Rian Johnson introduced her to us during *The Last Jedi* panel as the actress playing Rose Tico, a maintenance worker in the Resistance. At some point during Tran's moment in the spotlight on stage, I ended up sitting down on my heels with my face in my hands. I don't know if it was when they first showed a picture of her in costume or when Johnson drew a comparison between her character and Luke Skywalker, saying, "The notion that any of us can step up and turn into a hero, that's really where the character of Rose comes from." But at some point, I ended up so obviously emotionally overwhelmed at seeing an Asian woman prominently featured in a *Star Wars* film that a stranger felt the need to check on me. With the advent of the sequel trilogy came more diverse casting within the galaxy far, far away

than ever before. Seeing faces like Oscar Isaac's and John Boyega's were welcome indeed as had been the majority of the main cast of *Rogue One,* but with Kelly Marie Tran, I finally could see a woman in the Resistance whose face looked like my mother's. And I immediately loved Rose Tico with my entire heart.

The character of Rose Tico wasn't always quite like the one we ultimately saw on screen. She started life on the page as a "grumpy Eeyore type." According to his director's commentary on *The Last Jedi,* Johnson rewrote the role to reflect Tran's natural enthusiasm, making her "a much more open-hearted character that was a reflection of Kelly." In a world with lightsabers and starships, Rose is decidedly human. From her love of animals to her disappointment in one of her personal heroes after he doesn't quite live up to her expectations. When we first meet her in *The Last Jedi,* she's mourning the death of her older sister, Paige, who'd just given her life to take out a First Order dreadnaught. The sisters were presumed orphans from Hays Minor who joined the Resistance to try to help stop the First Order from ruining any other worlds like theirs.

Despite being mechanically gifted, Rose lived in her sister's shadow, often struggling to convince herself to step out even though Paige always knew she could be a hero. She just needed a push and the chance. Rose, along with her compatriots in the Resistance, is a reminder that we could all be that hero.

My answer to that concerned stranger at Celebration wasn't much more than some squeaked words about representation and being really happy to see Kelly Marie Tran on the stage. I have a far better one now though. In the years since, we've gotten to know both Rose and her actress better. We've watched the first part of Rose Tico's story and saw how emotional Tran was every step of the way, fully cognizant of what her character meant to so many Asian American women who hadn't previously seen themselves in the franchise they loved. "That's how we're going to win," Rose says to Finn, "not fighting what we hate, saving what we love." To me, Rose Tico is hope, and she is a hero, and she's just what *Star Wars* needed.

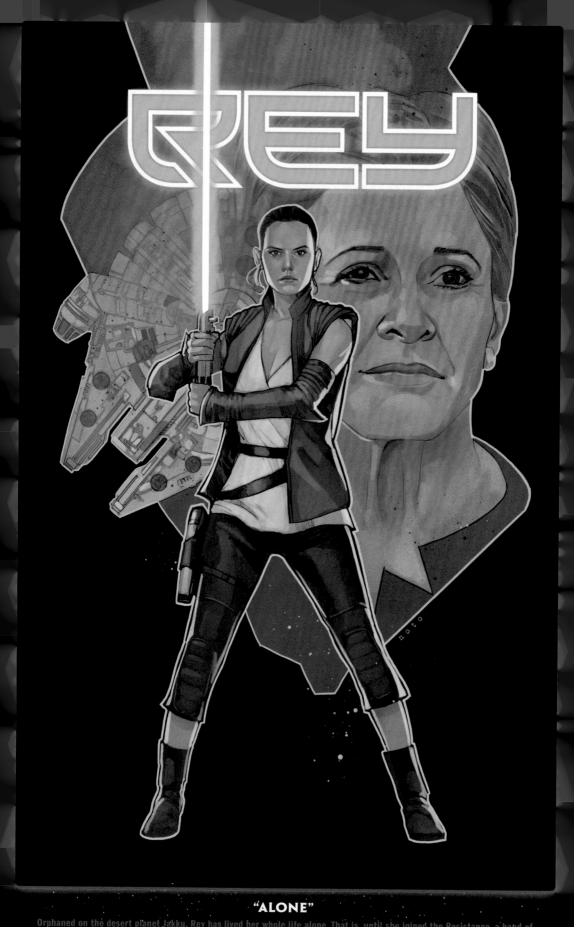

"ALONE"

Orphaned on the desert planet Jakku, Rey has lived her whole life alone. That is, until she joined the Resistance, a band of intergalactic freedom fighters who defend the galaxy from the villainous First Order. Now she may be the Resistance's last hope as

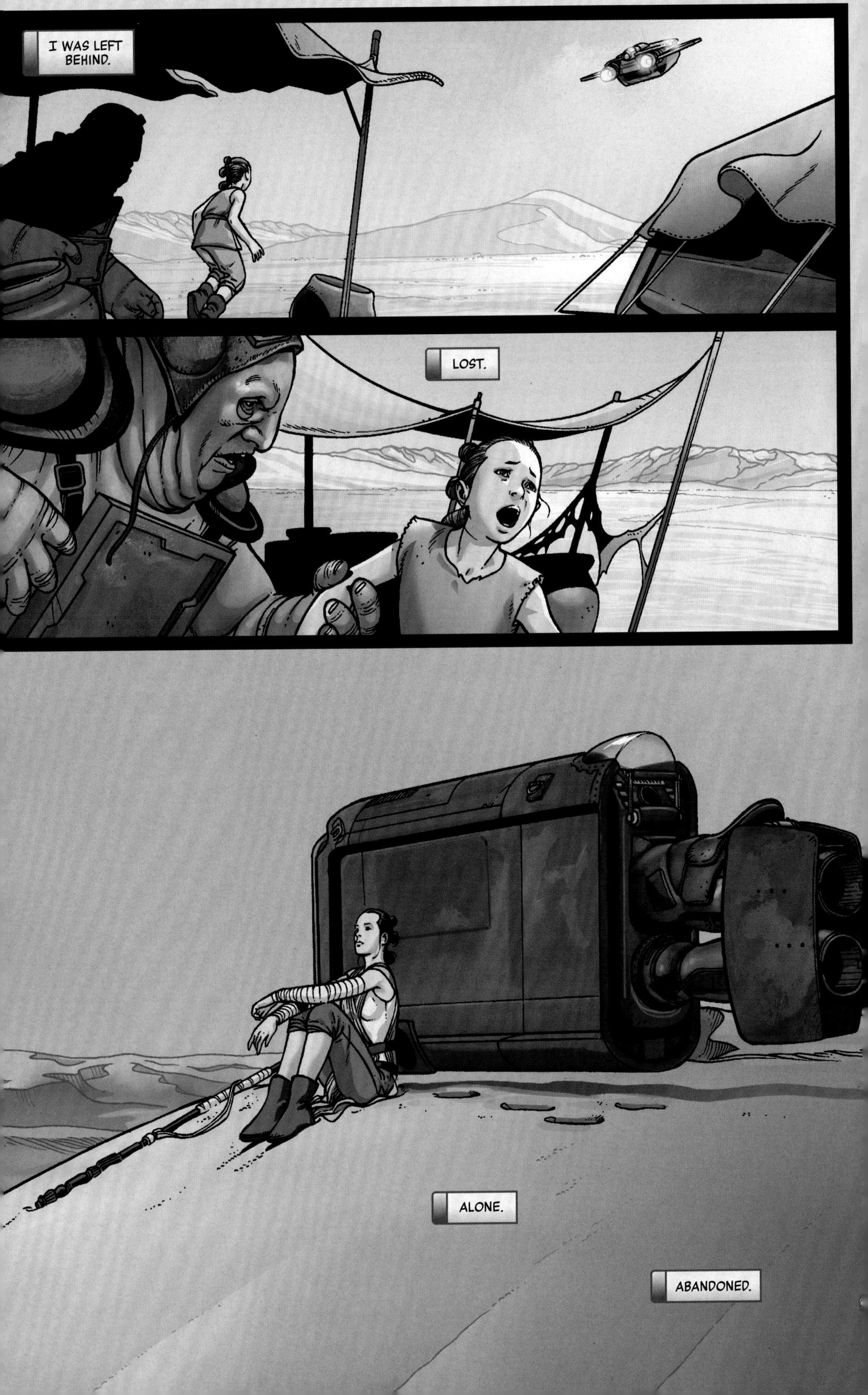
I WAS LEFT BEHIND.
LOST.
ALONE.
ABANDONED.

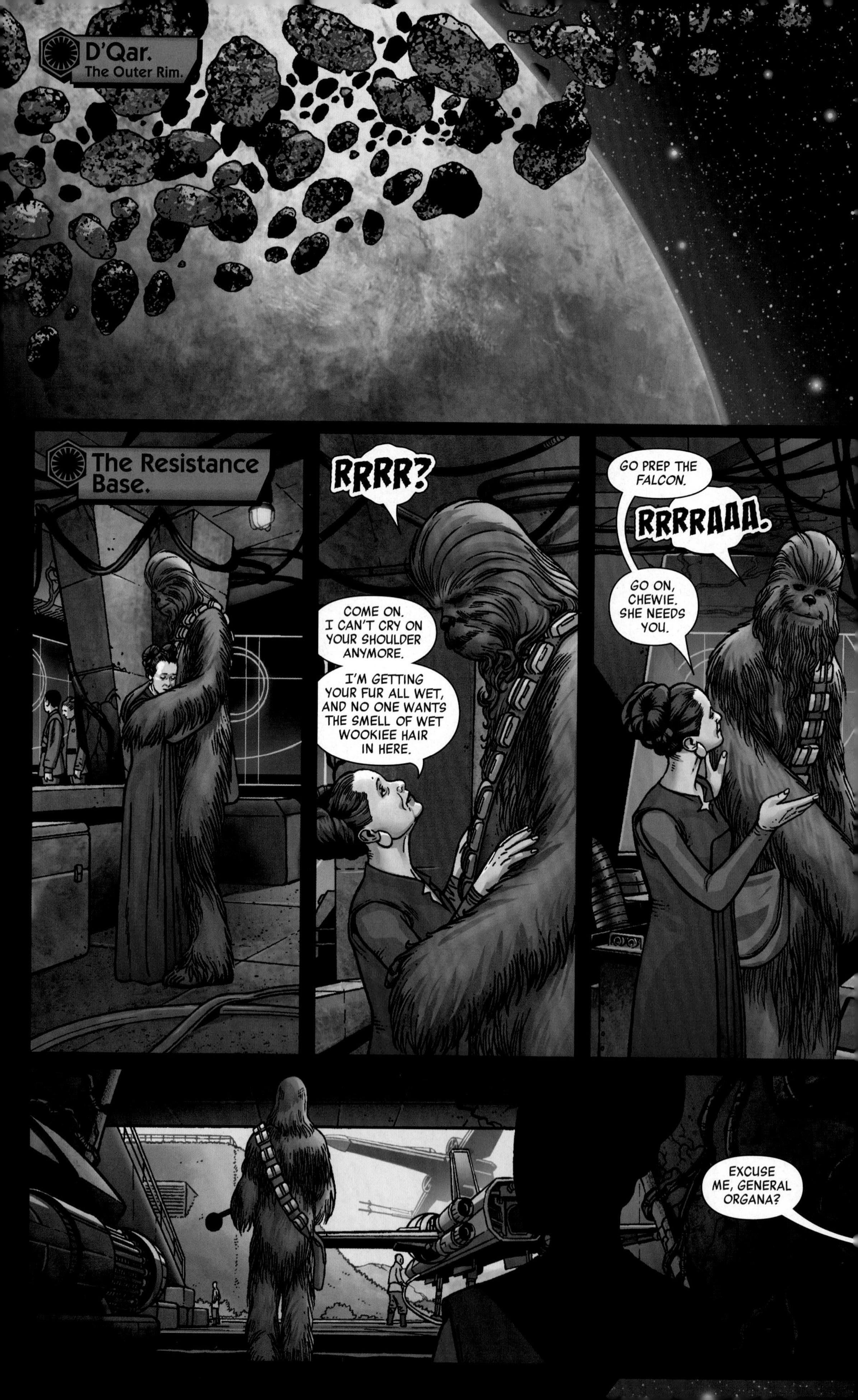
D'Qar.
The Outer Rim.
The Resistance Base.
RRRR?
COME ON. I CAN'T CRY ON YOUR SHOULDER ANYMORE.
I'M GETTING YOUR FUR ALL WET, AND NO ONE WANTS THE SMELL OF WET WOOKIEE HAIR IN HERE.
GO PREP THE FALCON.
RRRRAAA.
GO ON, CHEWIE. SHE NEEDS YOU.
EXCUSE ME, GENERAL ORGANA?

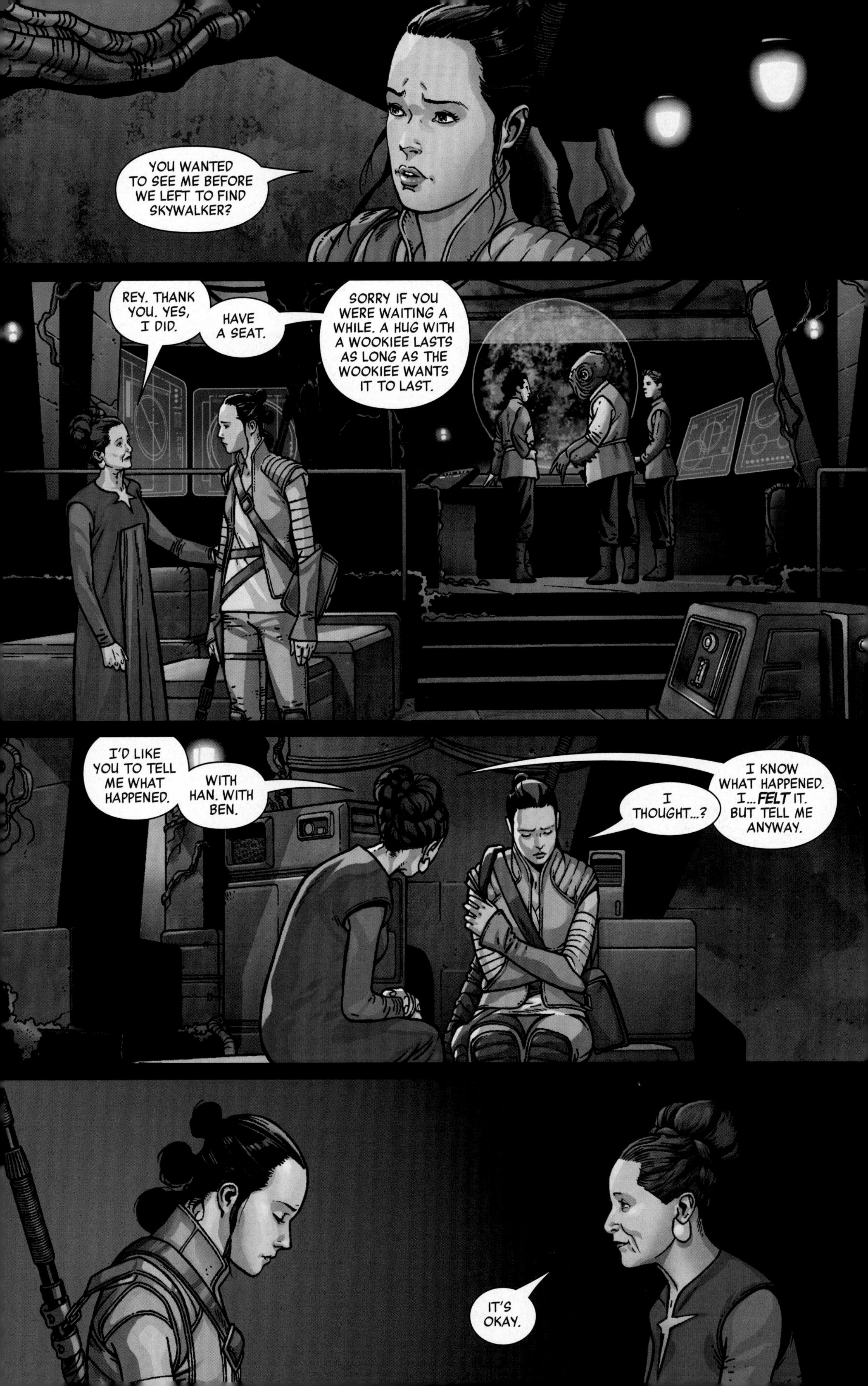
YOU WANTED TO SEE ME BEFORE WE LEFT TO FIND SKYWALKER?
REY. THANK YOU. YES, I DID.
HAVE A SEAT.
SORRY IF YOU WERE WAITING A WHILE. A HUG WITH A WOOKIEE LASTS AS LONG AS THE WOOKIEE WANTS IT TO LAST.
I'D LIKE YOU TO TELL ME WHAT HAPPENED.
WITH HAN. WITH BEN.
I THOUGHT...?
I KNOW WHAT HAPPENED. I...*FELT* IT. BUT TELL ME ANYWAY.
IT'S OKAY.

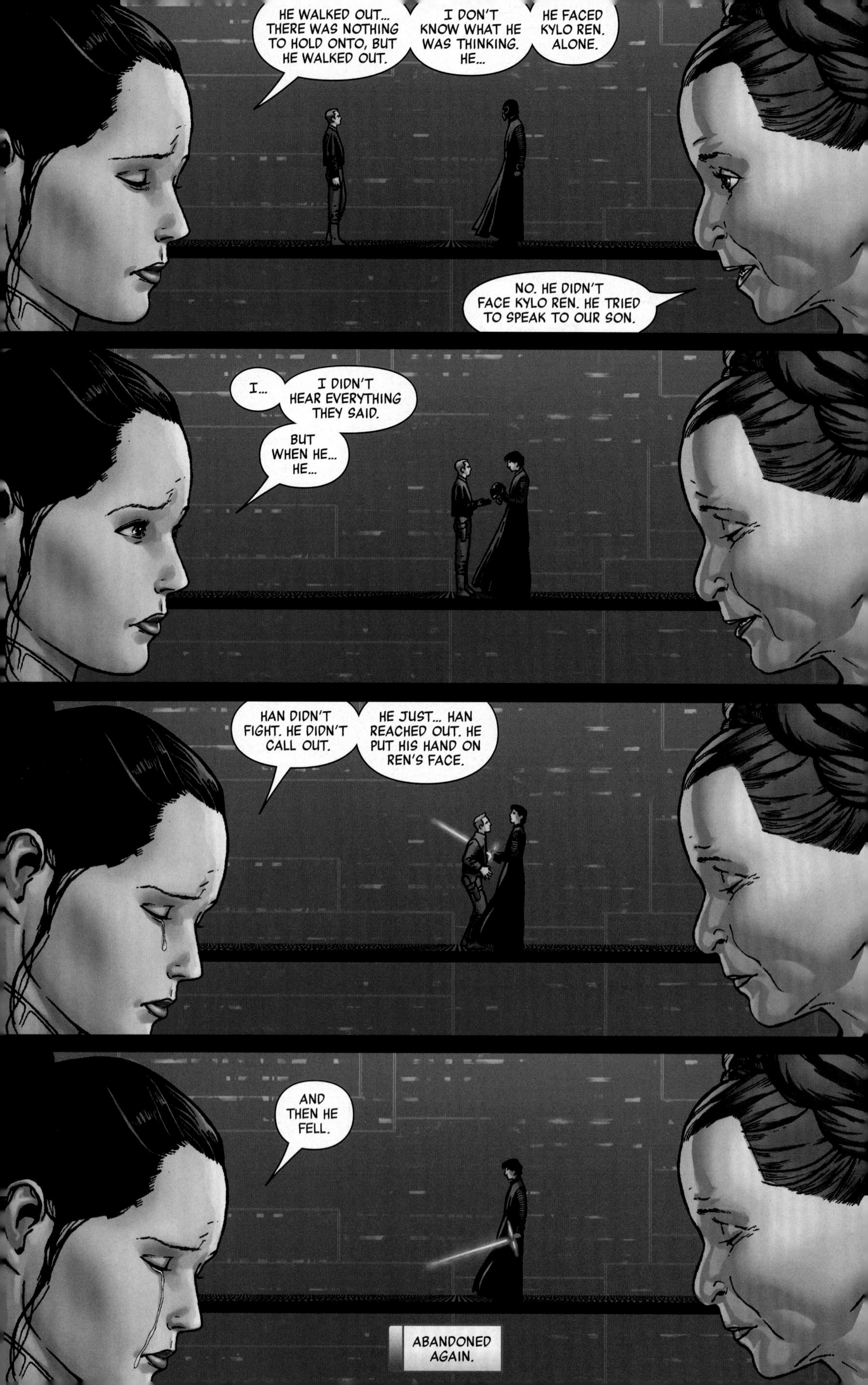
HE WALKED OUT... THERE WAS NOTHING TO HOLD ONTO, BUT HE WALKED OUT.
I DON'T KNOW WHAT HE WAS THINKING. HE...
HE FACED KYLO REN. ALONE.
NO. HE DIDN'T FACE KYLO REN. HE TRIED TO SPEAK TO OUR SON.
I...
I DIDN'T HEAR EVERYTHING THEY SAID.
BUT WHEN HE... HE...
HAN DIDN'T FIGHT. HE DIDN'T CALL OUT.
HE JUST... HAN REACHED OUT. HE PUT HIS HAND ON REN'S FACE.
AND THEN HE FELL.
ABANDONED AGAIN.

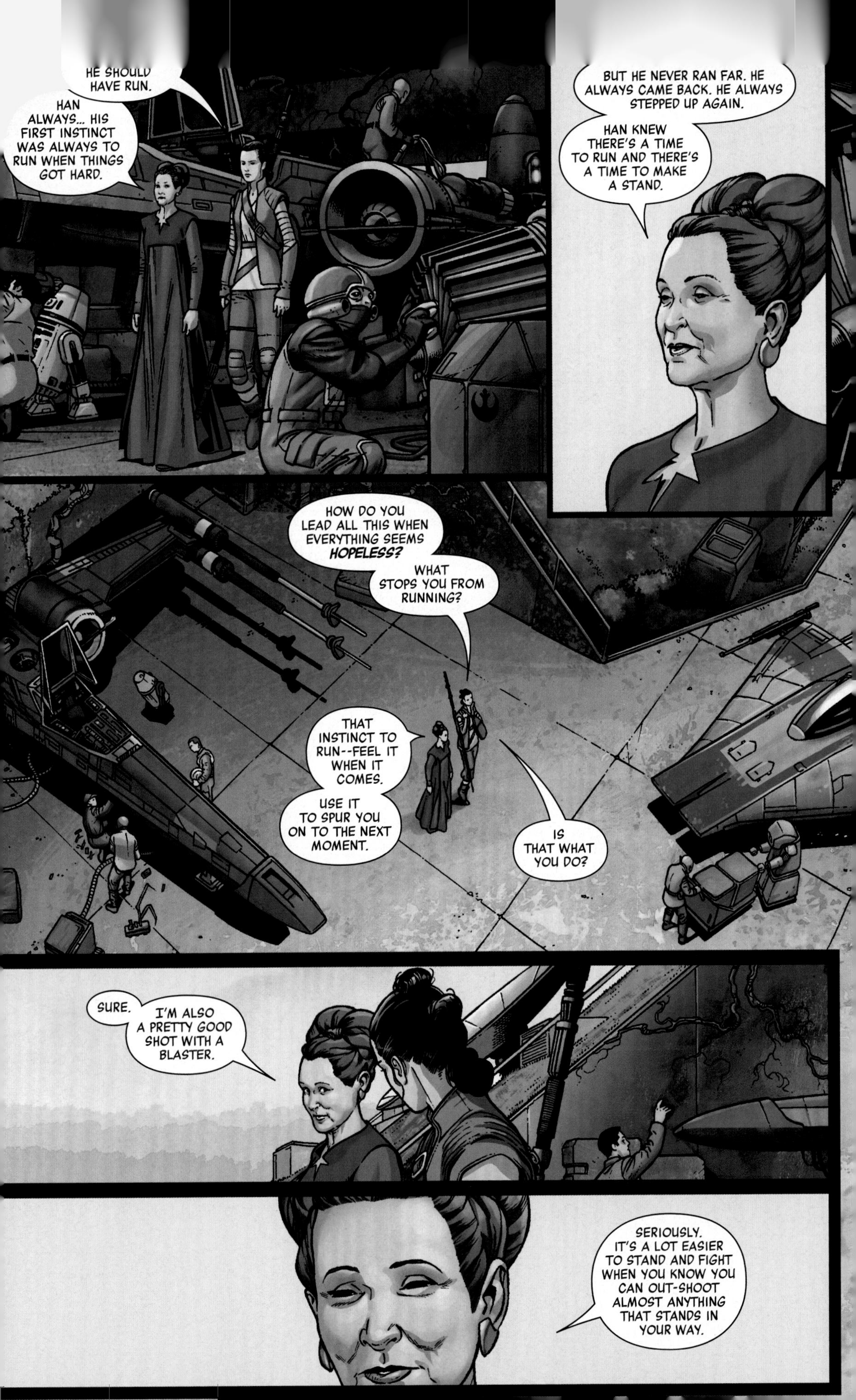
HE SHOULD HAVE RUN.
HAN ALWAYS... HIS FIRST INSTINCT WAS ALWAYS TO RUN WHEN THINGS GOT HARD.
BUT HE NEVER RAN FAR. HE ALWAYS CAME BACK. HE ALWAYS STEPPED UP AGAIN.
HAN KNEW THERE'S A TIME TO RUN AND THERE'S A TIME TO MAKE A STAND.
HOW DO YOU LEAD ALL THIS WHEN EVERYTHING SEEMS *HOPELESS?*
WHAT STOPS YOU FROM RUNNING?
THAT INSTINCT TO RUN--FEEL IT WHEN IT COMES.
USE IT TO SPUR YOU ON TO THE NEXT MOMENT.
IS THAT WHAT YOU DO?
SURE.
I'M ALSO A PRETTY GOOD SHOT WITH A BLASTER.
SERIOUSLY. IT'S A LOT EASIER TO STAND AND FIGHT WHEN YOU KNOW YOU CAN OUT-SHOOT ALMOST ANYTHING THAT STANDS IN YOUR WAY.

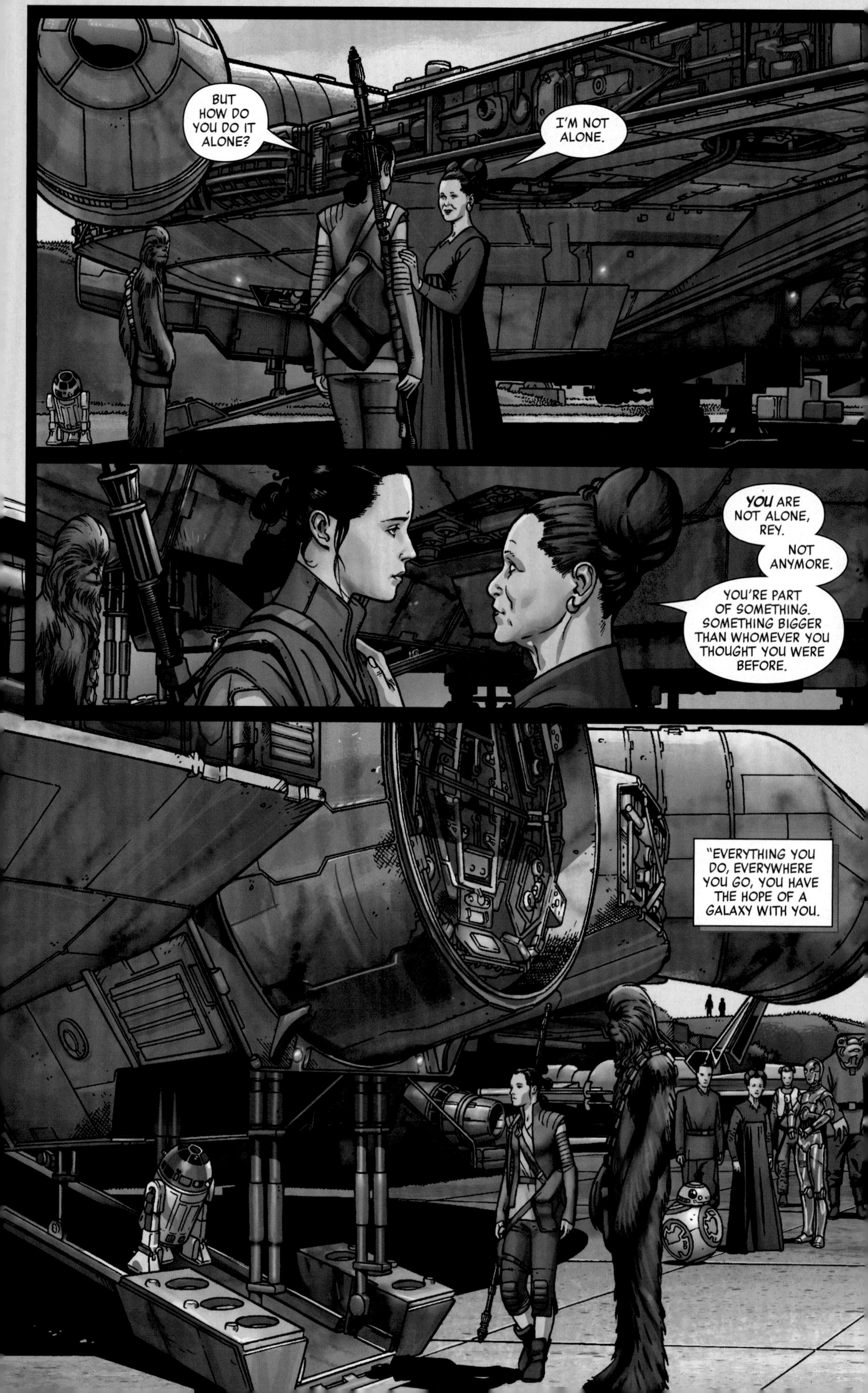
BUT HOW DO YOU DO IT ALONE?
I'M NOT ALONE.
YOU ARE NOT ALONE, REY.
NOT ANYMORE.
YOU'RE PART OF SOMETHING. SOMETHING BIGGER THAN WHOMEVER YOU THOUGHT YOU WERE BEFORE.
"EVERYTHING YOU DO, EVERYWHERE YOU GO, YOU HAVE THE HOPE OF A GALAXY WITH YOU.

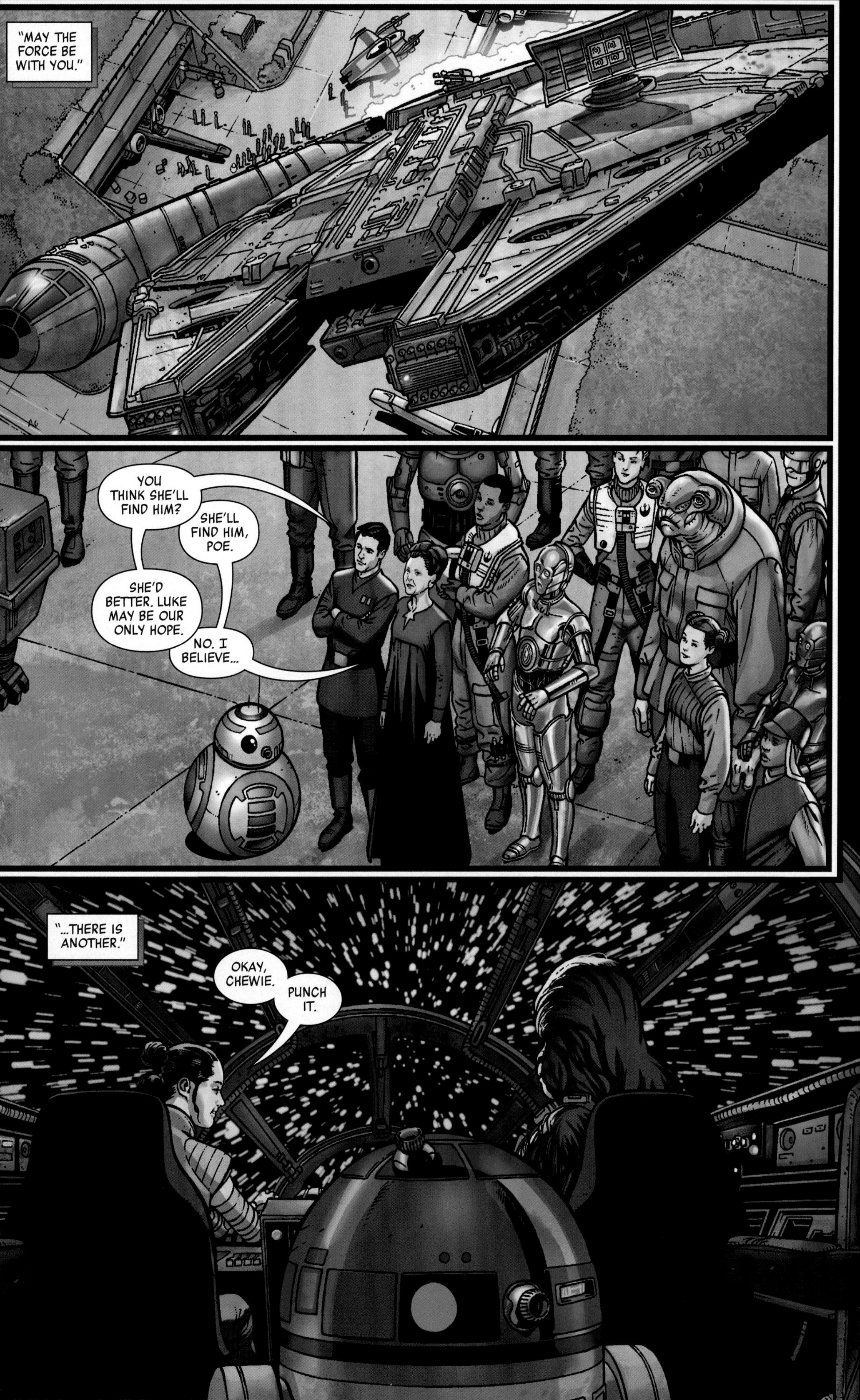
"MAY THE FORCE BE WITH YOU."
YOU THINK SHE'LL FIND HIM?
SHE'LL FIND HIM, POE.
SHE'D BETTER. LUKE MAY BE OUR ONLY HOPE.
NO. I BELIEVE...
"...THERE IS ANOTHER."
OKAY, CHEWIE.
PUNCH IT.

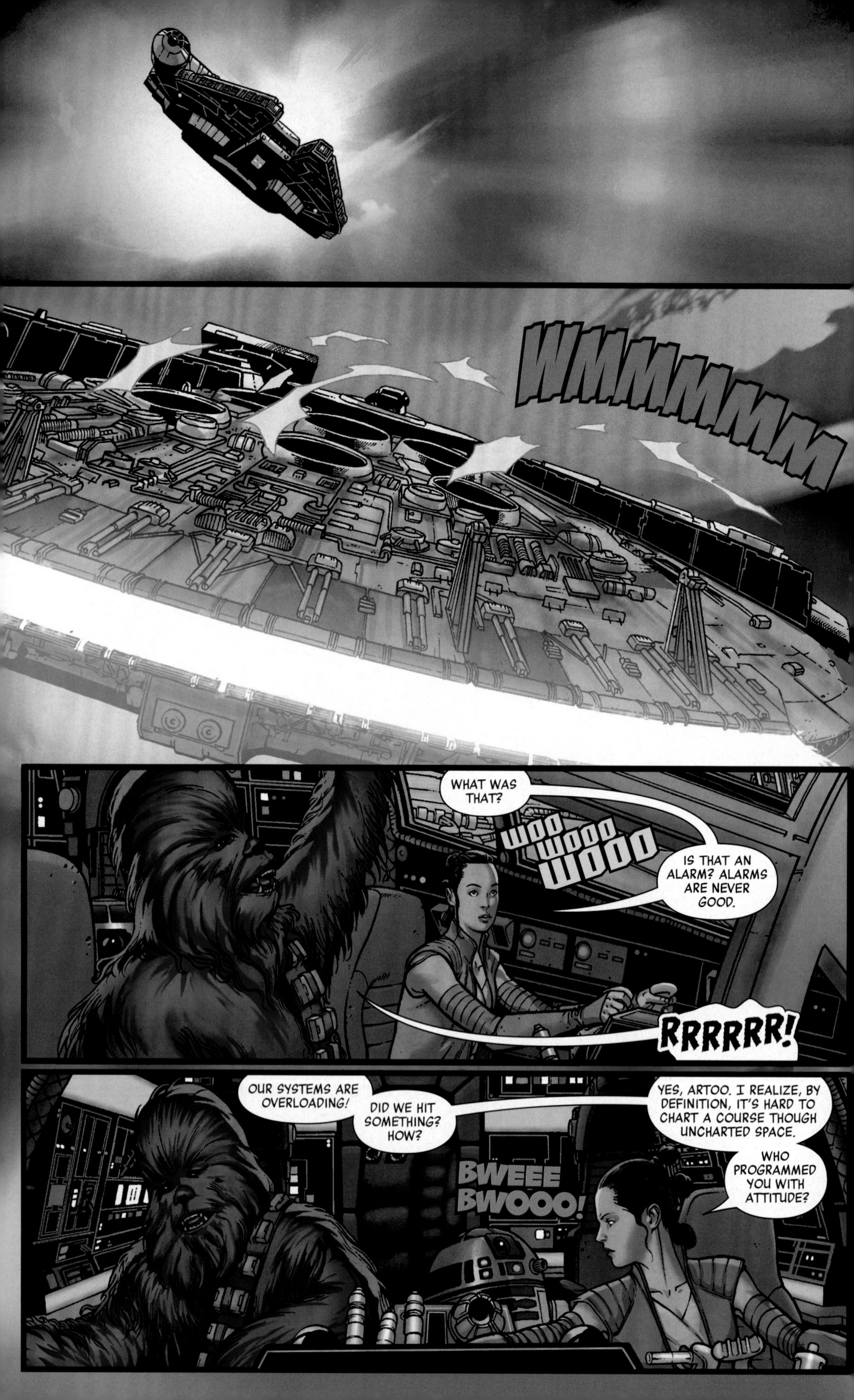
WMMMMMM
WHAT WAS THAT?
WOO WOOO WOOO
IS THAT AN ALARM? ALARMS ARE NEVER GOOD.
RRRRRR!
OUR SYSTEMS ARE OVERLOADING!
DID WE HIT SOMETHING? HOW?
YES, ARTOO. I REALIZE, BY DEFINITION, IT'S HARD TO CHART A COURSE THOUGH UNCHARTED SPACE.
WHO PROGRAMMED YOU WITH ATTITUDE?
BWEEE BWOOO!

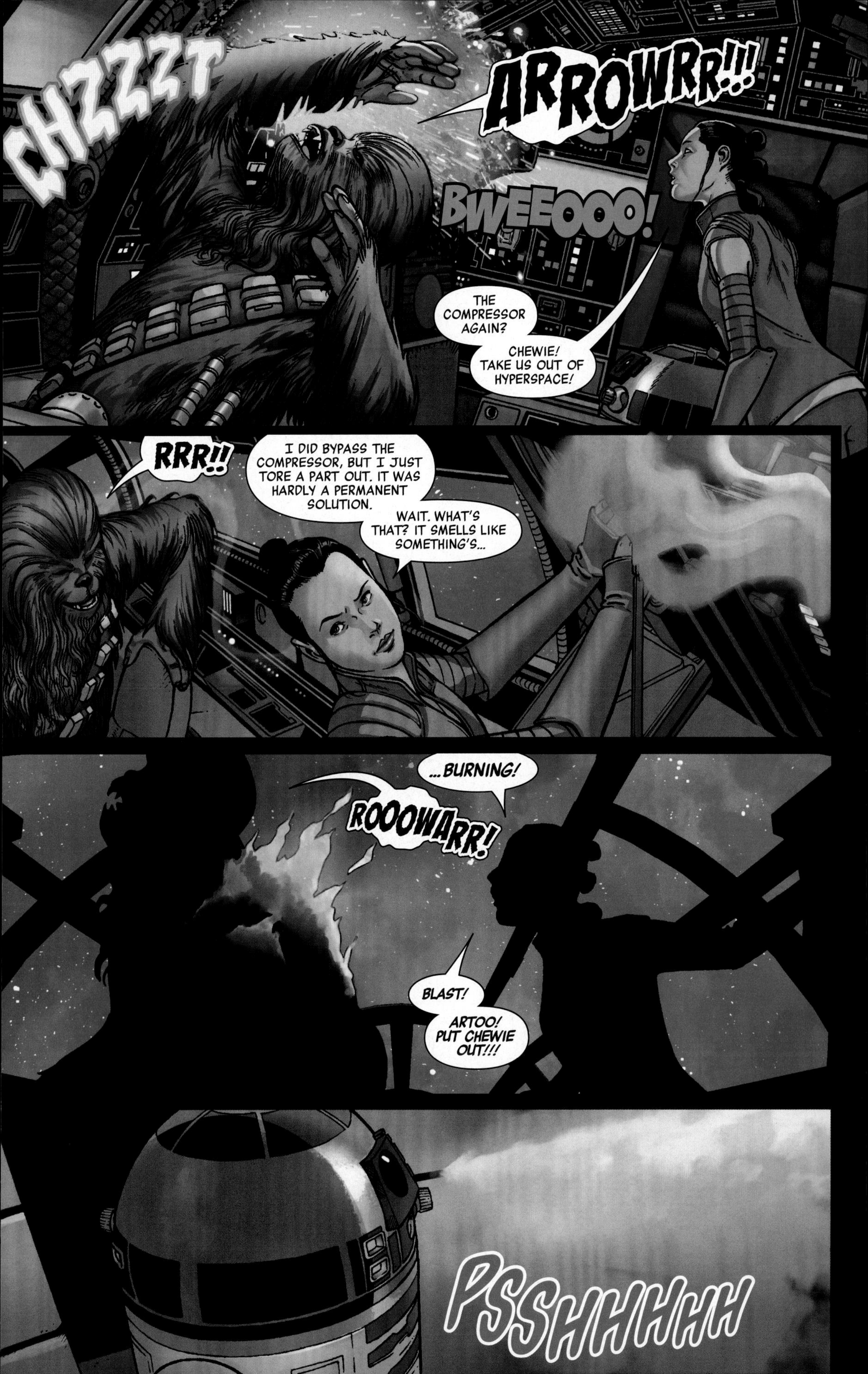
CHZZZT
ARROWRR!!!
BWEEOOO!
THE COMPRESSOR AGAIN?
CHEWIE! TAKE US OUT OF HYPERSPACE!
RRR!!
I DID BYPASS THE COMPRESSOR, BUT I JUST TORE A PART OUT. IT WAS HARDLY A PERMANENT SOLUTION.
WAIT. WHAT'S THAT? IT SMELLS LIKE SOMETHING'S...
...BURNING!
ROOOWARR!
BLAST!
ARTOO! PUT CHEWIE OUT!!!
PSSHHHHH

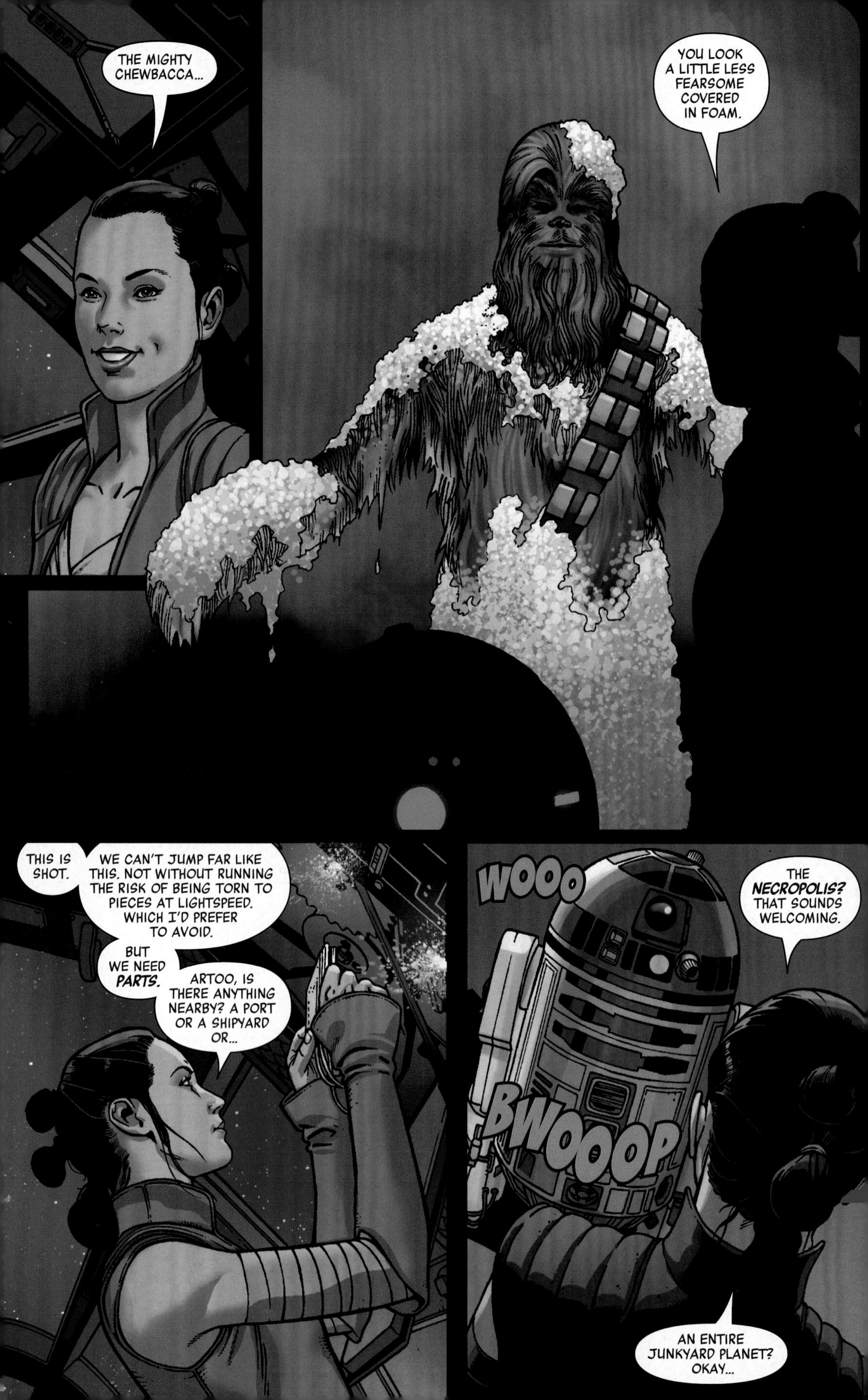
THE MIGHTY CHEWBACCA...
YOU LOOK A LITTLE LESS FEARSOME COVERED IN FOAM.
THIS IS SHOT.
WE CAN'T JUMP FAR LIKE THIS. NOT WITHOUT RUNNING THE RISK OF BEING TORN TO PIECES AT LIGHTSPEED. WHICH I'D PREFER TO AVOID.
BUT WE NEED *PARTS.*
ARTOO, IS THERE ANYTHING NEARBY? A PORT OR A SHIPYARD OR...
WOOO
BWOOOP
THE *NECROPOLIS?* THAT SOUNDS WELCOMING.
AN ENTIRE JUNKYARD PLANET? OKAY...

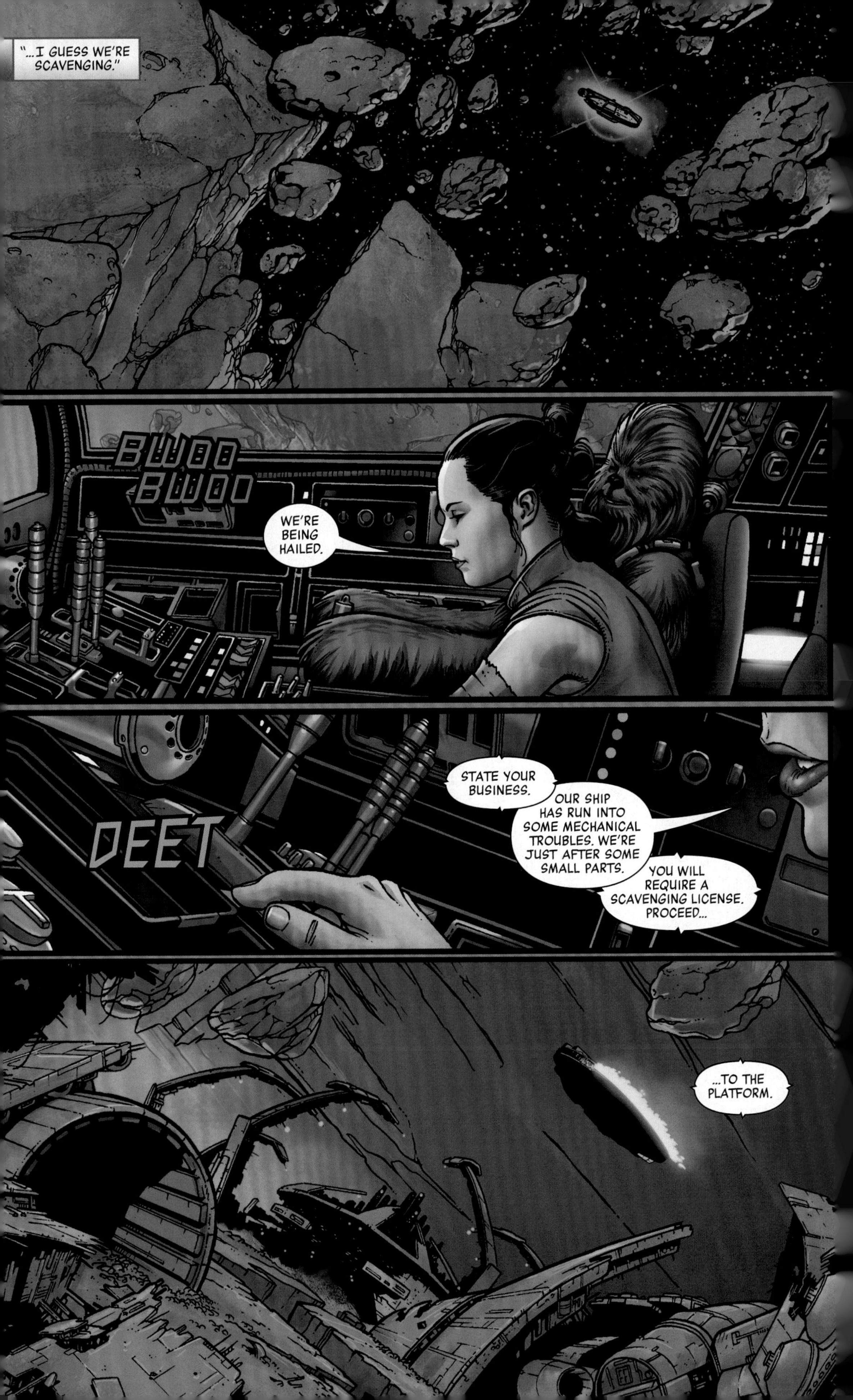
"...I GUESS WE'RE SCAVENGING."
BWOO BWOO
WE'RE BEING HAILED.
DEET
STATE YOUR BUSINESS.
OUR SHIP HAS RUN INTO SOME MECHANICAL TROUBLES. WE'RE JUST AFTER SOME SMALL PARTS.
YOU WILL REQUIRE A SCAVENGING LICENSE. PROCEED...
...TO THE PLATFORM.

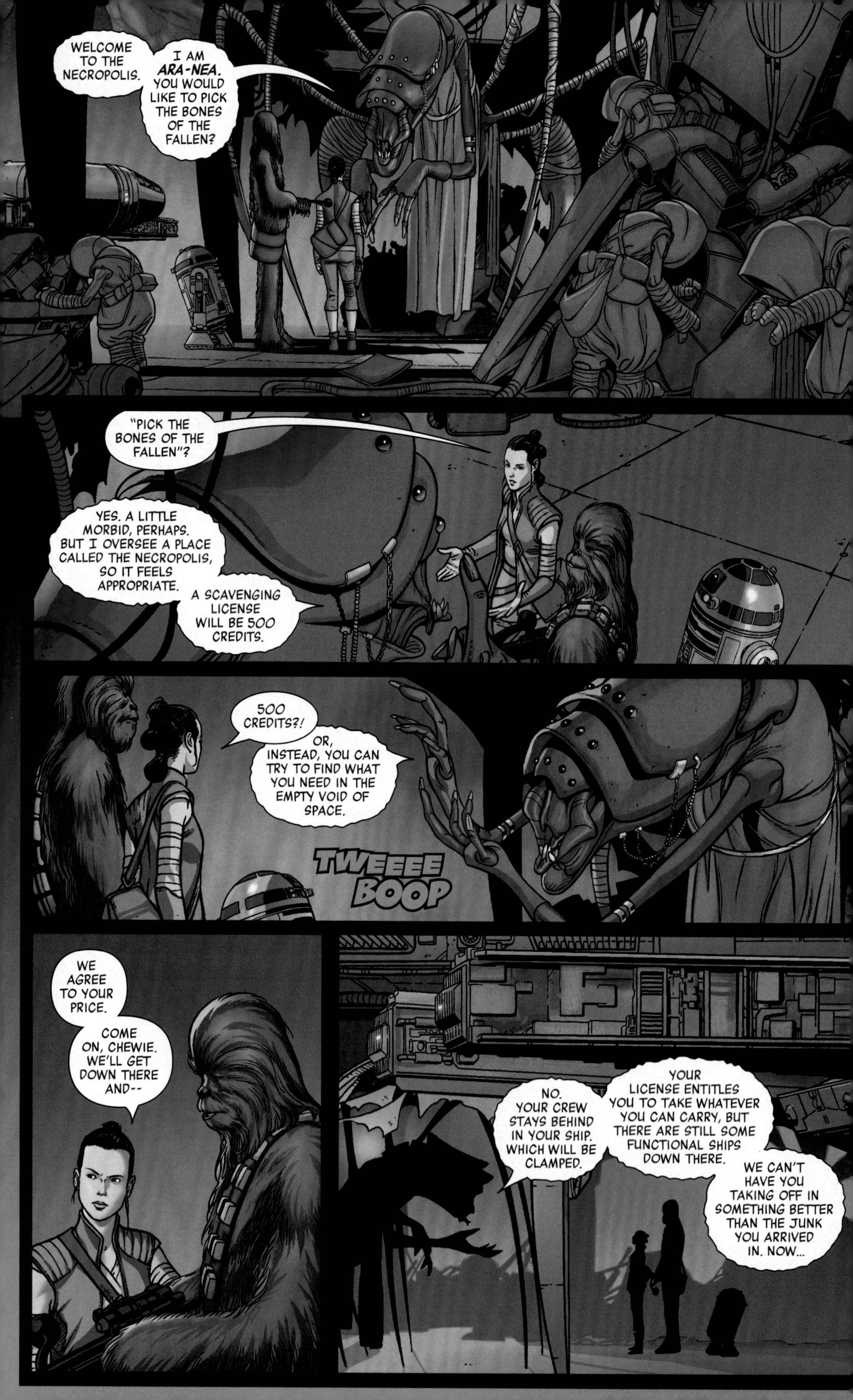
WELCOME TO THE NECROPOLIS.
I AM **ARA-NEA.** YOU WOULD LIKE TO PICK THE BONES OF THE FALLEN?
"PICK THE BONES OF THE FALLEN"?
YES. A LITTLE MORBID, PERHAPS. BUT I OVERSEE A PLACE CALLED THE NECROPOLIS, SO IT FEELS APPROPRIATE.
A SCAVENGING LICENSE WILL BE 500 CREDITS.
500 CREDITS?!
OR, INSTEAD, YOU CAN TRY TO FIND WHAT YOU NEED IN THE EMPTY VOID OF SPACE.
TWEEEE BOOP
WE AGREE TO YOUR PRICE.
COME ON, CHEWIE. WE'LL GET DOWN THERE AND--
NO. YOUR CREW STAYS BEHIND IN YOUR SHIP. WHICH WILL BE CLAMPED.
YOUR LICENSE ENTITLES YOU TO TAKE WHATEVER YOU CAN CARRY, BUT THERE ARE STILL SOME FUNCTIONAL SHIPS DOWN THERE.
WE CAN'T HAVE YOU TAKING OFF IN SOMETHING BETTER THAN THE JUNK YOU ARRIVED IN. NOW...

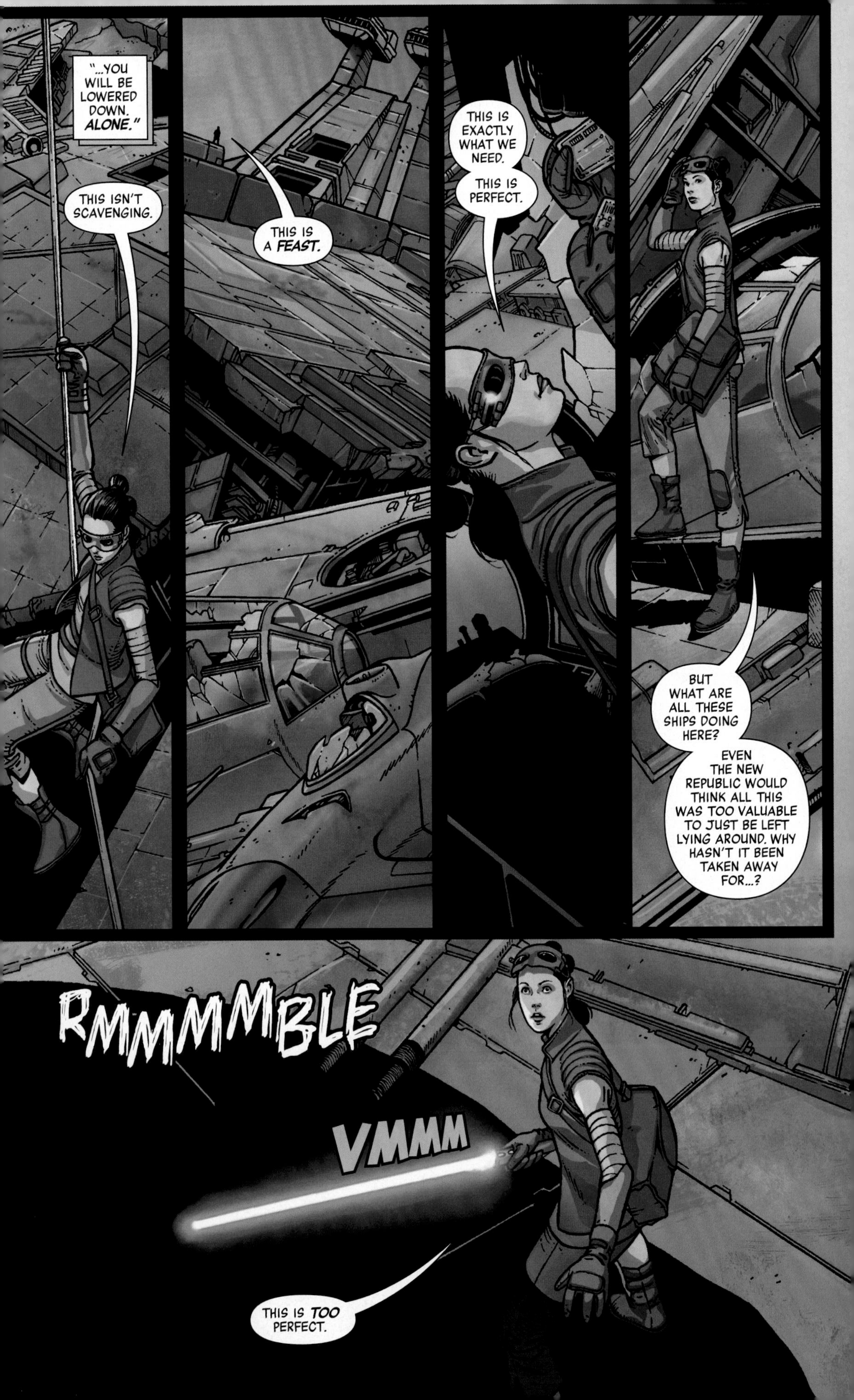
"...YOU WILL BE LOWERED DOWN. *ALONE.*"
THIS ISN'T SCAVENGING.
THIS IS A *FEAST.*
THIS IS EXACTLY WHAT WE NEED.
THIS IS PERFECT.
BUT WHAT ARE ALL THESE SHIPS DOING HERE?
EVEN THE NEW REPUBLIC WOULD THINK ALL THIS WAS TOO VALUABLE TO JUST BE LEFT LYING AROUND. WHY HASN'T IT BEEN TAKEN AWAY FOR...?
RMMMMBLE
VMMM
THIS IS *TOO* PERFECT.

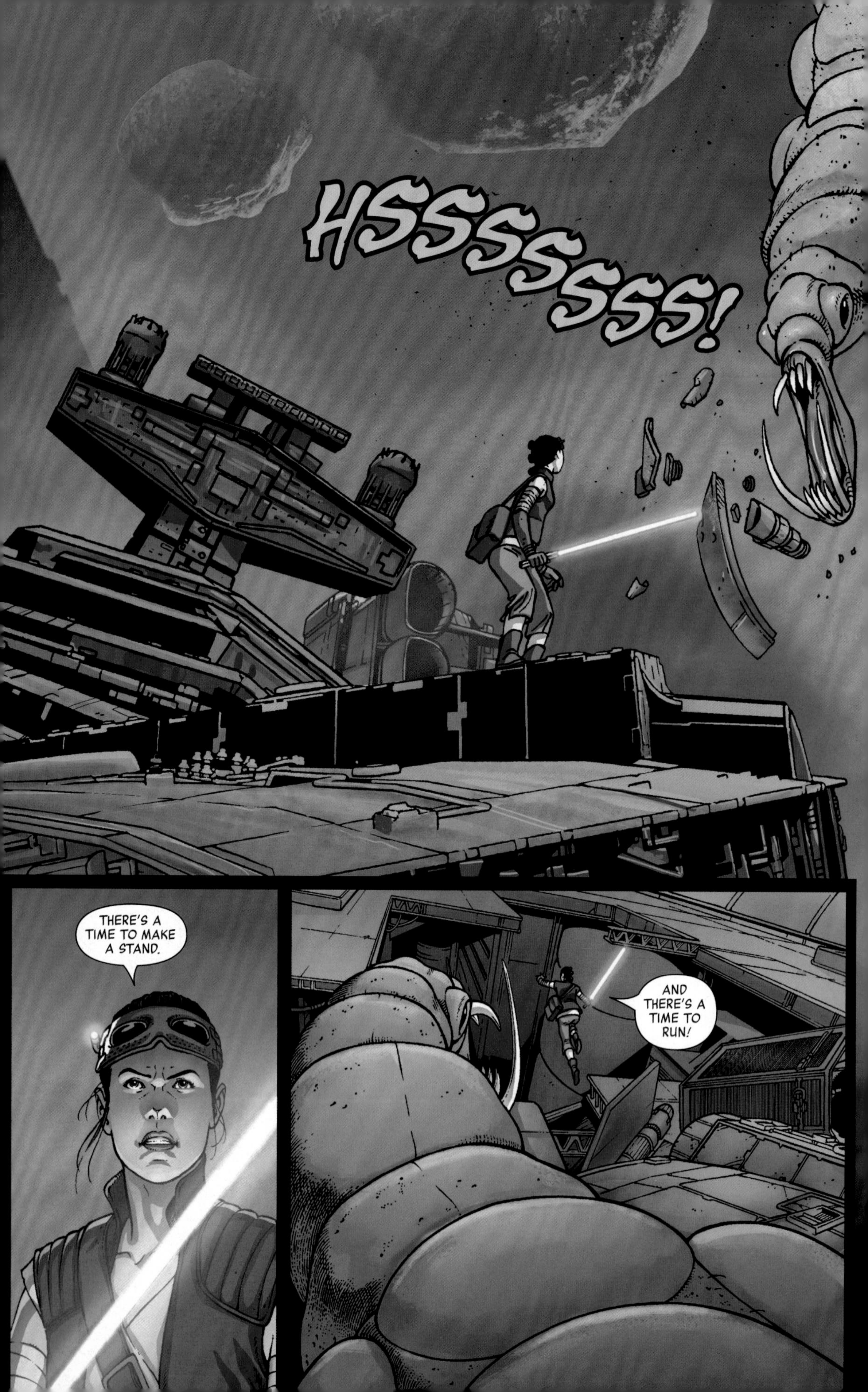
HSSSSSSS!
THERE'S A TIME TO MAKE A STAND.
AND THERE'S A TIME TO RUN!

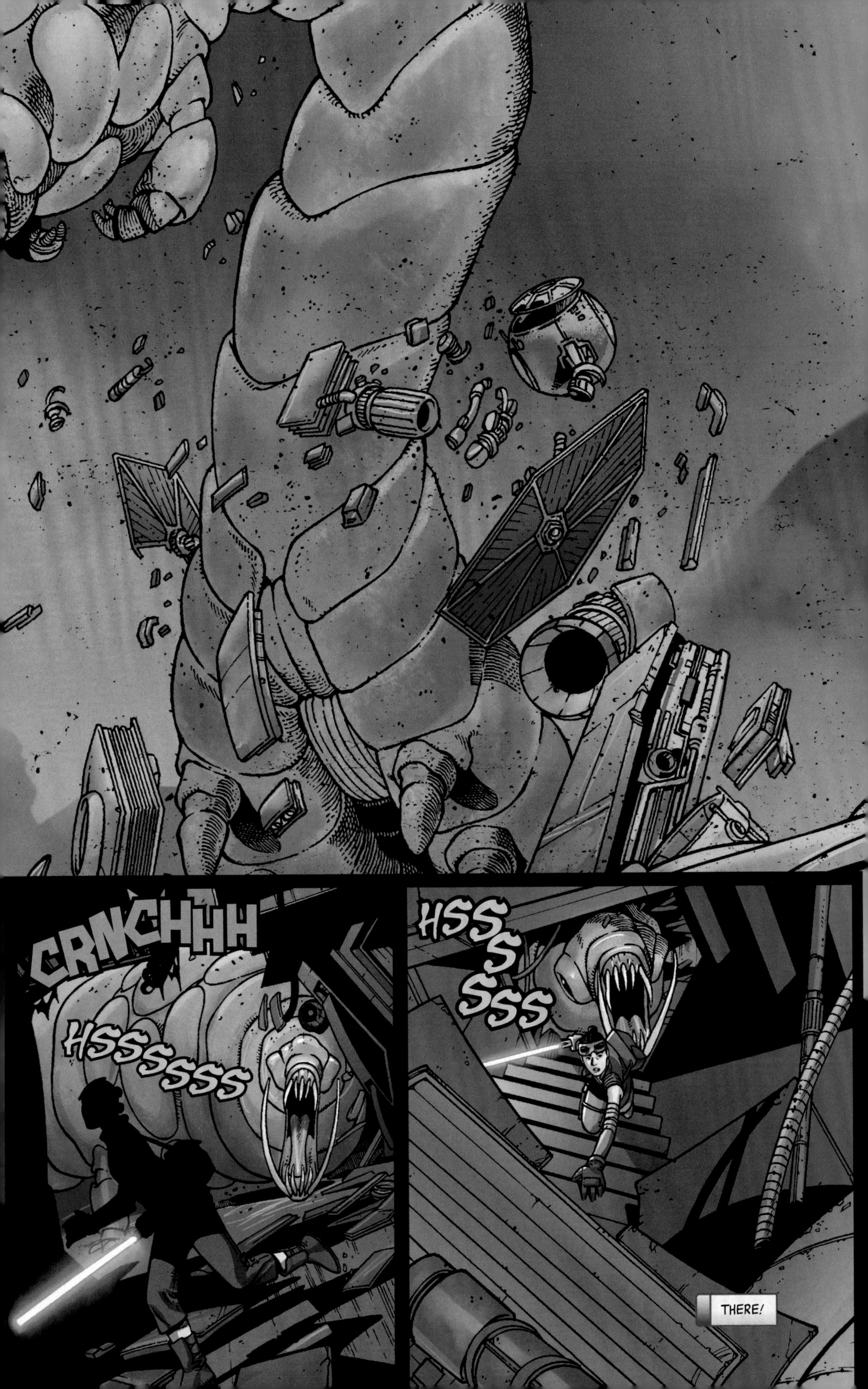
CRNCHHH
HSSSSSS
HSS S SSS
THERE!

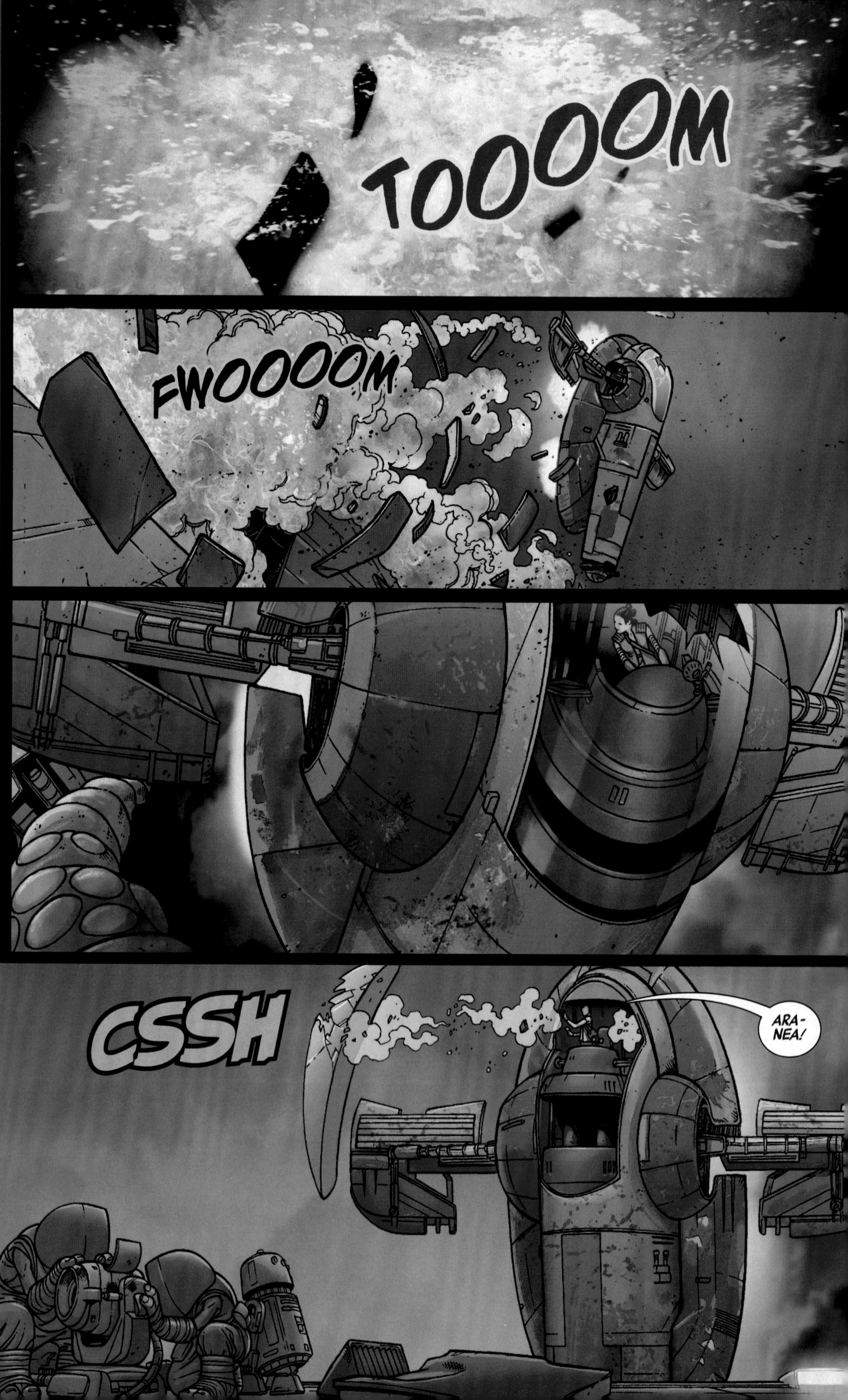
TOOOOOM
FWOOOOOM
CSSH
ARA-NEA!

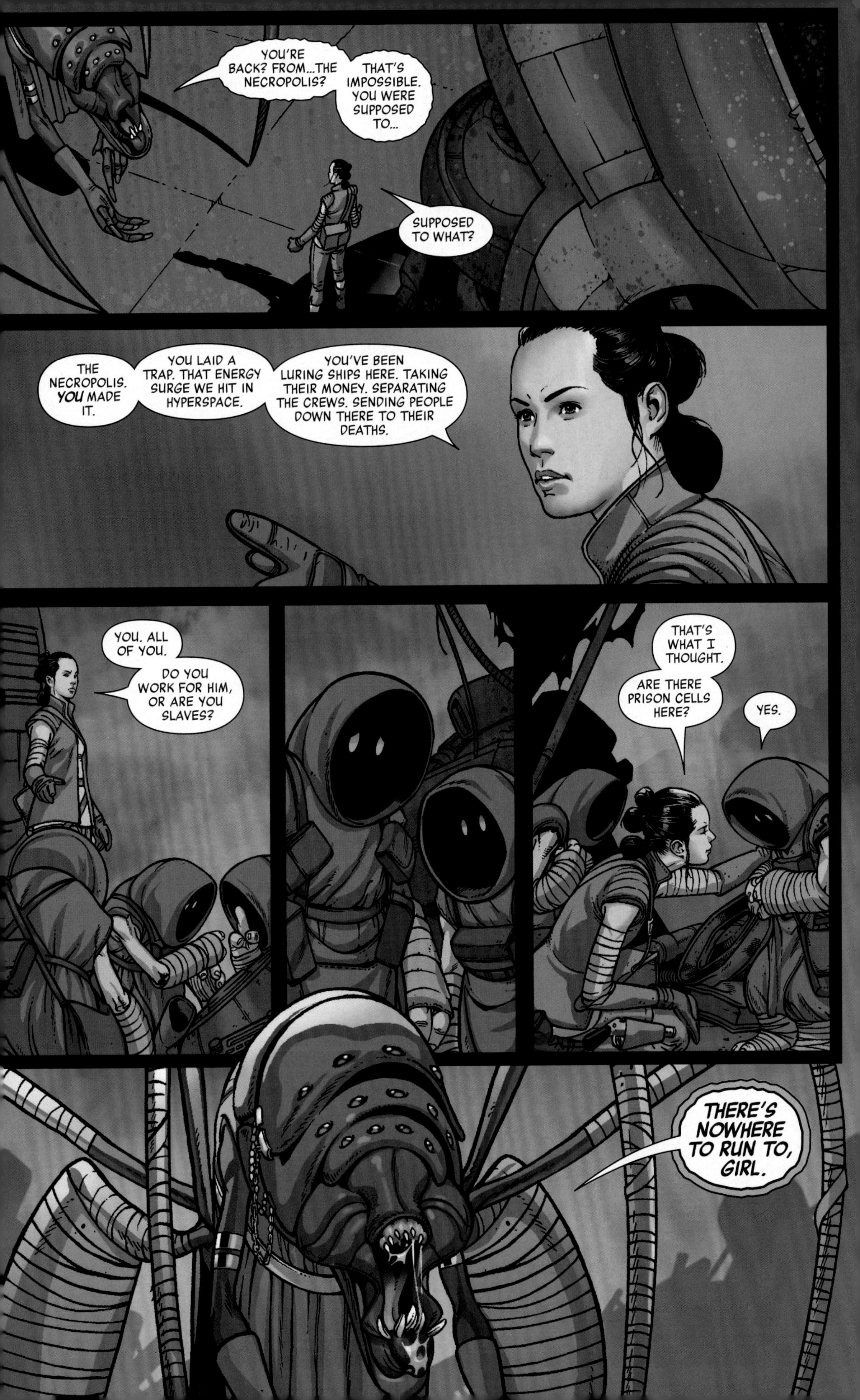

YOU'RE BACK? FROM...THE NECROPOLIS?
THAT'S IMPOSSIBLE. YOU WERE SUPPOSED TO...
SUPPOSED TO WHAT?
THE NECROPOLIS. YOU MADE IT.
YOU LAID A TRAP. THAT ENERGY SURGE WE HIT IN HYPERSPACE.
YOU'VE BEEN LURING SHIPS HERE. TAKING THEIR MONEY. SEPARATING THE CREWS. SENDING PEOPLE DOWN THERE TO THEIR DEATHS.
YOU. ALL OF YOU.
DO YOU WORK FOR HIM, OR ARE YOU SLAVES?
THAT'S WHAT I THOUGHT.
ARE THERE PRISON CELLS HERE?
YES.
THERE'S NOWHERE TO RUN TO, GIRL.

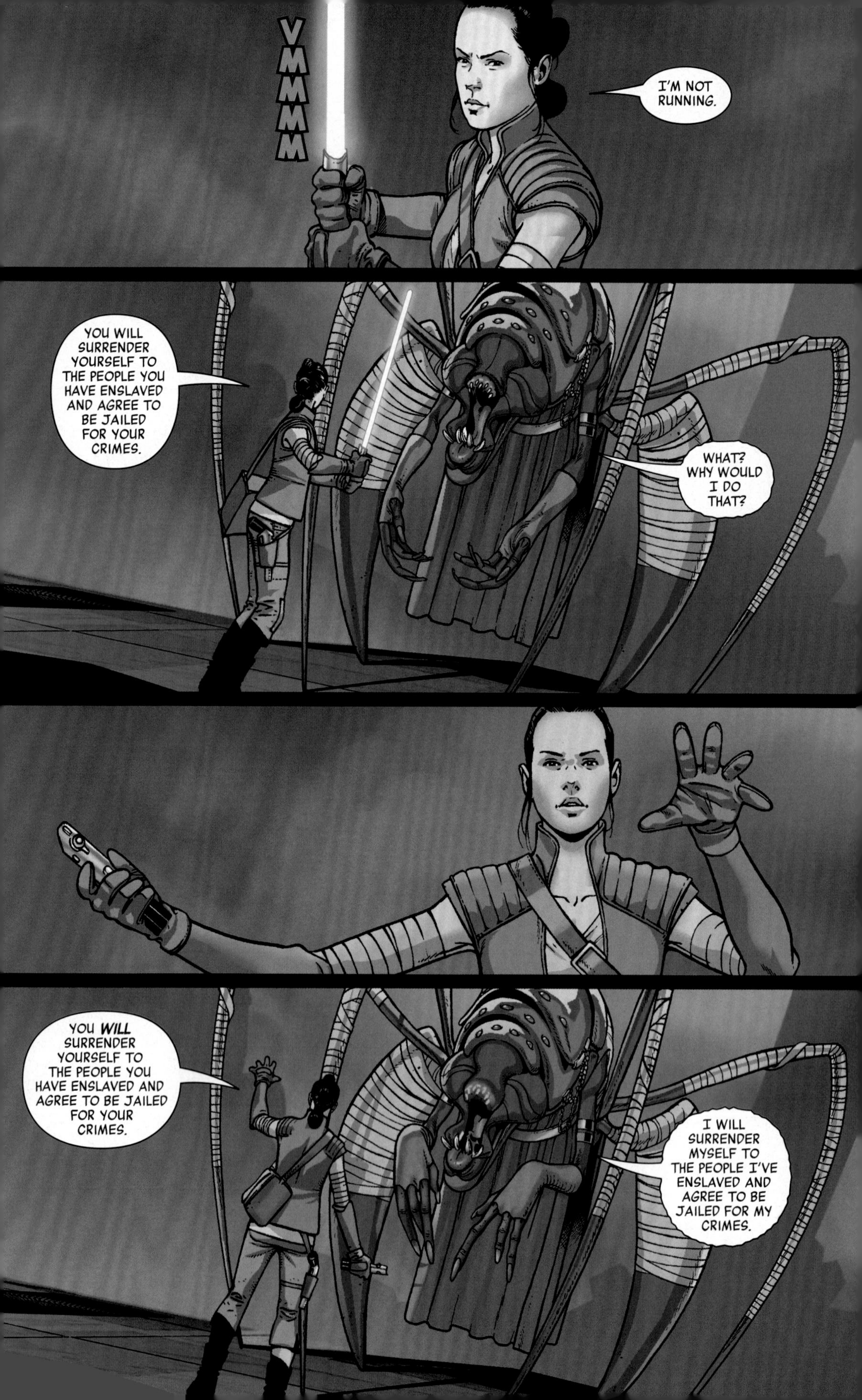

VMMMM
I'M NOT RUNNING.
YOU WILL SURRENDER YOURSELF TO THE PEOPLE YOU HAVE ENSLAVED AND AGREE TO BE JAILED FOR YOUR CRIMES.
WHAT? WHY WOULD I DO THAT?
YOU *WILL* SURRENDER YOURSELF TO THE PEOPLE YOU HAVE ENSLAVED AND AGREE TO BE JAILED FOR YOUR CRIMES.
I WILL SURRENDER MYSELF TO THE PEOPLE I'VE ENSLAVED AND AGREE TO BE JAILED FOR MY CRIMES.

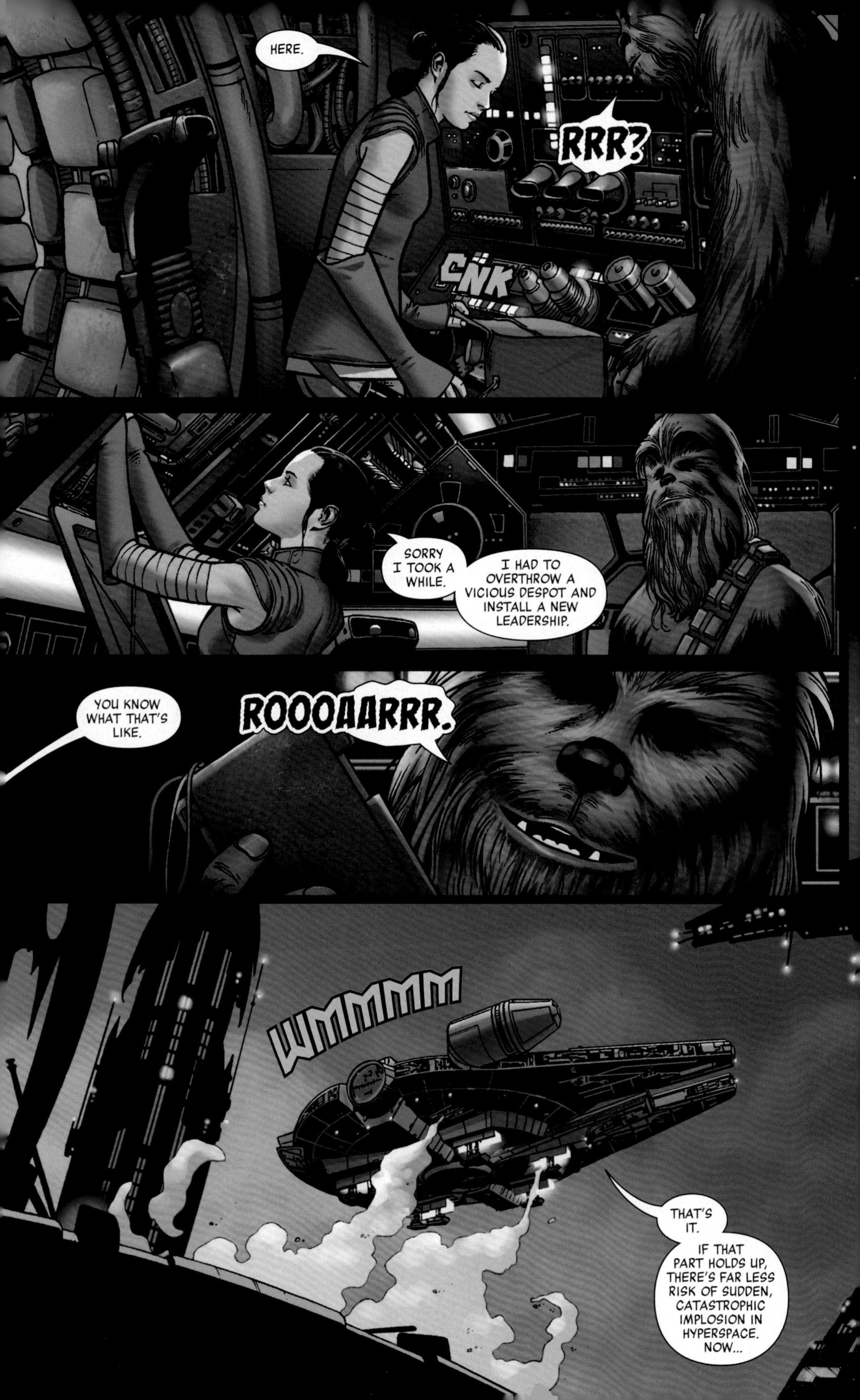
HERE.
RRR?
CNK
SORRY I TOOK A WHILE.
I HAD TO OVERTHROW A VICIOUS DESPOT AND INSTALL A NEW LEADERSHIP.
YOU KNOW WHAT THAT'S LIKE.
ROOOAARRR.
WMMMMM
THAT'S IT.
IF THAT PART HOLDS UP, THERE'S FAR LESS RISK OF SUDDEN, CATASTROPHIC IMPLOSION IN HYPERSPACE. NOW...

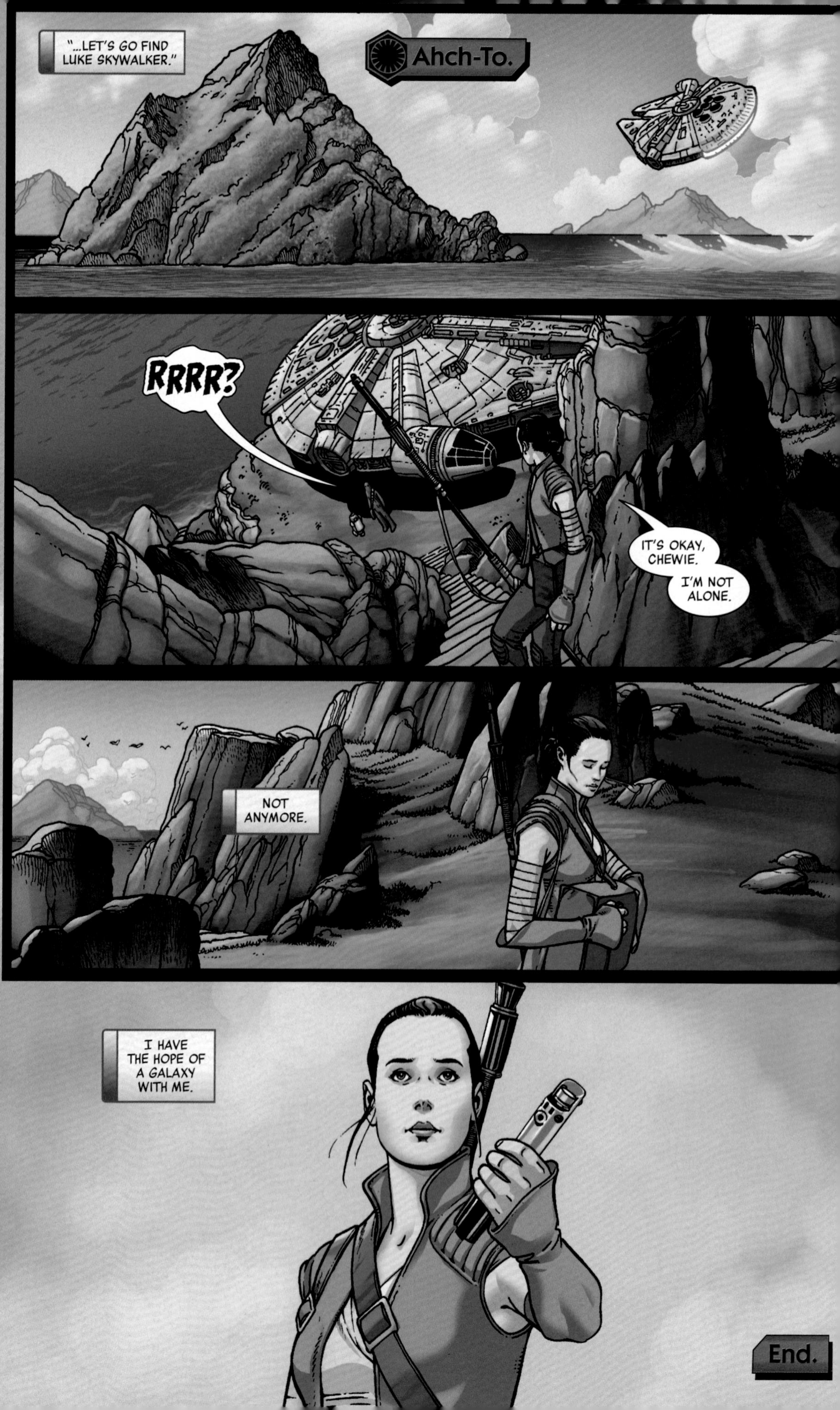

"...LET'S GO FIND LUKE SKYWALKER."
Ahch-To.
RRRR?
IT'S OKAY, CHEWIE.
I'M NOT ALONE.
NOT ANYMORE.
I HAVE THE HOPE OF A GALAXY WITH ME.
End.

AGE OF RESISTANCE

Art by Glyn Dillon

AGE OF RESISTANCE
Rey – Hope for the Next Generation and Ours
By Bria LaVorgna

Before I sat down to write this essay, I tweeted one simple question: "What does Rey mean to you?" The first two answers I received were "how much time do you have?", followed by an emphatic "Everything!" As the responses continued for the next few days, people poured their hearts out and the themes of hope, resilience and goodness quickly emerged. I couldn't possibly think of three better words to sum up not only who Rey is as a person and a character but also the unbelievably positive impact she's had on the *Star Wars* community as a whole.

While *Star Wars* has a long tradition of capable female characters like Leia and Padmé who fight right alongside the men, Rey became something different at that moment in *The Force Awakens* when Luke Skywalker's lightsaber flew right past Kylo and into her hand. She became *the* hero of the sequel trilogy and for the first time, we had a female Force user at the heart of a *Star Wars* movie. She was what so many of us had been waiting for; a chance to feel like the center of the story.

Rey is inspiring for far more than her gender though. The galaxy presented Rey with every opportunity to embrace the dark side but she never did.

Separated from her parents and left to live in a desert wasteland as a child, she became a scavenger by necessity, making a home for herself in a downed AT-AT. Kindnesses from others were few and far between. Every skill she picked up, from languages to flying, were ones she had to teach herself. The sands of Jakku weren't an ideal place to learn about trust and friendship especially when other scavengers were more likely to steal a ship she'd worked to restore to flight condition than to offer genuine help without a hidden agenda. And yet, Rey stayed a good person, helping others when she could have easily walked away. "My favorite thing about [her] is that strong moral compass. Even having grown up quite lonely, she meets people and immediately tries to do the right thing," said actress Daisy Ridley in an interview with *Rolling Stone*. Rey says no to the dark because it's the right thing to do.

In an interview with the *Los Angeles Times*, Kathleen Kennedy described Rey as "[embodying] that sense of self-reliance and independence," both traits which partially define Rey especially when audiences first met her in *The Force Awakens*. She is a woman who can take care of herself and perseveres even when everything and everyone

around her tells her no. But now she doesn't have to rely on just herself. By helping a stranger in need and a curious little round droid, the loner scavenger girl became a part of something bigger and now has people who truly care about her and see her value in more than quarter portions. Rey found the belonging Maz Kanata knew she sought in Finn, Poe, Chewbacca, Leia and the rest of the Resistance.

It's impossible for any one character to be everything to everyone, but Rey's positive impact cannot be overstated. Walk around any convention and you'll see dozens of women and girls dressed up as Rey, ranging in age from toddlers to parents, but all with their faces lit up with a pure love of *Star Wars*. Rey has brought new fans to the *Star Wars* franchise and reinvigorated a love for it in others. While we don't yet know how Rey's story ends, we do know that she has inspired people both in a galaxy far, far away and in ours. She is hope, she is resilience, she is the light. Rey from nowhere is the hero we need and deserve.

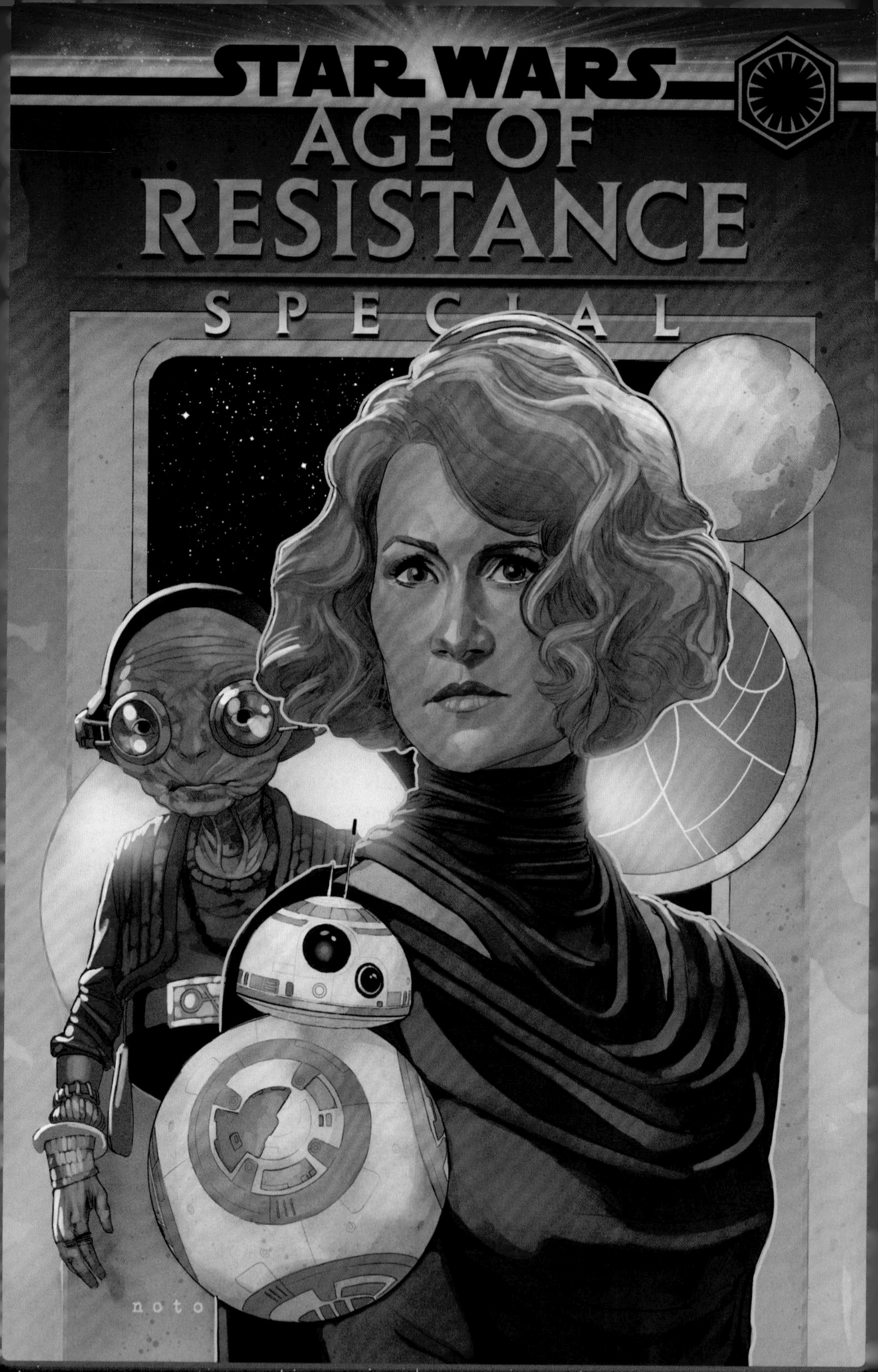
STAR WARS
AGE OF
RESISTANCE
SPECIAL
noto

"MAZ'S SCOUNDRELS"

Maz Kanata is the most well-connected underworld smuggler in the galaxy. Crossing her would not be wise. . . .

"THE BRIDGE"

Flying with the heroic Rebel Alliance might give the young minister Amilyn Holdo the chance she needs to prove all that she is capable of. . . .

"ROBOT RESISTANCE"

Infiltrating the First Order has become second nature to Poe Dameron. But controlling BB-8 could be a

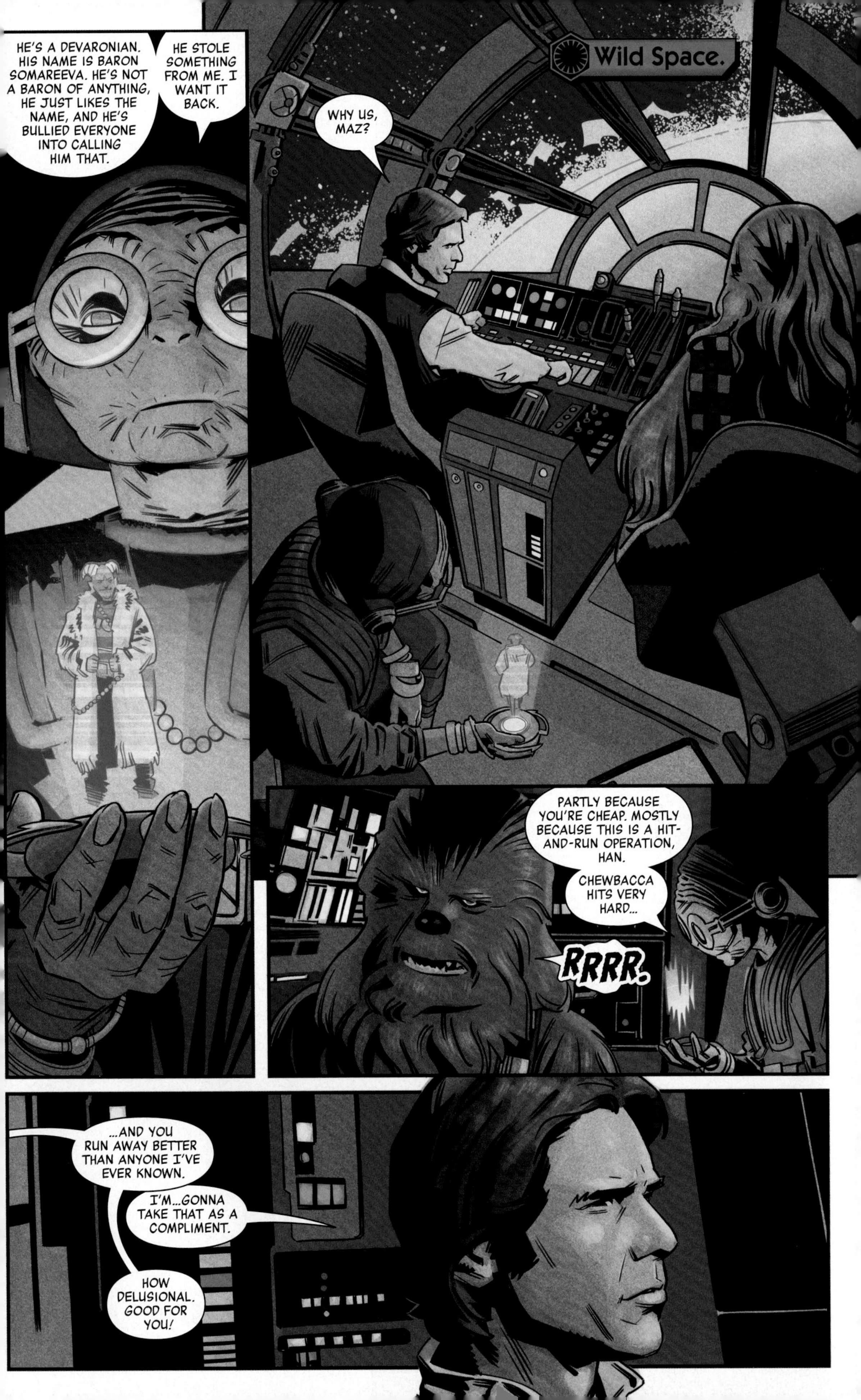
Wild Space.
HE'S A DEVARONIAN. HIS NAME IS BARON SOMAREEVA. HE'S NOT A BARON OF ANYTHING, HE JUST LIKES THE NAME, AND HE'S BULLIED EVERYONE INTO CALLING HIM THAT.
HE STOLE SOMETHING FROM ME. I WANT IT BACK.
WHY US, MAZ?
PARTLY BECAUSE YOU'RE CHEAP. MOSTLY BECAUSE THIS IS A HIT-AND-RUN OPERATION, HAN.
CHEWBACCA HITS VERY HARD...
RRRR.
...AND YOU RUN AWAY BETTER THAN ANYONE I'VE EVER KNOWN.
I'M...GONNA TAKE THAT AS A COMPLIMENT.
HOW DELUSIONAL. GOOD FOR YOU!

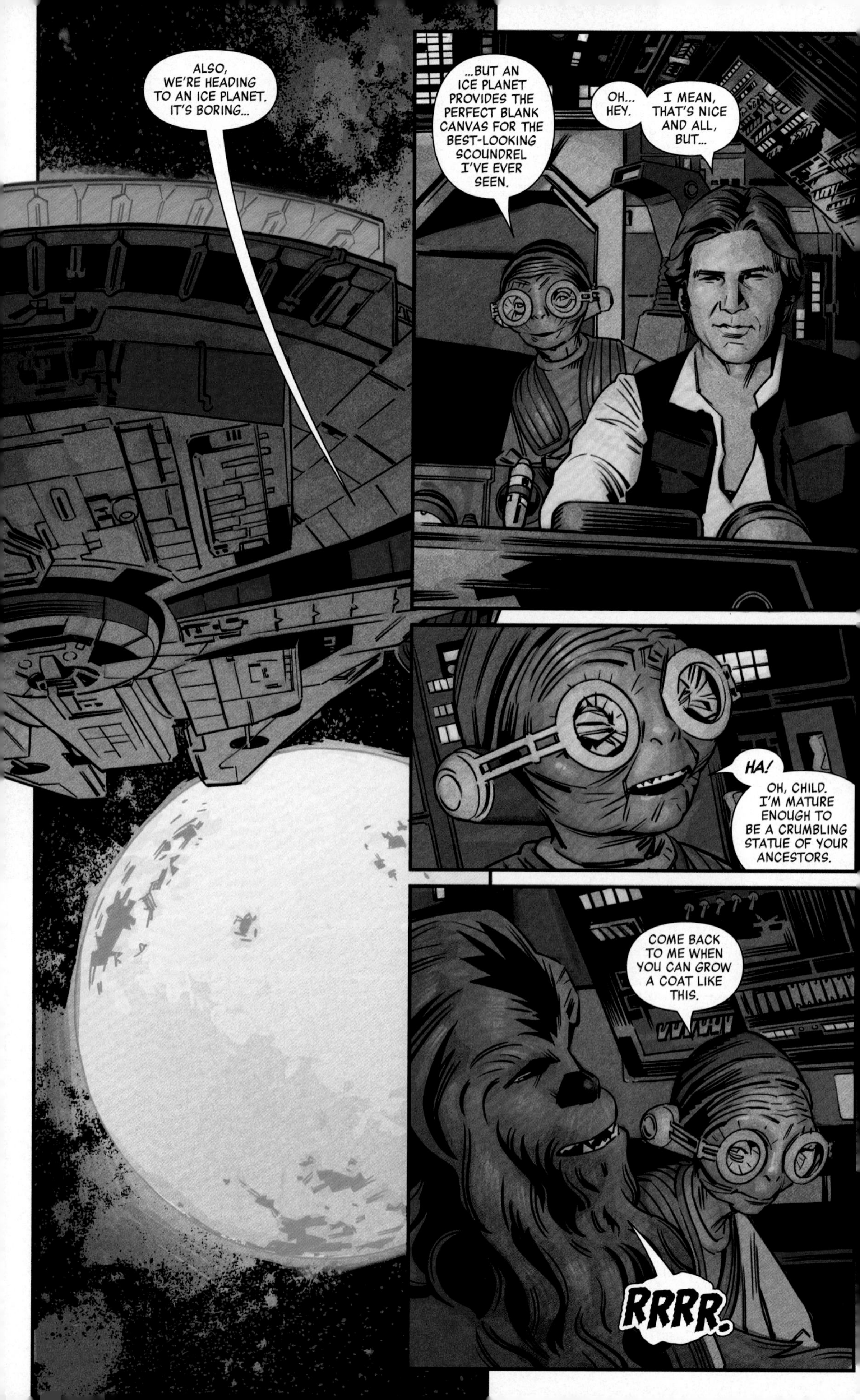
ALSO, WE'RE HEADING TO AN ICE PLANET. IT'S BORING...
...BUT AN ICE PLANET PROVIDES THE PERFECT BLANK CANVAS FOR THE BEST-LOOKING SCOUNDREL I'VE EVER SEEN.
OH... HEY.
I MEAN, THAT'S NICE AND ALL, BUT...
HA!
OH, CHILD. I'M MATURE ENOUGH TO BE A CRUMBLING STATUE OF YOUR ANCESTORS.
COME BACK TO ME WHEN YOU CAN GROW A COAT LIKE THIS.
RRRR.

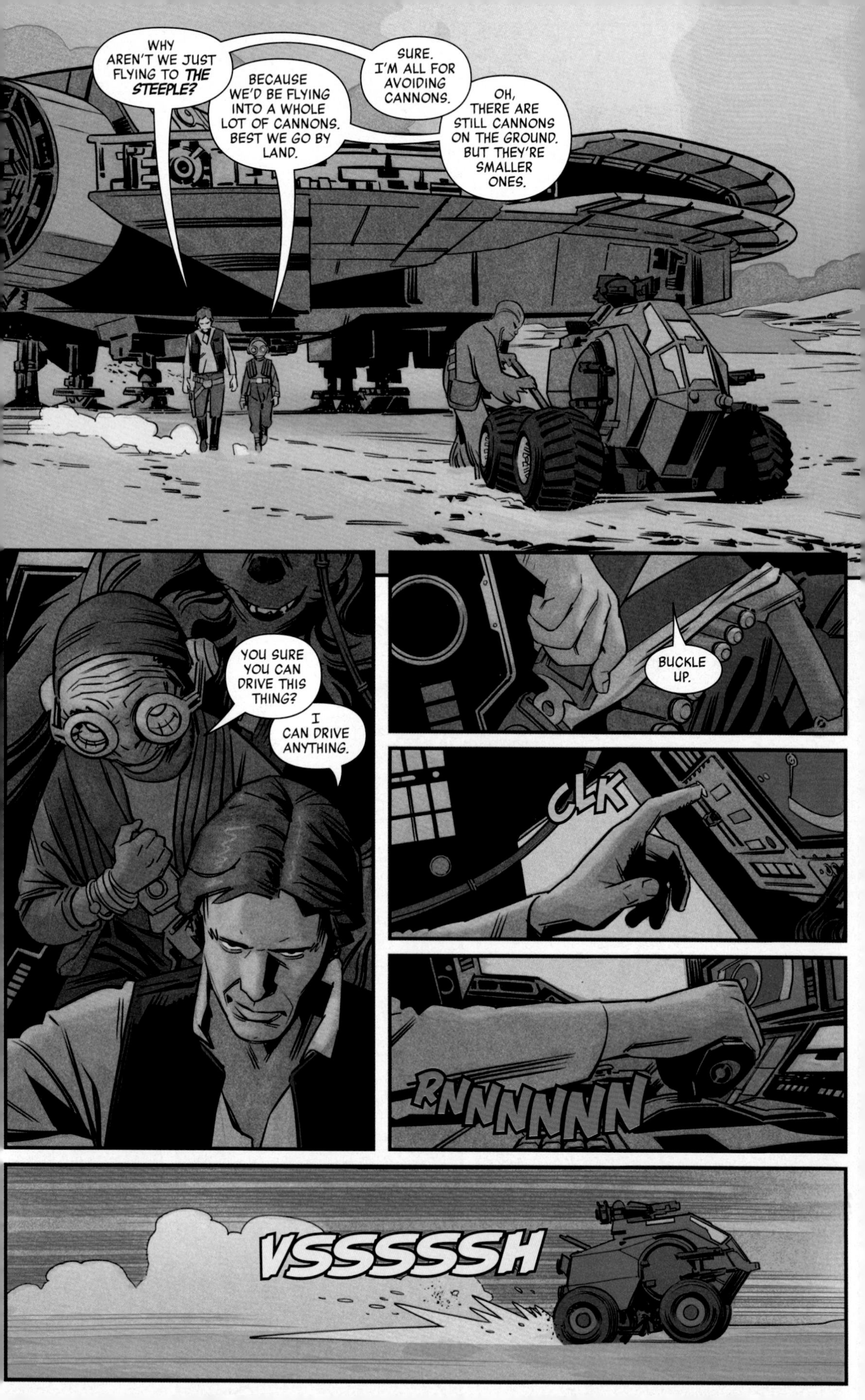
WHY AREN'T WE JUST FLYING TO ***THE STEEPLE?***
BECAUSE WE'D BE FLYING INTO A WHOLE LOT OF CANNONS. BEST WE GO BY LAND.
SURE. I'M ALL FOR AVOIDING CANNONS.
OH, THERE ARE STILL CANNONS ON THE GROUND. BUT THEY'RE SMALLER ONES.
YOU SURE YOU CAN DRIVE THIS THING?
I CAN DRIVE ANYTHING.
BUCKLE UP.
CLK
RNNNNNNN
VSSSSSH

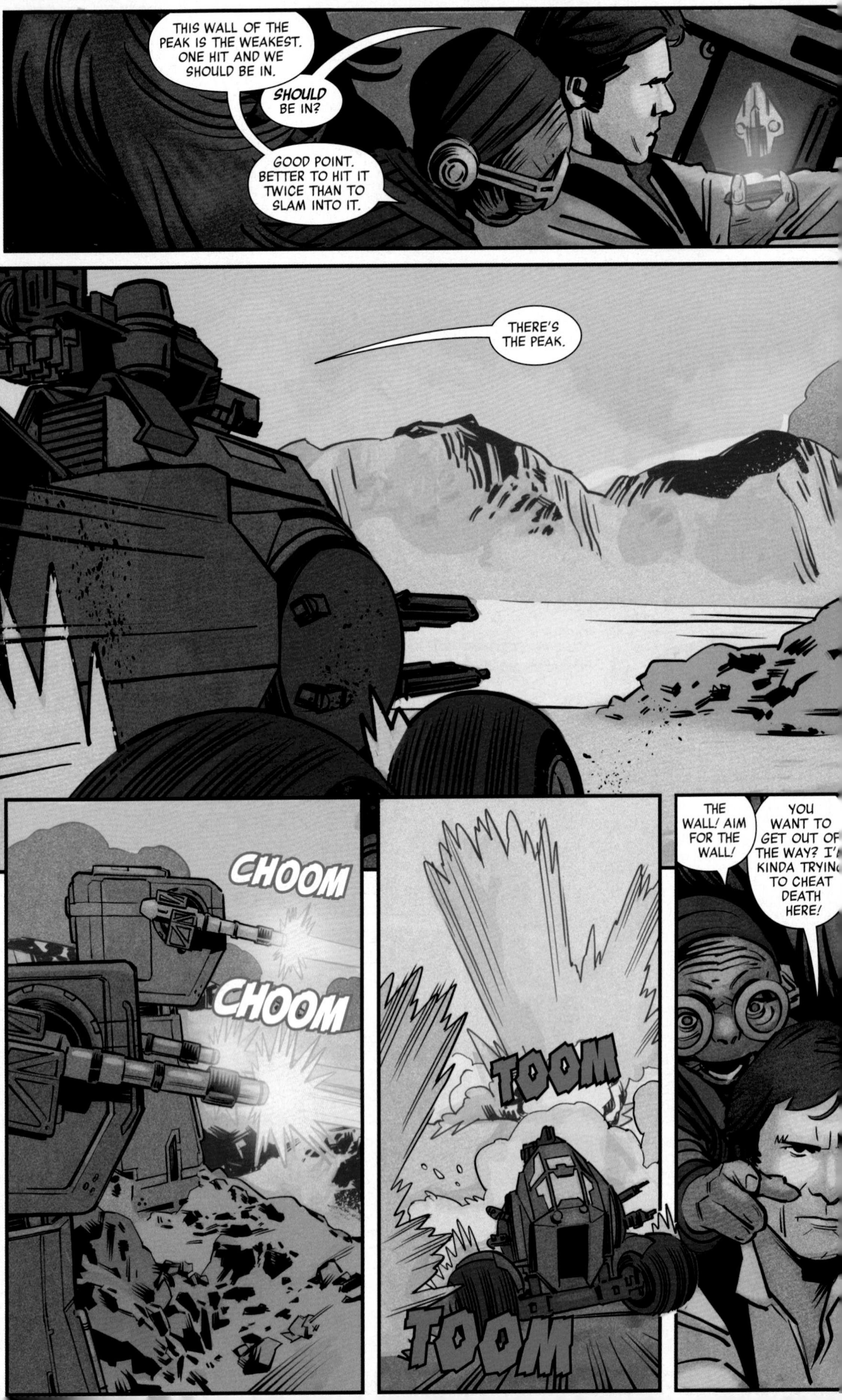

THIS WALL OF THE PEAK IS THE WEAKEST. ONE HIT AND WE SHOULD BE IN.
SHOULD BE IN?
GOOD POINT. BETTER TO HIT IT TWICE THAN TO SLAM INTO IT.
THERE'S THE PEAK.
CHOOM
CHOOM
TOOM
TOOM
THE WALL! AIM FOR THE WALL!
YOU WANT TO GET OUT OF THE WAY? I' KINDA TRYIN TO CHEAT DEATH HERE!

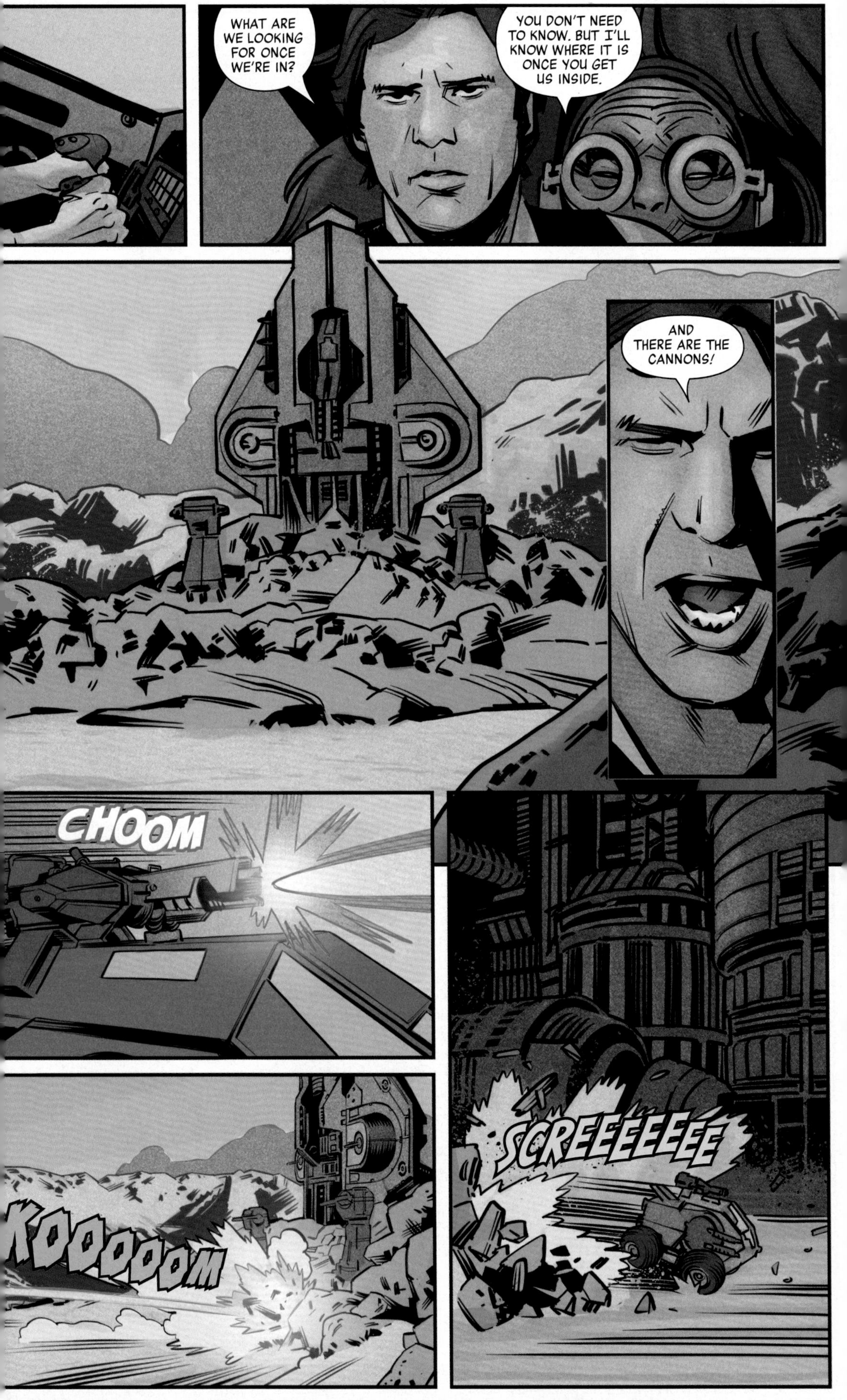
WHAT ARE WE LOOKING FOR ONCE WE'RE IN?
YOU DON'T NEED TO KNOW. BUT I'LL KNOW WHERE IT IS ONCE YOU GET US INSIDE.
AND THERE ARE THE CANNONS!
CHOOM
KOOOOOM
SCREEEEEEE

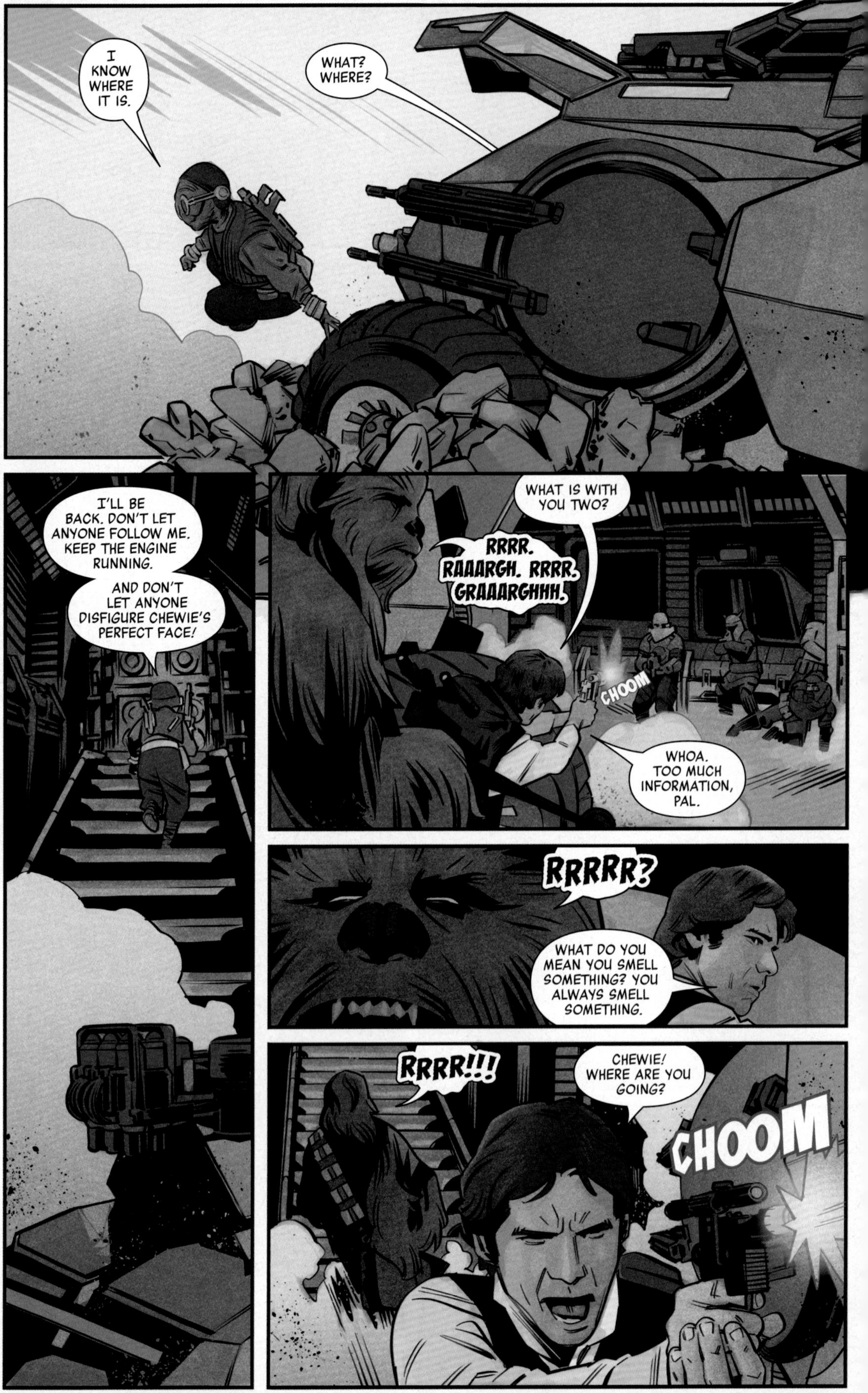

I KNOW WHERE IT IS.
WHAT? WHERE?
I'LL BE BACK. DON'T LET ANYONE FOLLOW ME. KEEP THE ENGINE RUNNING.
AND DON'T LET ANYONE DISFIGURE CHEWIE'S PERFECT FACE!
WHAT IS WITH YOU TWO?
RRRR. RAAARGH. RRRR. GRAAARGHHH.
CHOOM
WHOA. TOO MUCH INFORMATION, PAL.
RRRRR?
WHAT DO YOU MEAN YOU SMELL SOMETHING? YOU ALWAYS SMELL SOMETHING.
RRRR!!!
CHEWIE! WHERE ARE YOU GOING?
CHOOM

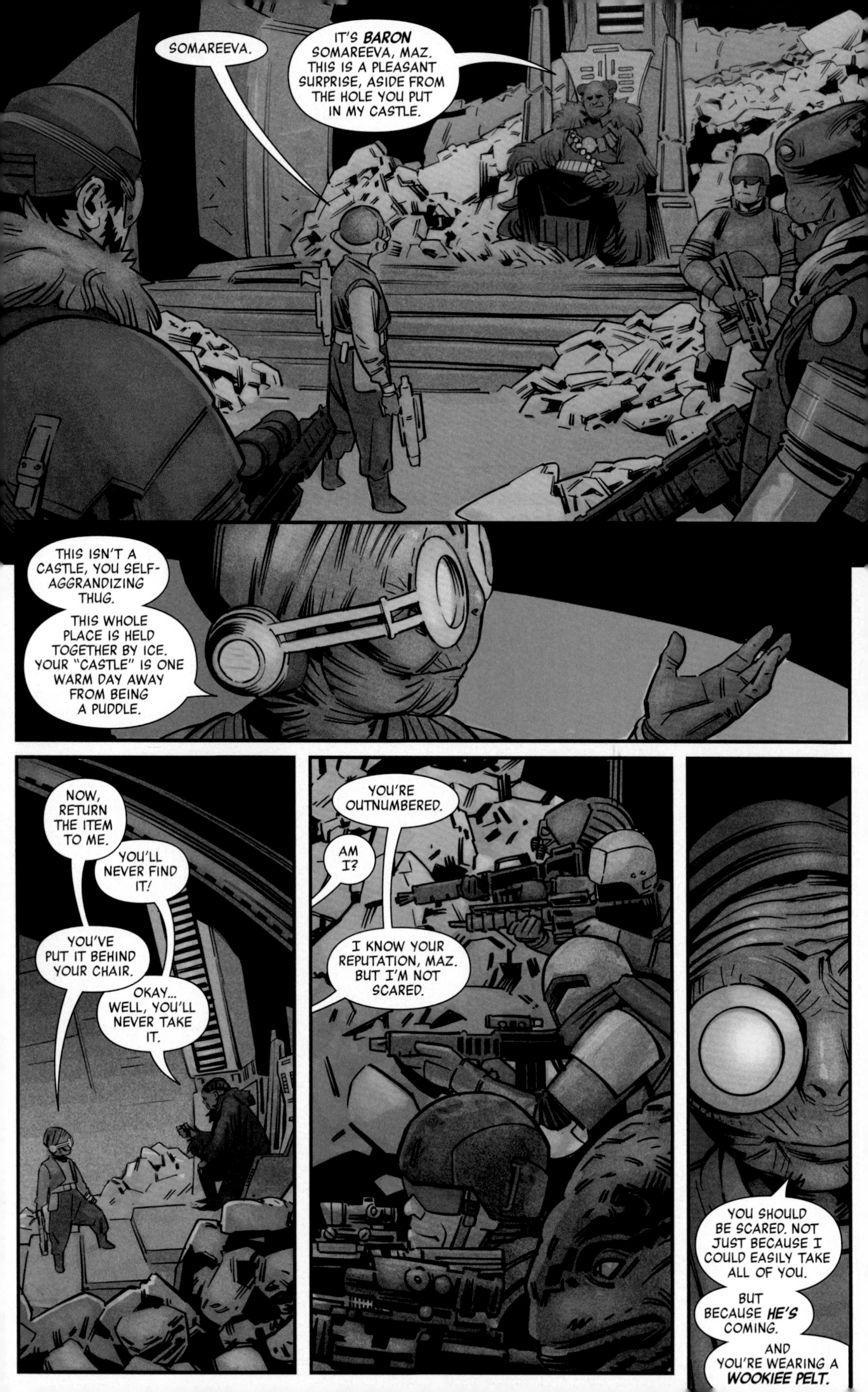
SOMAREEVA.
IT'S BARON SOMAREEVA, MAZ. THIS IS A PLEASANT SURPRISE, ASIDE FROM THE HOLE YOU PUT IN MY CASTLE.
THIS ISN'T A CASTLE, YOU SELF-AGGRANDIZING THUG.
THIS WHOLE PLACE IS HELD TOGETHER BY ICE. YOUR "CASTLE" IS ONE WARM DAY AWAY FROM BEING A PUDDLE.
NOW, RETURN THE ITEM TO ME.
YOU'LL NEVER FIND IT!
YOU'VE PUT IT BEHIND YOUR CHAIR.
OKAY... WELL, YOU'LL NEVER TAKE IT.
YOU'RE OUTNUMBERED.
AM I?
I KNOW YOUR REPUTATION, MAZ. BUT I'M NOT SCARED.
YOU SHOULD BE SCARED. NOT JUST BECAUSE I COULD EASILY TAKE ALL OF YOU.
BUT BECAUSE HE'S COMING.
AND YOU'RE WEARING A WOOKIEE PELT.

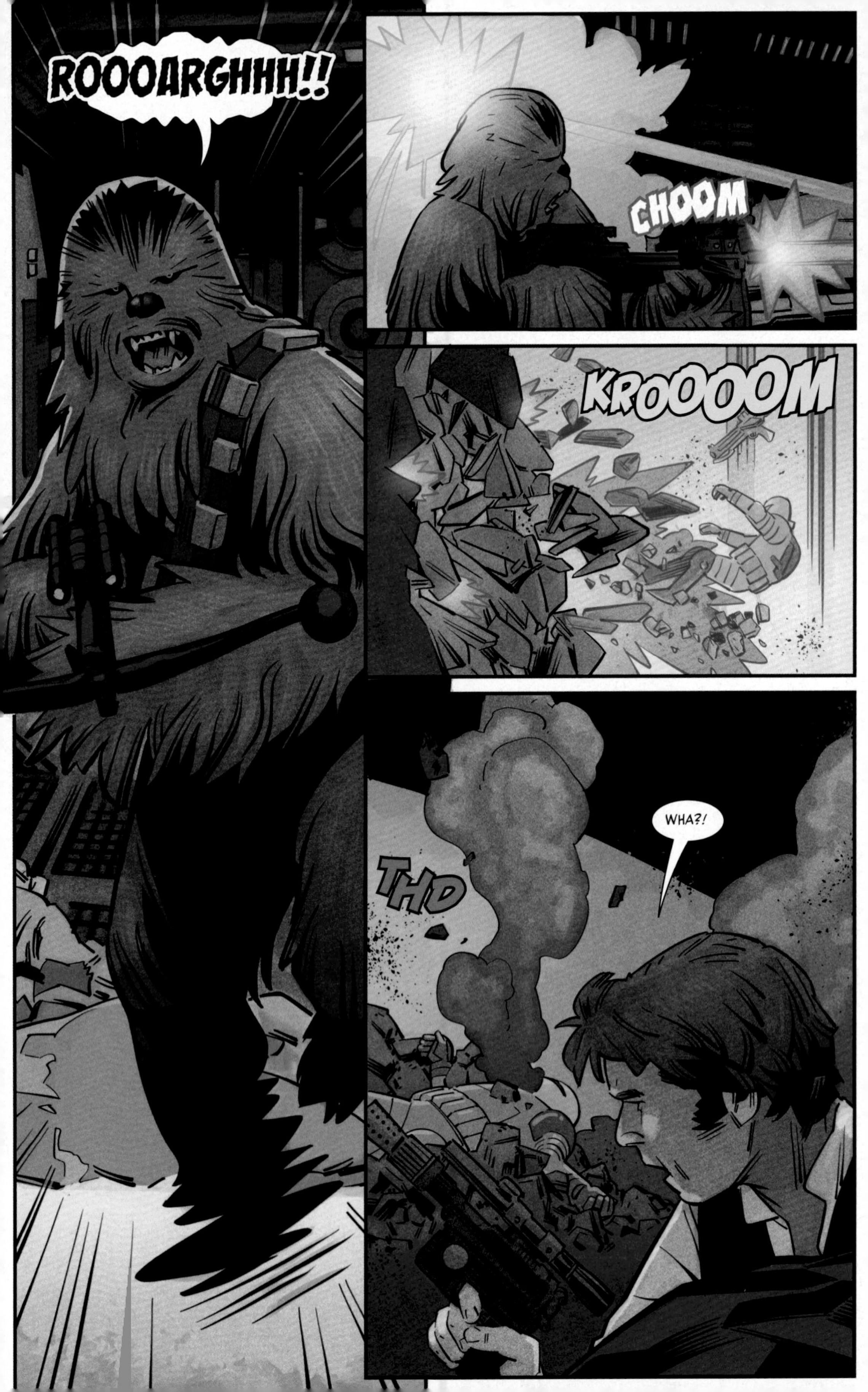
ROOOARGHHH!!
CHOOM
KROOOOOM
THD
WHA?!

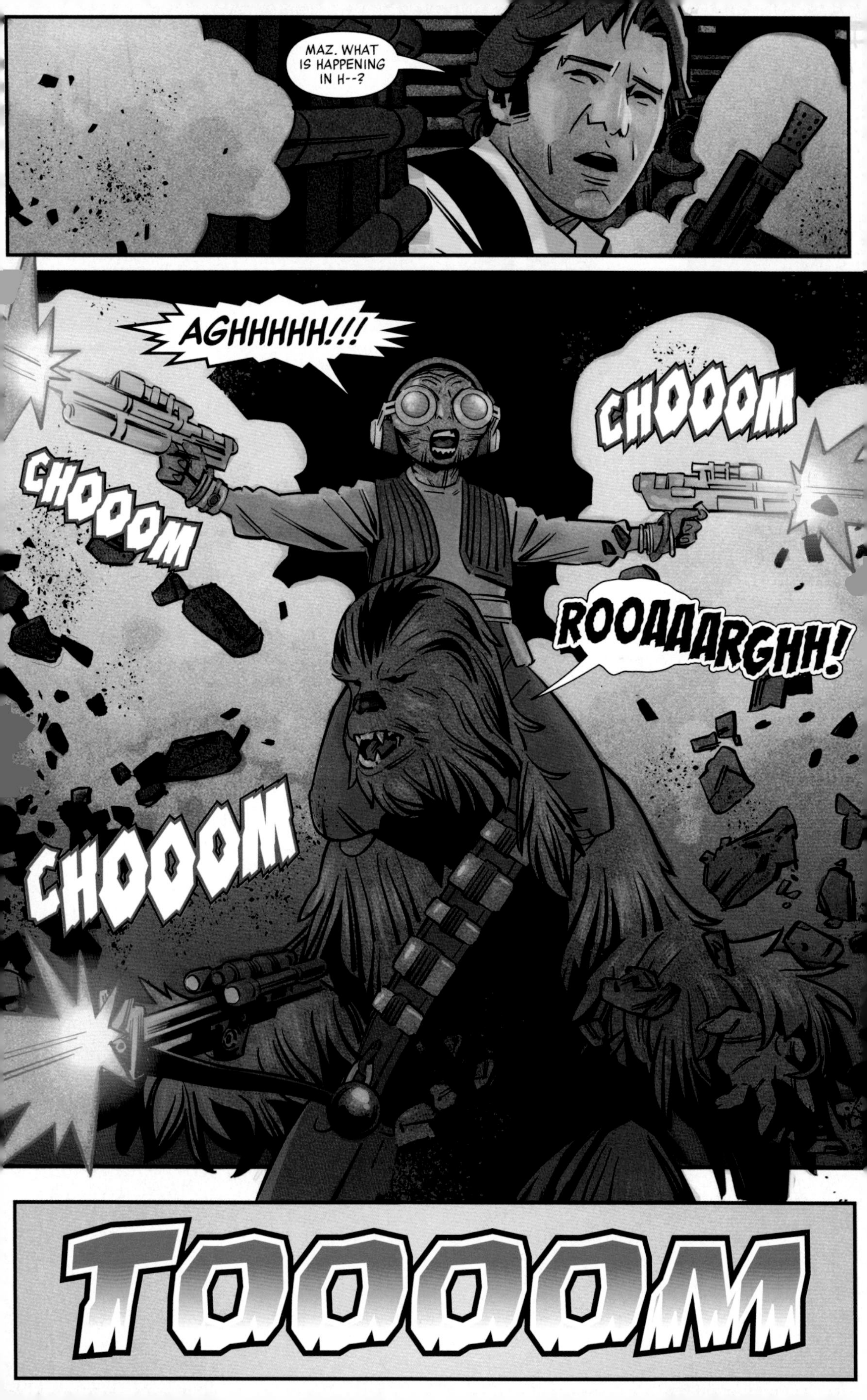
MAZ. WHAT IS HAPPENING IN H--?
AGHHHHH!!!
CHOOOM
CHOOOM
ROOAAAARGHH!
CHOOOM
TOOOOM

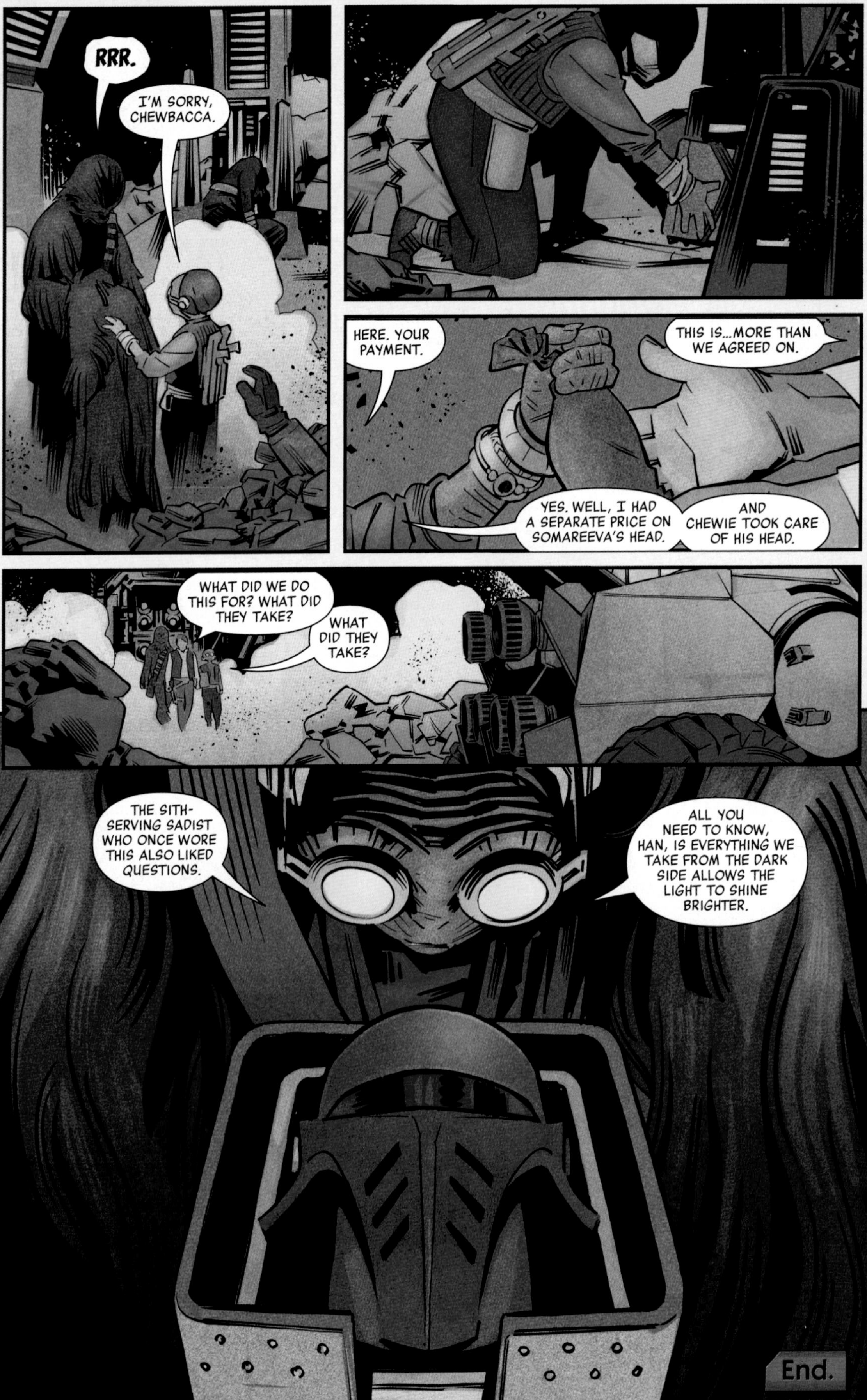
RRR.
I'M SORRY, CHEWBACCA.
HERE. YOUR PAYMENT.
THIS IS...MORE THAN WE AGREED ON.
YES. WELL, I HAD A SEPARATE PRICE ON SOMAREEVA'S HEAD.
AND CHEWIE TOOK CARE OF HIS HEAD.
WHAT DID WE DO THIS FOR? WHAT DID THEY TAKE?
WHAT DID THEY TAKE?
THE SITH-SERVING SADIST WHO ONCE WORE THIS ALSO LIKED QUESTIONS.
ALL YOU NEED TO KNOW, HAN, IS EVERYTHING WE TAKE FROM THE DARK SIDE ALLOWS THE LIGHT TO SHINE BRIGHTER.
End.

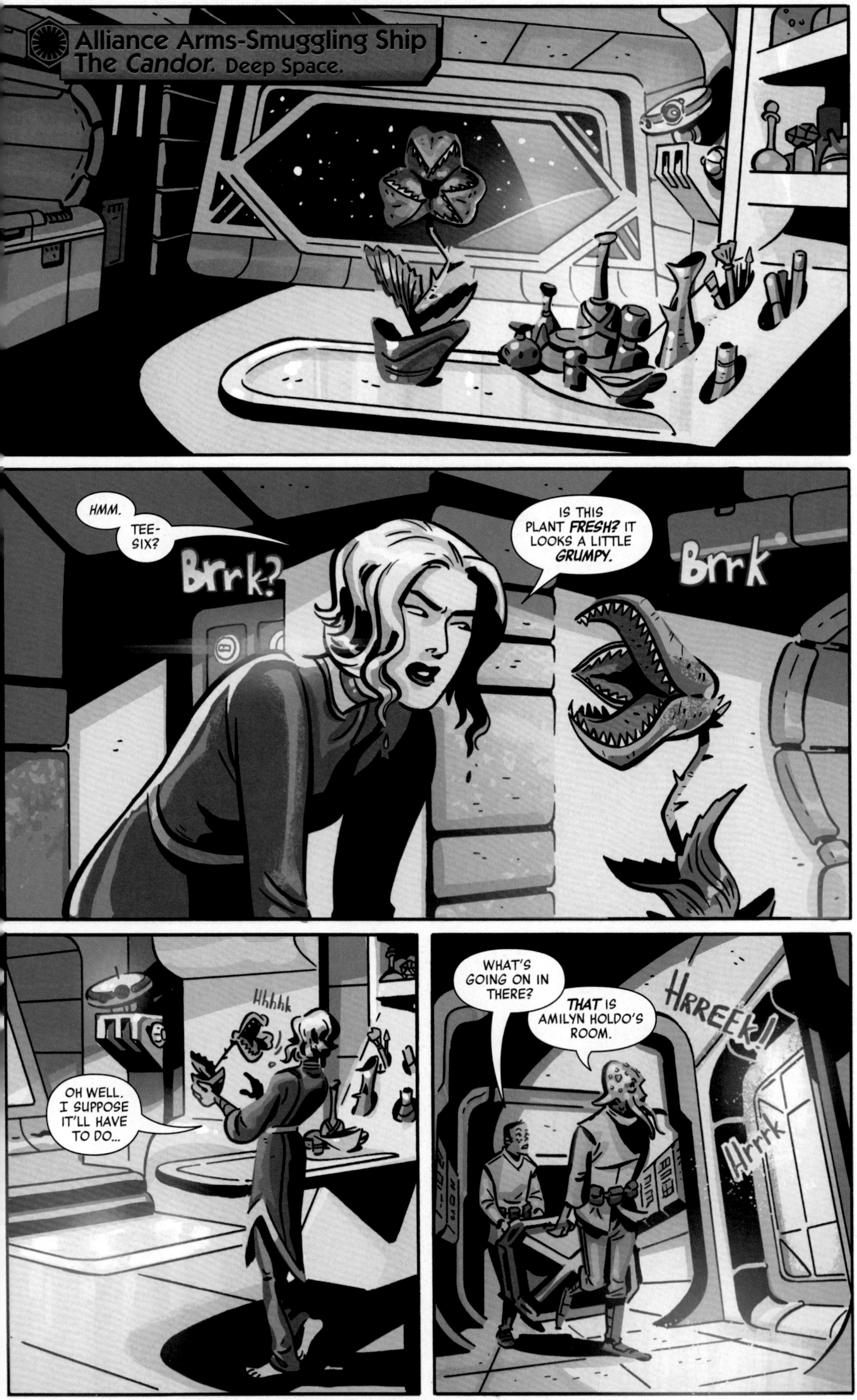

Alliance Arms-Smuggling Ship The Candor. Deep Space.
HMM. TEE-SIX?
Brrk?
IS THIS PLANT FRESH? IT LOOKS A LITTLE GRUMPY.
Brrk
Hhhhk
OH WELL. I SUPPOSE IT'LL HAVE TO DO...
WHAT'S GOING ON IN THERE?
THAT IS AMILYN HOLDO'S ROOM.
HRREEK!!
Hrrrk

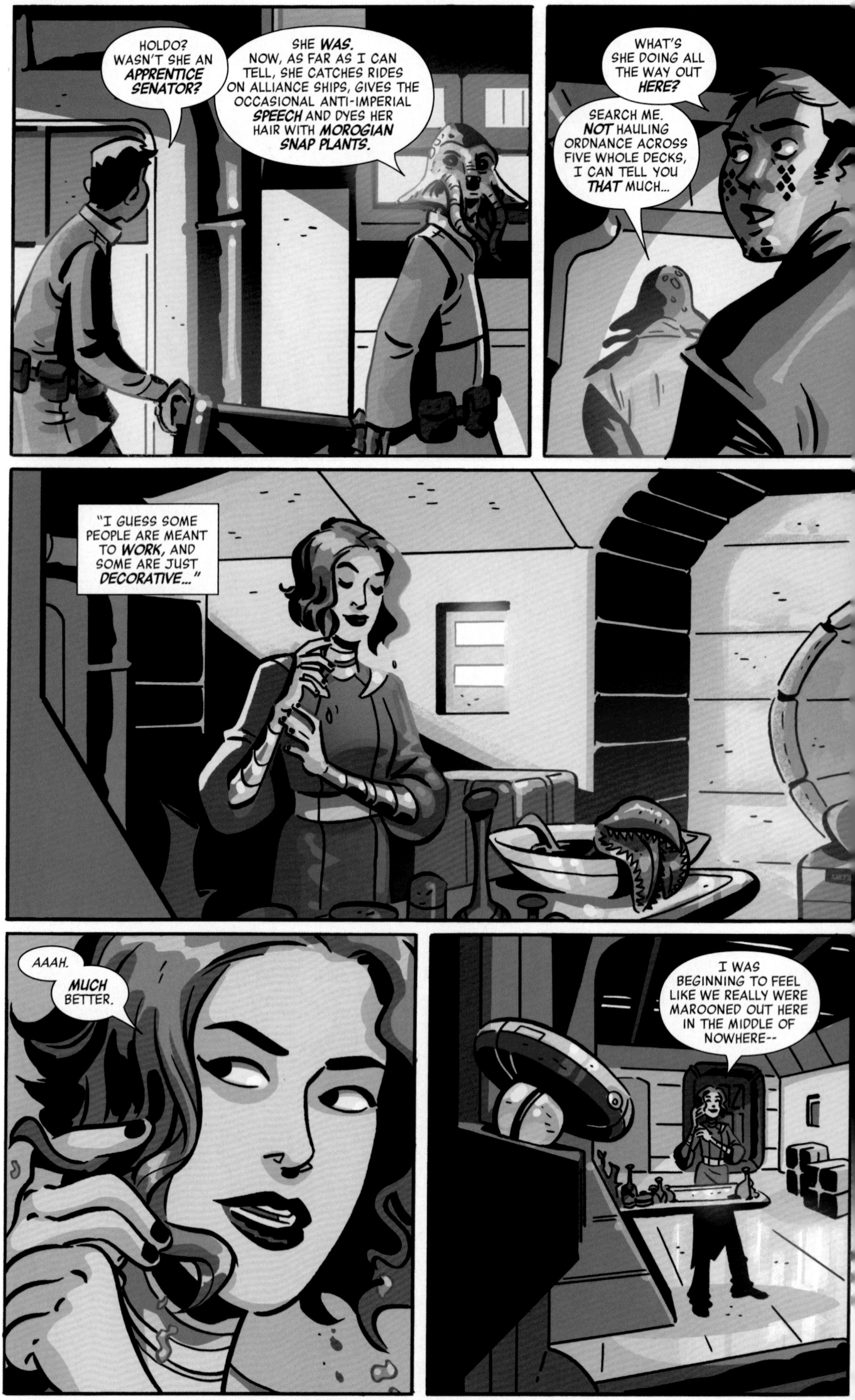
HOLDO? WASN'T SHE AN APPRENTICE SENATOR?
SHE WAS. NOW, AS FAR AS I CAN TELL, SHE CATCHES RIDES ON ALLIANCE SHIPS, GIVES THE OCCASIONAL ANTI-IMPERIAL SPEECH AND DYES HER HAIR WITH MOROGIAN SNAP PLANTS.
WHAT'S SHE DOING ALL THE WAY OUT HERE?
SEARCH ME. NOT HAULING ORDNANCE ACROSS FIVE WHOLE DECKS, I CAN TELL YOU THAT MUCH...
"I GUESS SOME PEOPLE ARE MEANT TO WORK, AND SOME ARE JUST DECORATIVE..."
AAAH. MUCH BETTER.
I WAS BEGINNING TO FEEL LIKE WE REALLY WERE MAROONED OUT HERE IN THE MIDDLE OF NOWHERE--

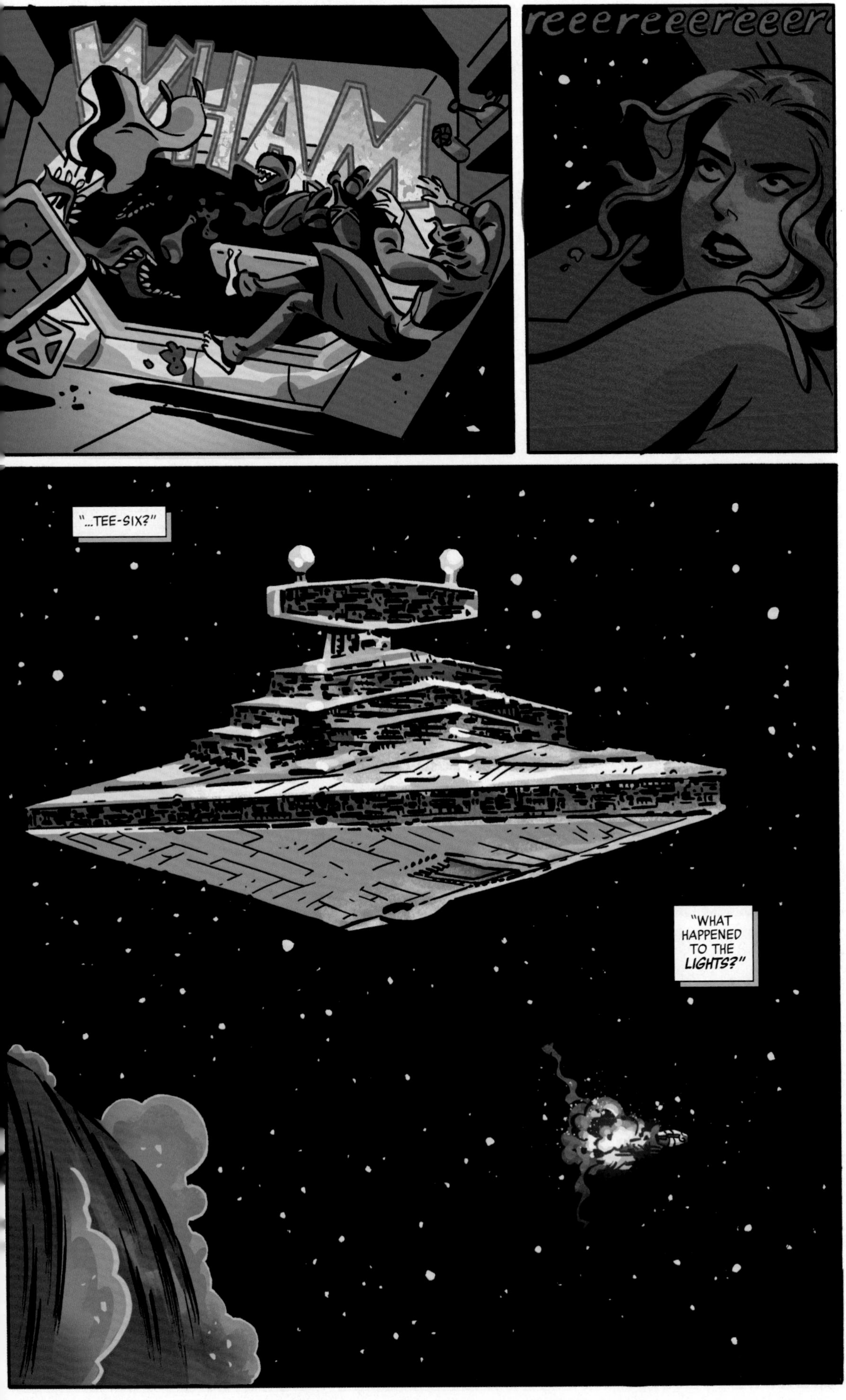
WHAM
reeereeeereeeer
"...TEE-SIX?"
"WHAT HAPPENED TO THE LIGHTS?"

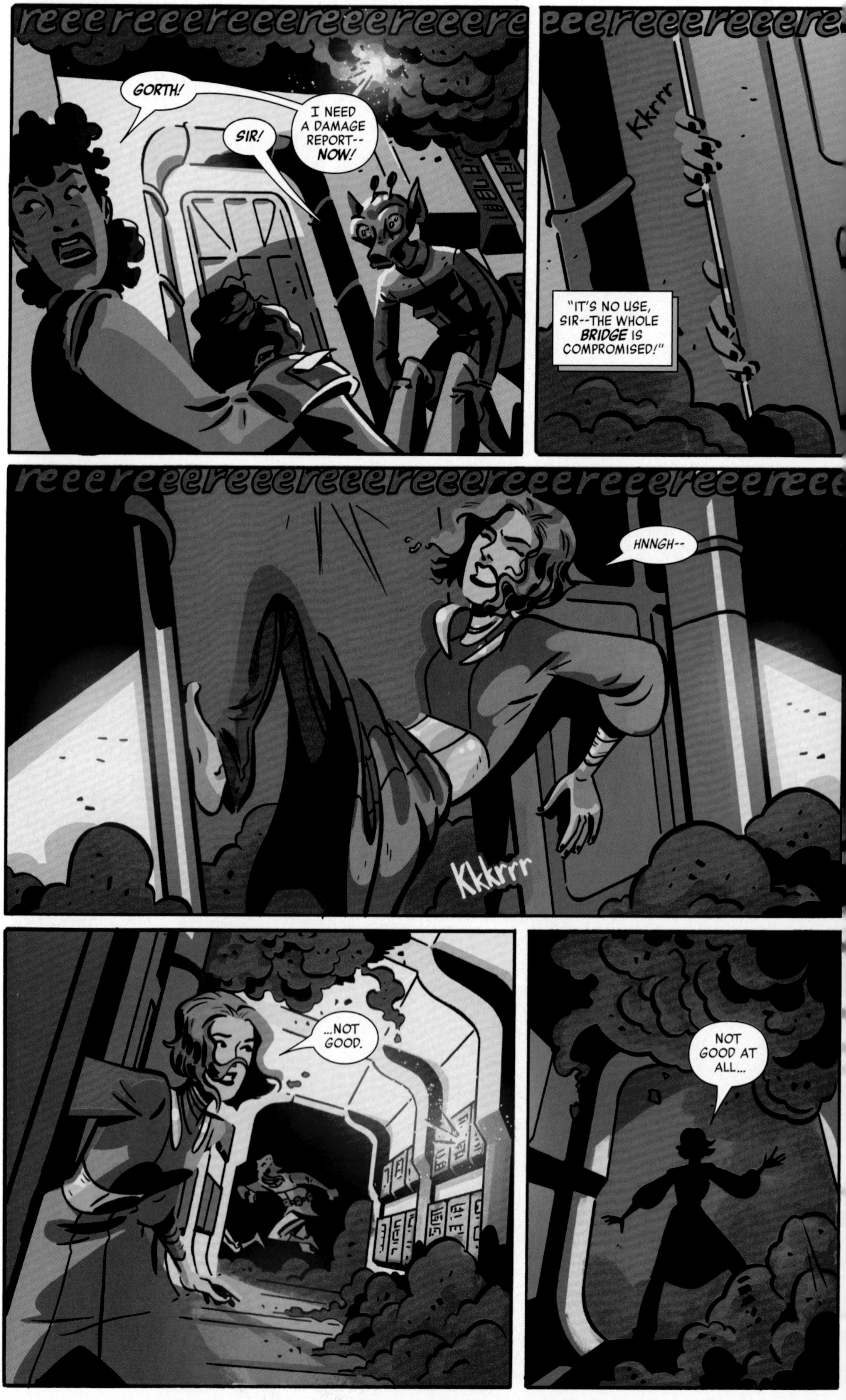
reeereeereeereeere
GORTH!
I NEED A DAMAGE REPORT-- NOW!
SIR!
eeereeereeere
Kkrrr
"IT'S NO USE, SIR--THE WHOLE BRIDGE IS COMPROMISED!"
reeereeereeereeereeereeereeereee
HNNGH--
Kkkrrr
...NOT GOOD.
NOT GOOD AT ALL...

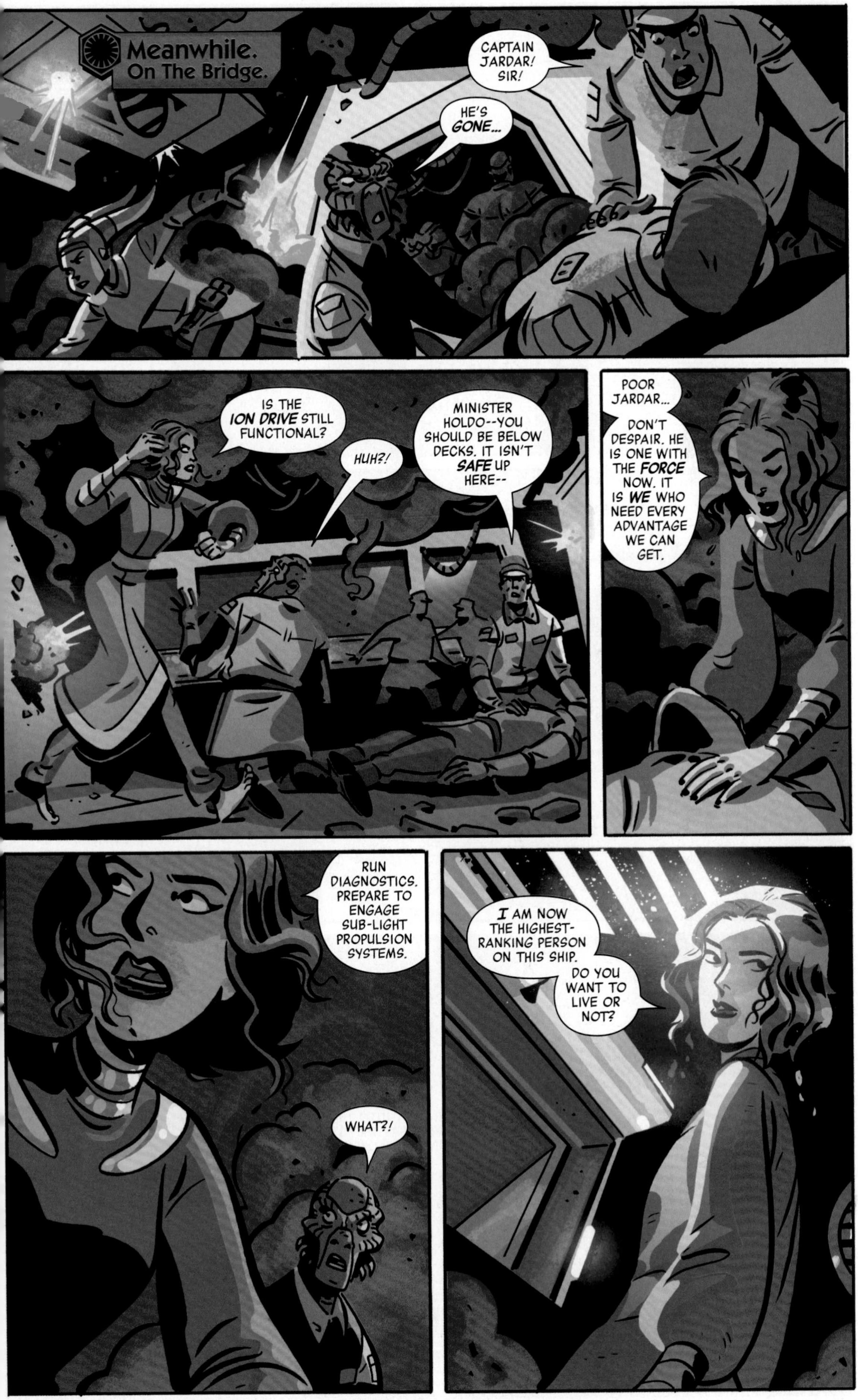
Meanwhile. On The Bridge.
CAPTAIN JARDAR! SIR!
HE'S GONE...
IS THE ION DRIVE STILL FUNCTIONAL?
HUH?!
MINISTER HOLDO--YOU SHOULD BE BELOW DECKS. IT ISN'T SAFE UP HERE--
POOR JARDAR...
DON'T DESPAIR. HE IS ONE WITH THE FORCE NOW. IT IS WE WHO NEED EVERY ADVANTAGE WE CAN GET.
RUN DIAGNOSTICS. PREPARE TO ENGAGE SUB-LIGHT PROPULSION SYSTEMS.
WHAT?!
I AM NOW THE HIGHEST-RANKING PERSON ON THIS SHIP.
DO YOU WANT TO LIVE OR NOT?

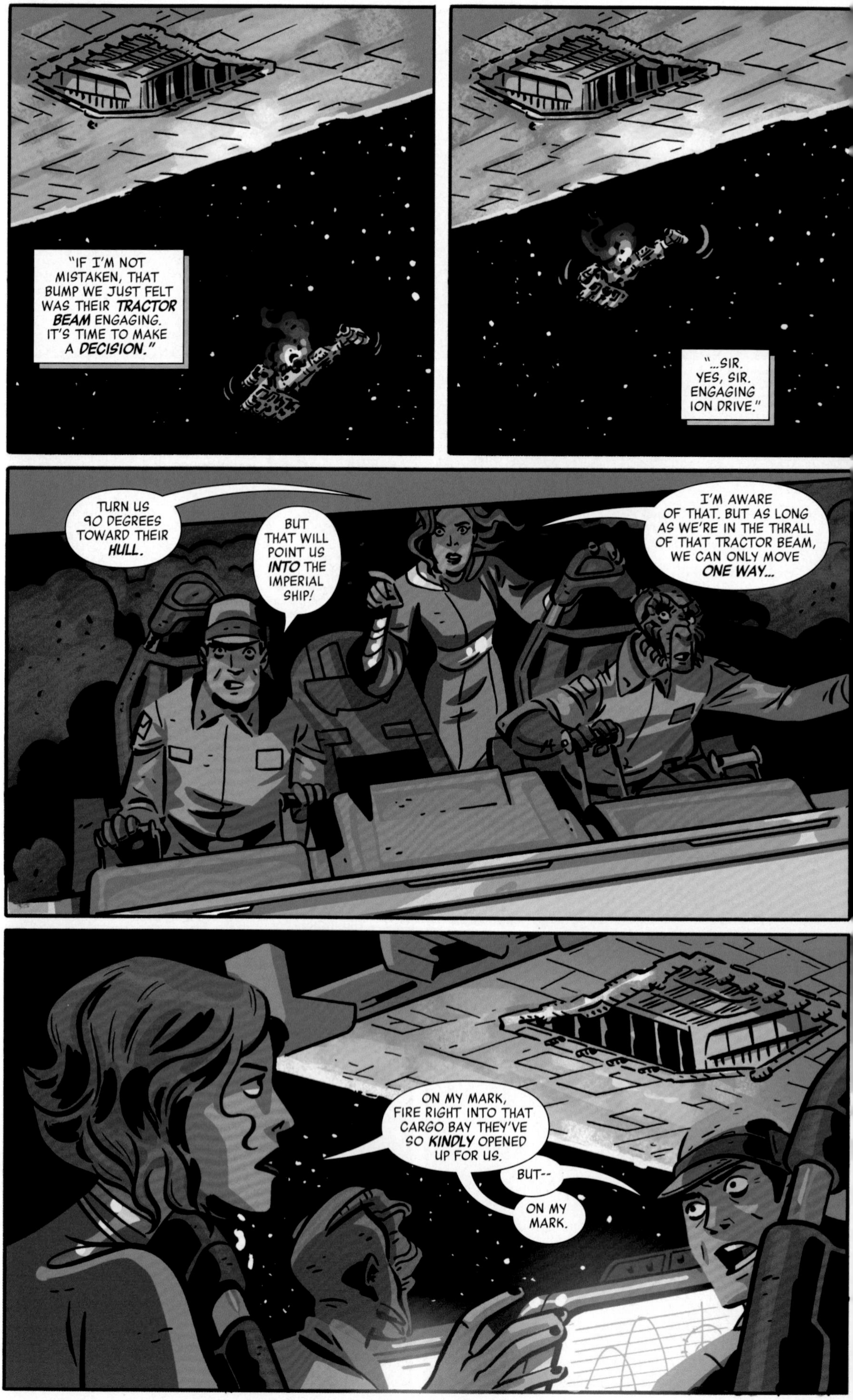
"IF I'M NOT MISTAKEN, THAT BUMP WE JUST FELT WAS THEIR *TRACTOR BEAM* ENGAGING. IT'S TIME TO MAKE A *DECISION.*"
"...SIR. YES, SIR. ENGAGING ION DRIVE."
TURN US 90 DEGREES TOWARD THEIR *HULL.*
BUT THAT WILL POINT US *INTO* THE IMPERIAL SHIP!
I'M AWARE OF THAT. BUT AS LONG AS WE'RE IN THE THRALL OF THAT TRACTOR BEAM, WE CAN ONLY MOVE *ONE WAY...*
ON MY MARK, FIRE RIGHT INTO THAT CARGO BAY THEY'VE SO *KINDLY* OPENED UP FOR US.
BUT--
ON MY MARK.

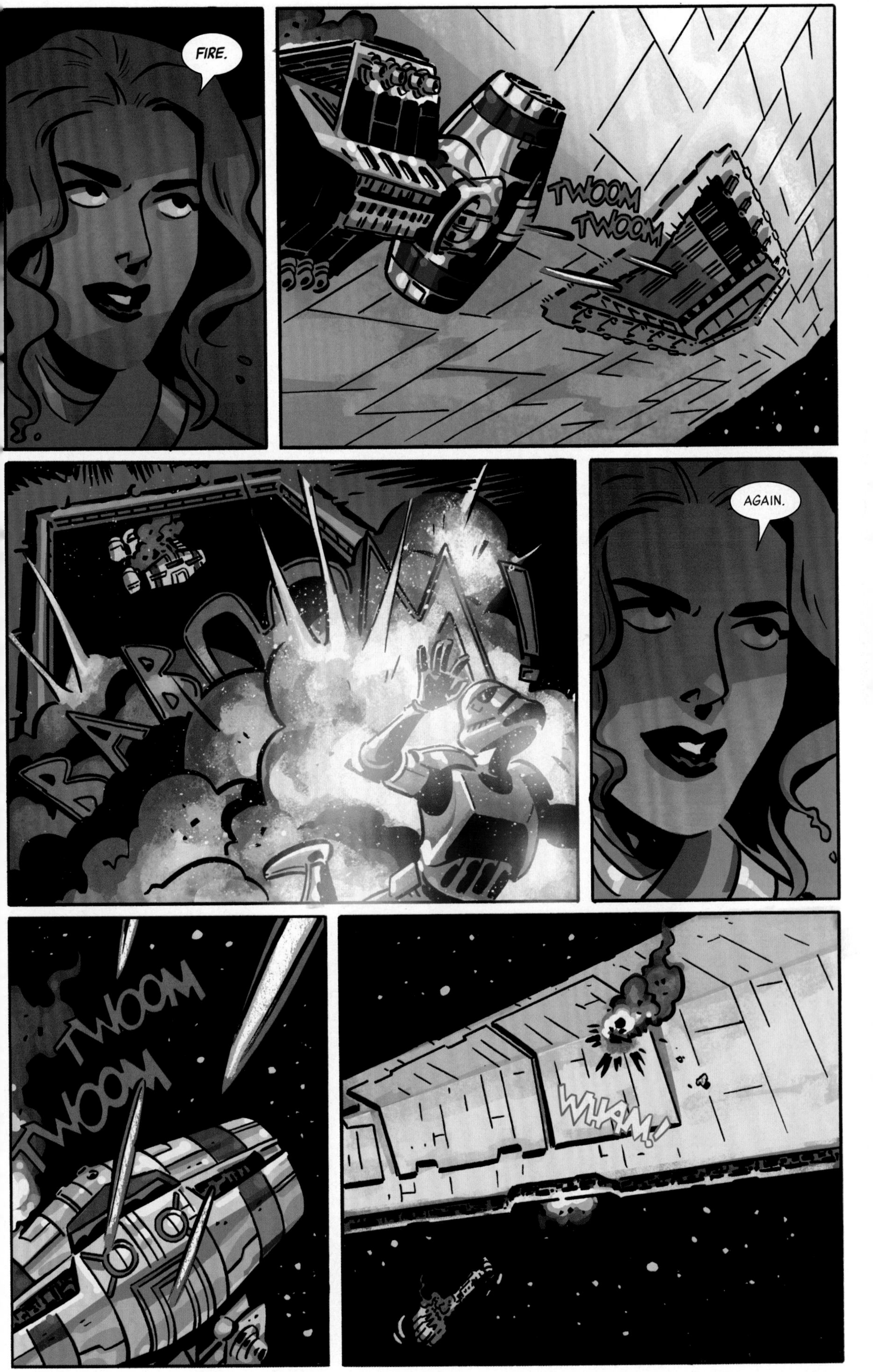
FIRE.
TWOOM
TWOOM
RABOOM!
AGAIN.
TWOOM
TWOOM
WHAM!

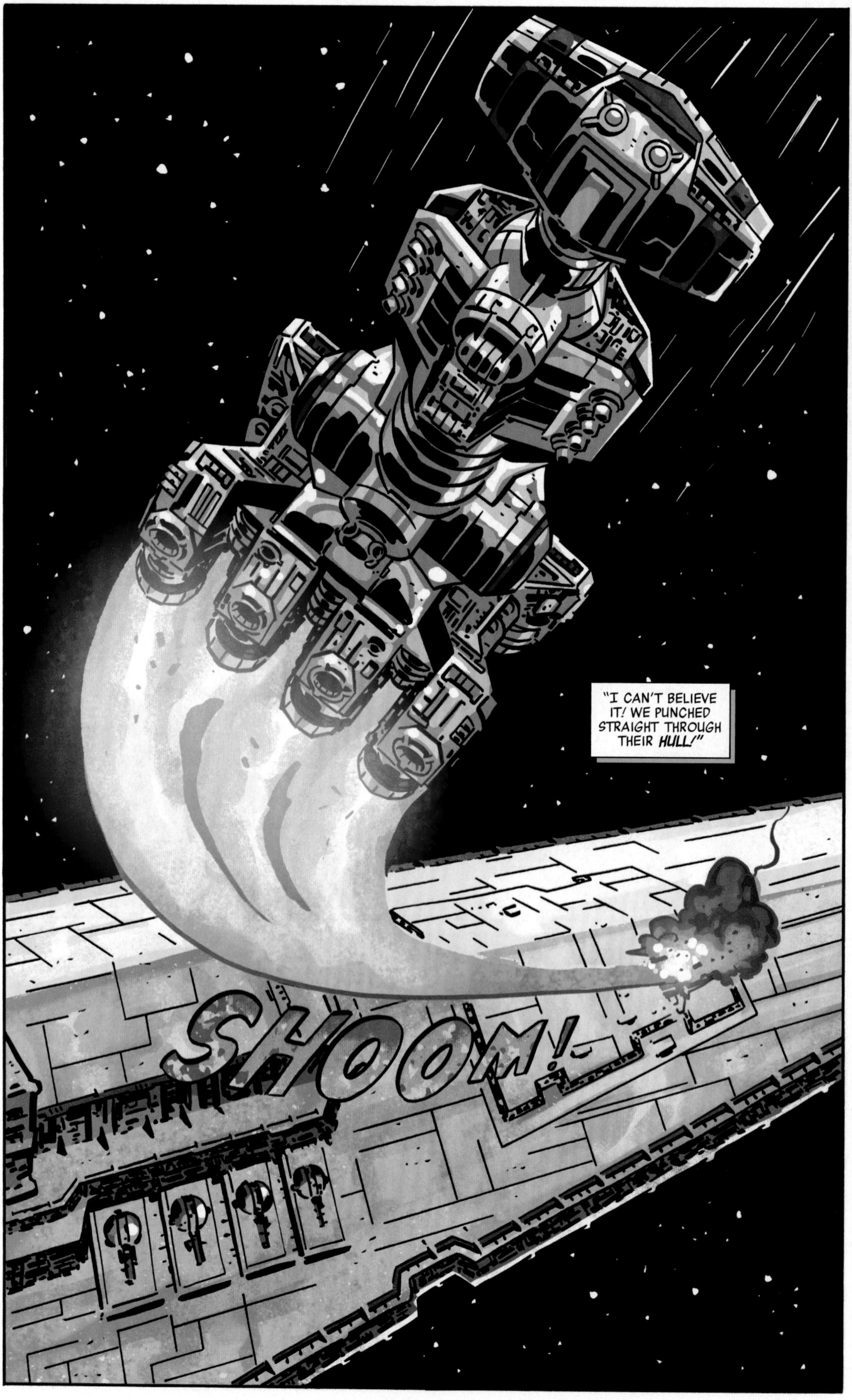
"I CAN'T BELIEVE IT! WE PUNCHED STRAIGHT THROUGH THEIR HULL!"
SHOOM!

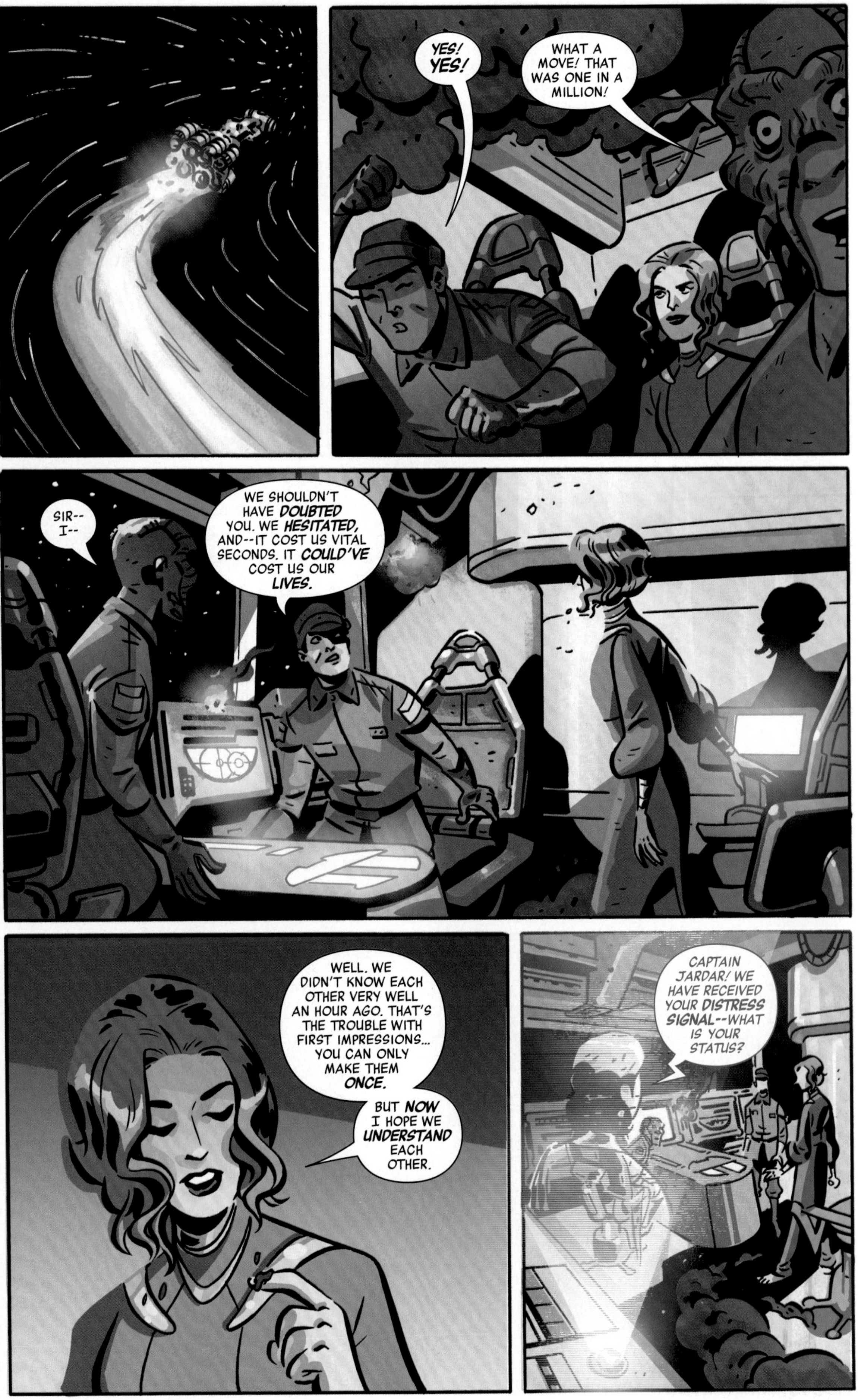
YES! YES!
WHAT A MOVE! THAT WAS ONE IN A MILLION!
SIR-- I--
WE SHOULDN'T HAVE DOUBTED YOU. WE HESITATED, AND--IT COST US VITAL SECONDS. IT COULD'VE COST US OUR LIVES.
WELL. WE DIDN'T KNOW EACH OTHER VERY WELL AN HOUR AGO. THAT'S THE TROUBLE WITH FIRST IMPRESSIONS... YOU CAN ONLY MAKE THEM ONCE.
BUT NOW I HOPE WE UNDERSTAND EACH OTHER.
CAPTAIN JARDAR! WE HAVE RECEIVED YOUR DISTRESS SIGNAL--WHAT IS YOUR STATUS?

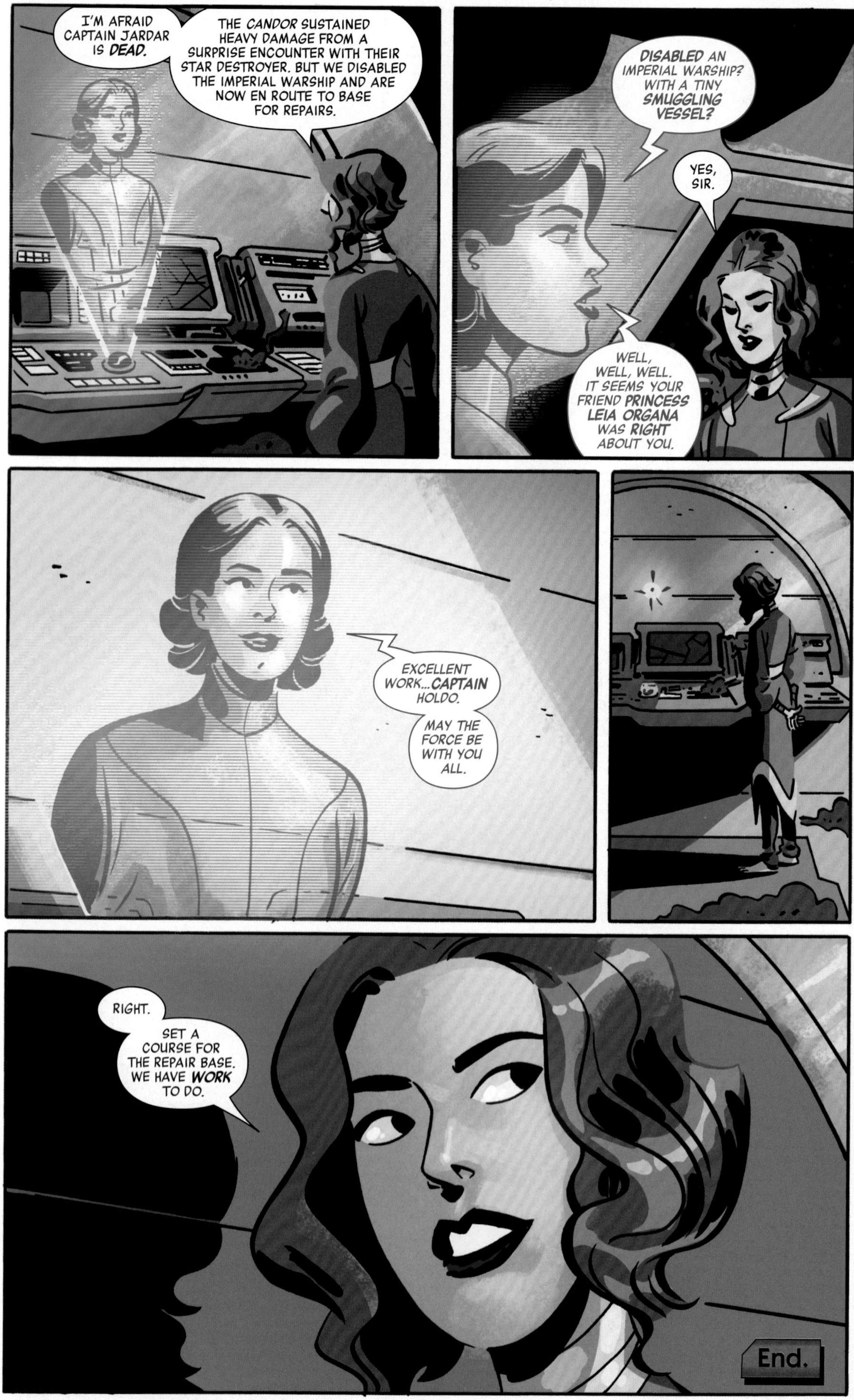
I'M AFRAID CAPTAIN JARDAR IS **DEAD.**
THE *CANDOR* SUSTAINED HEAVY DAMAGE FROM A SURPRISE ENCOUNTER WITH THEIR STAR DESTROYER. BUT WE DISABLED THE IMPERIAL WARSHIP AND ARE NOW EN ROUTE TO BASE FOR REPAIRS.
DISABLED AN IMPERIAL WARSHIP? WITH A TINY **SMUGGLING VESSEL?**
YES, SIR.
WELL, WELL, WELL. IT SEEMS YOUR FRIEND **PRINCESS LEIA ORGANA** WAS **RIGHT** ABOUT YOU.
EXCELLENT WORK...**CAPTAIN** HOLDO.
MAY THE FORCE BE WITH YOU ALL.
RIGHT.
SET A COURSE FOR THE REPAIR BASE. WE HAVE **WORK** TO DO.
End.

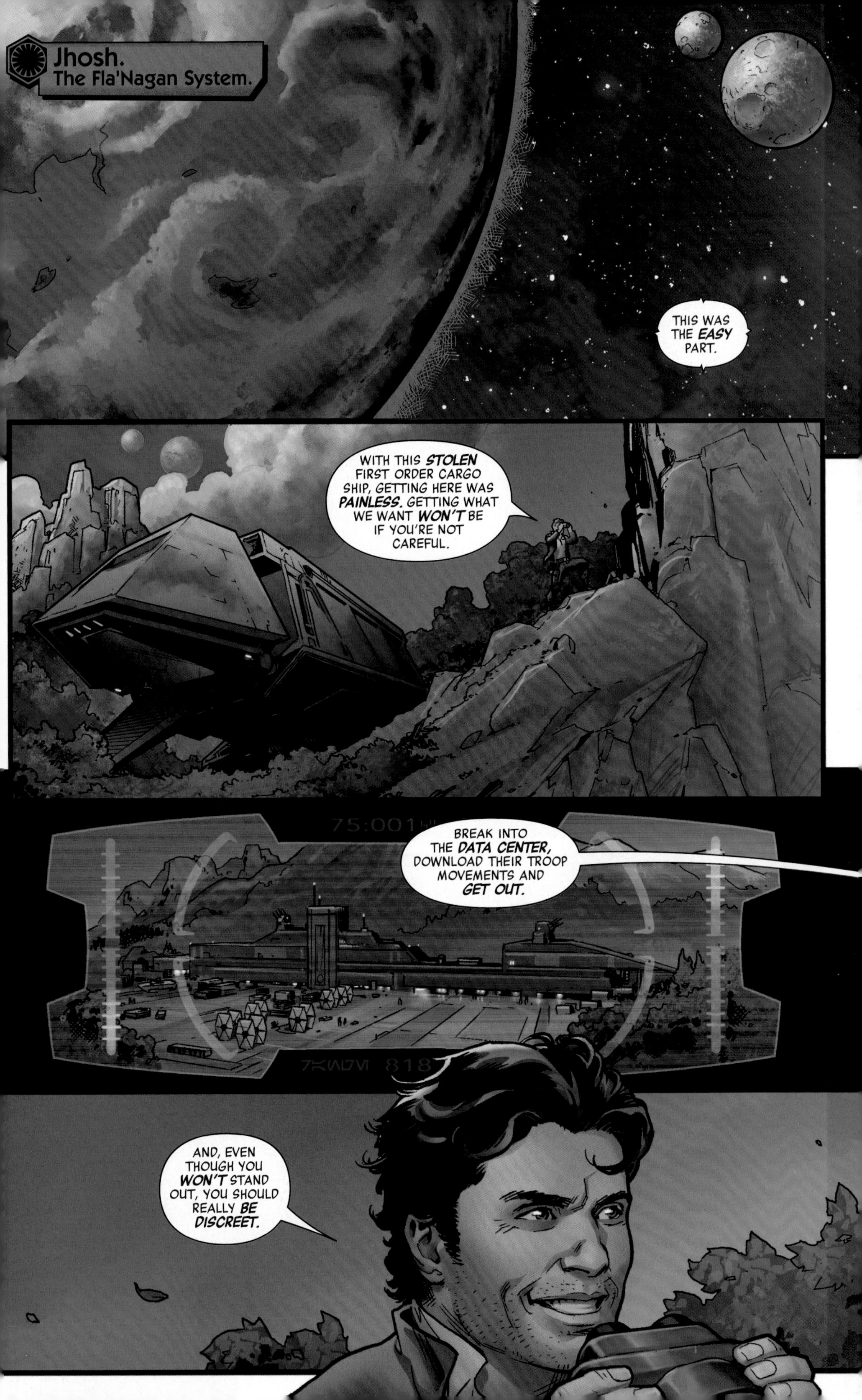
Jhosh.
The Fla'Nagan System.
THIS WAS THE EASY PART.
WITH THIS STOLEN FIRST ORDER CARGO SHIP, GETTING HERE WAS PAINLESS. GETTING WHAT WE WANT WON'T BE IF YOU'RE NOT CAREFUL.
75:001
BREAK INTO THE DATA CENTER, DOWNLOAD THEIR TROOP MOVEMENTS AND GET OUT.
818
AND, EVEN THOUGH YOU WON'T STAND OUT, YOU SHOULD REALLY BE DISCREET.

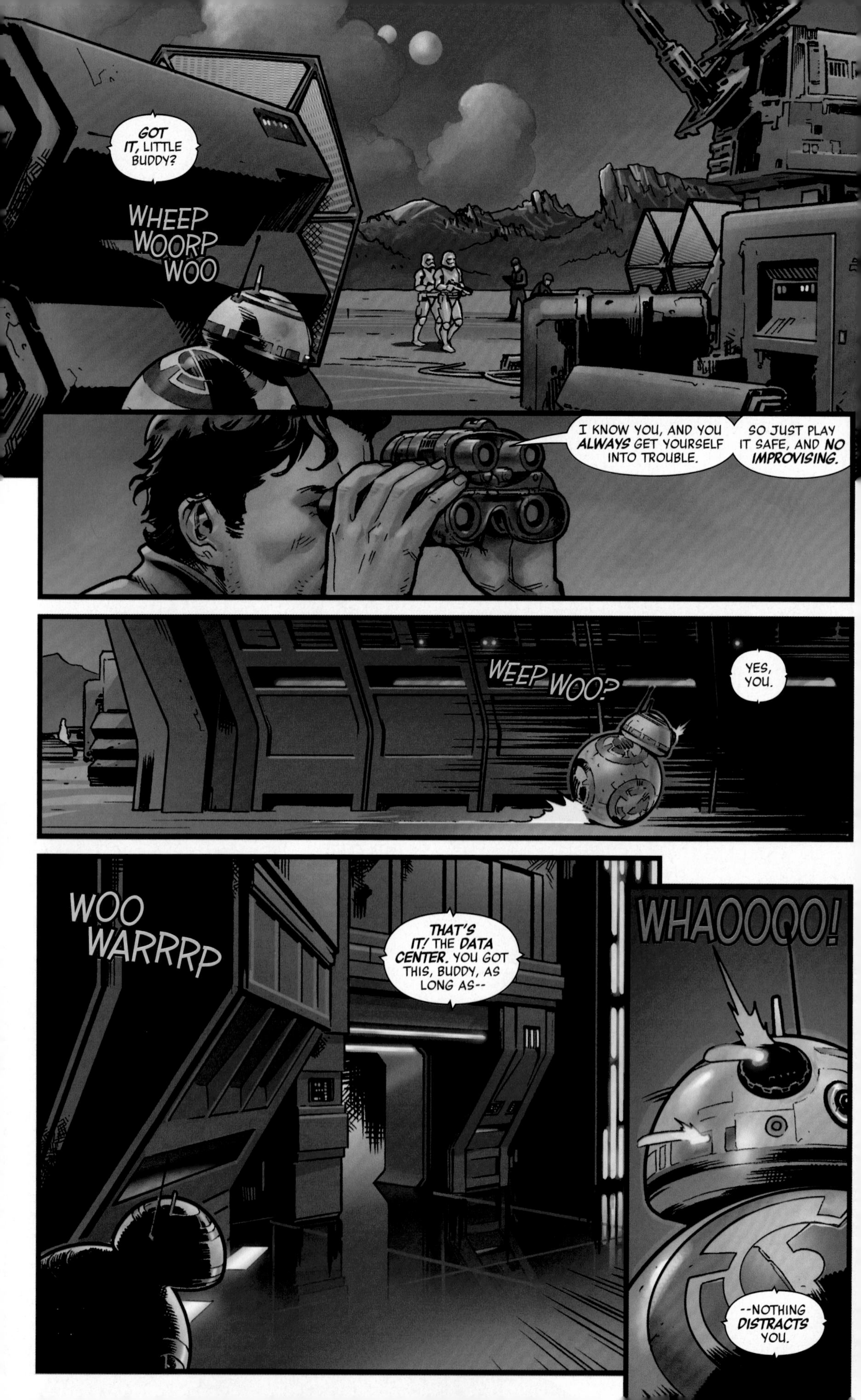
GOT IT, LITTLE BUDDY?
WHEEP WOORP WOO
I KNOW YOU, AND YOU ALWAYS GET YOURSELF INTO TROUBLE.
SO JUST PLAY IT SAFE, AND NO IMPROVISING.
WEEP WOO?
YES, YOU.
WOO WARRRP
THAT'S IT! THE DATA CENTER. YOU GOT THIS, BUDDY, AS LONG AS--
WHAOOQO!
--NOTHING DISTRACTS YOU.

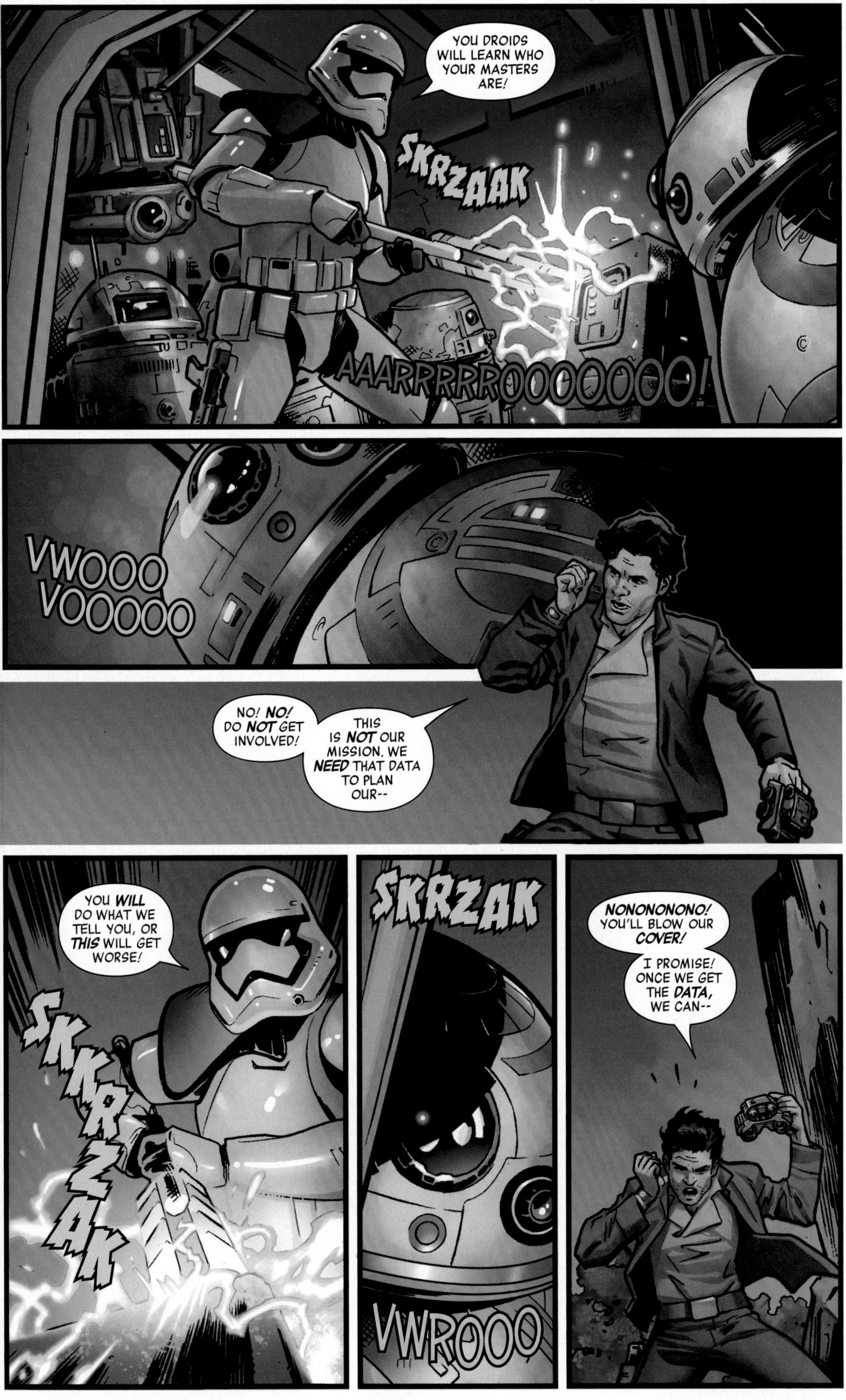
YOU DROIDS WILL LEARN WHO YOUR MASTERS ARE!
SKRZAAK
AAARRRRROOOOOOOO!
VWOOO VOOOOO
NO! NO! DO NOT GET INVOLVED!
THIS IS NOT OUR MISSION. WE NEED THAT DATA TO PLAN OUR--
YOU WILL DO WHAT WE TELL YOU, OR THIS WILL GET WORSE!
SKKRRZZAK
SKRZAK
VWROOO
NONONONONO! YOU'LL BLOW OUR COVER!
I PROMISE! ONCE WE GET THE DATA, WE CAN--

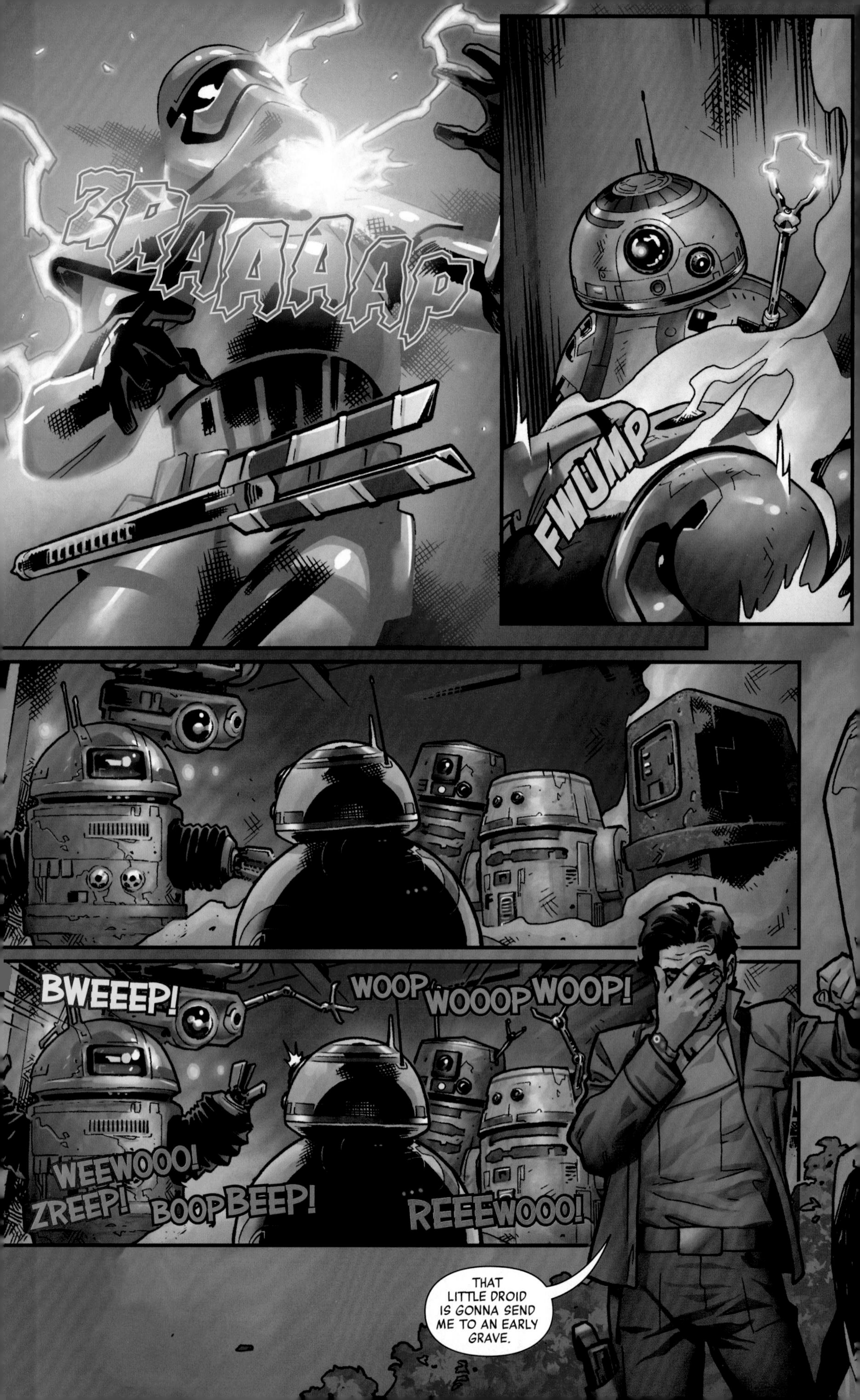
ZRAAAAAP
FWUMP
BWEEEP!
WOOP WOOOP WOOP!
WEEWOOO!
ZREEP!
BOOP BEEP!
REEEWOOO!
THAT LITTLE DROID IS GONNA SEND ME TO AN EARLY GRAVE.

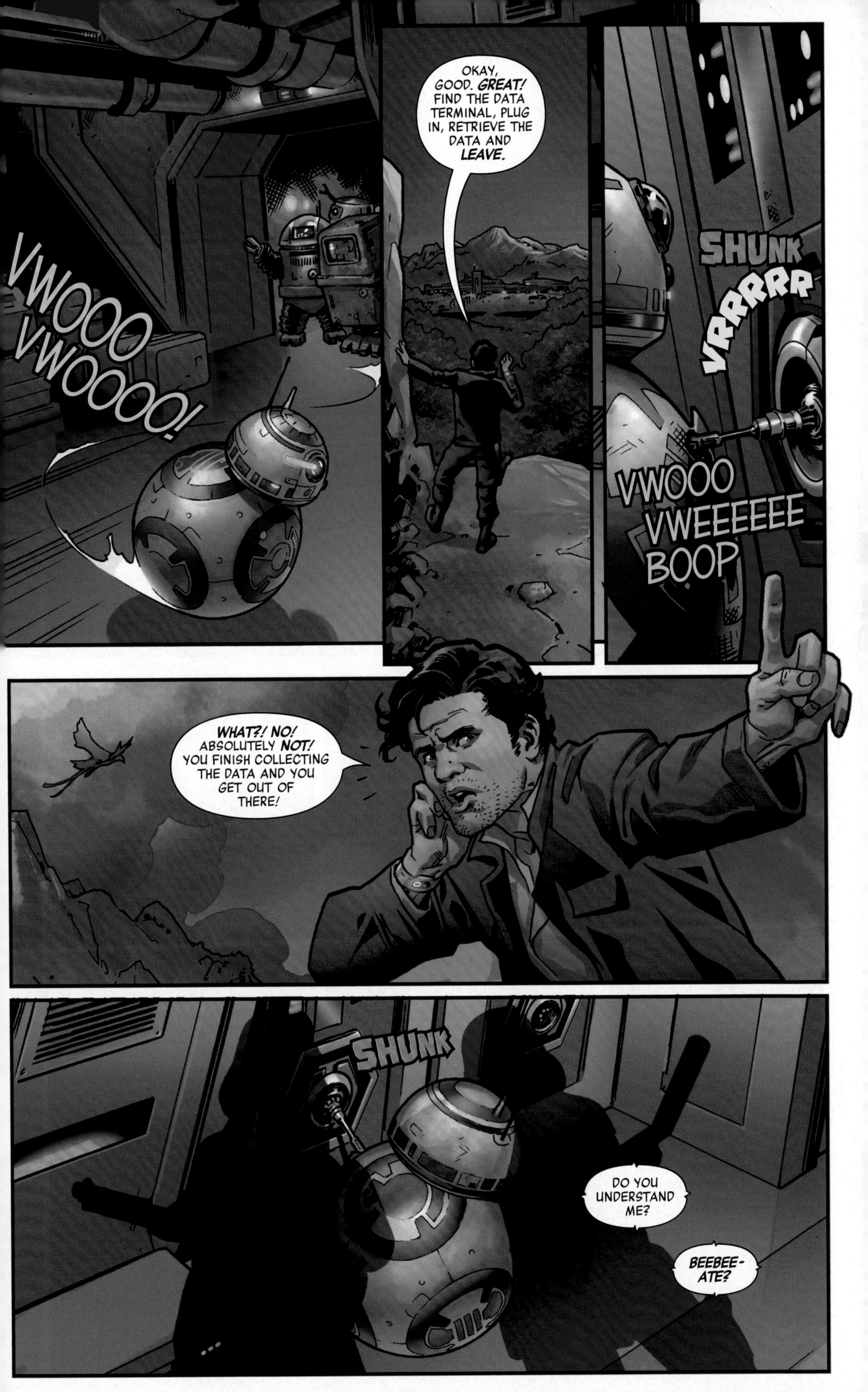
VWOOO VWOOOO!
OKAY, GOOD. GREAT! FIND THE DATA TERMINAL, PLUG IN, RETRIEVE THE DATA AND LEAVE.
SHUNK
VRRRRR
VWOOO VWEEEEEE BOOP
WHAT?! NO! ABSOLUTELY NOT! YOU FINISH COLLECTING THE DATA AND YOU GET OUT OF THERE!
SHUNK
DO YOU UNDERSTAND ME?
BEEBEE-ATE?

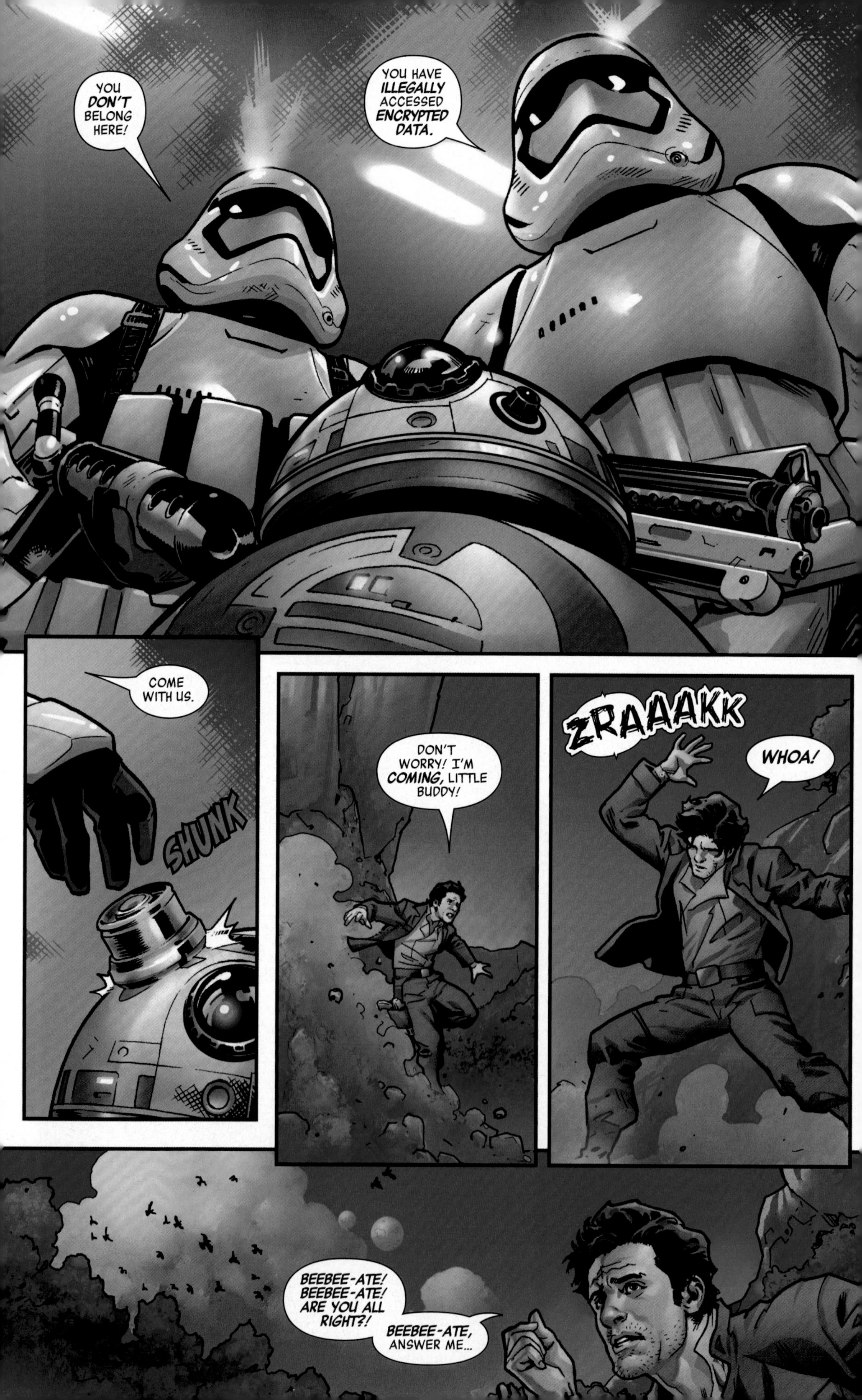
YOU DON'T BELONG HERE!
YOU HAVE ILLEGALLY ACCESSED ENCRYPTED DATA.
COME WITH US.
SHUNK
DON'T WORRY! I'M COMING, LITTLE BUDDY!
ZRAAAKK
WHOA!
BEEBEE-ATE! BEEBEE-ATE! ARE YOU ALL RIGHT?!
BEEBEE-ATE, ANSWER ME...

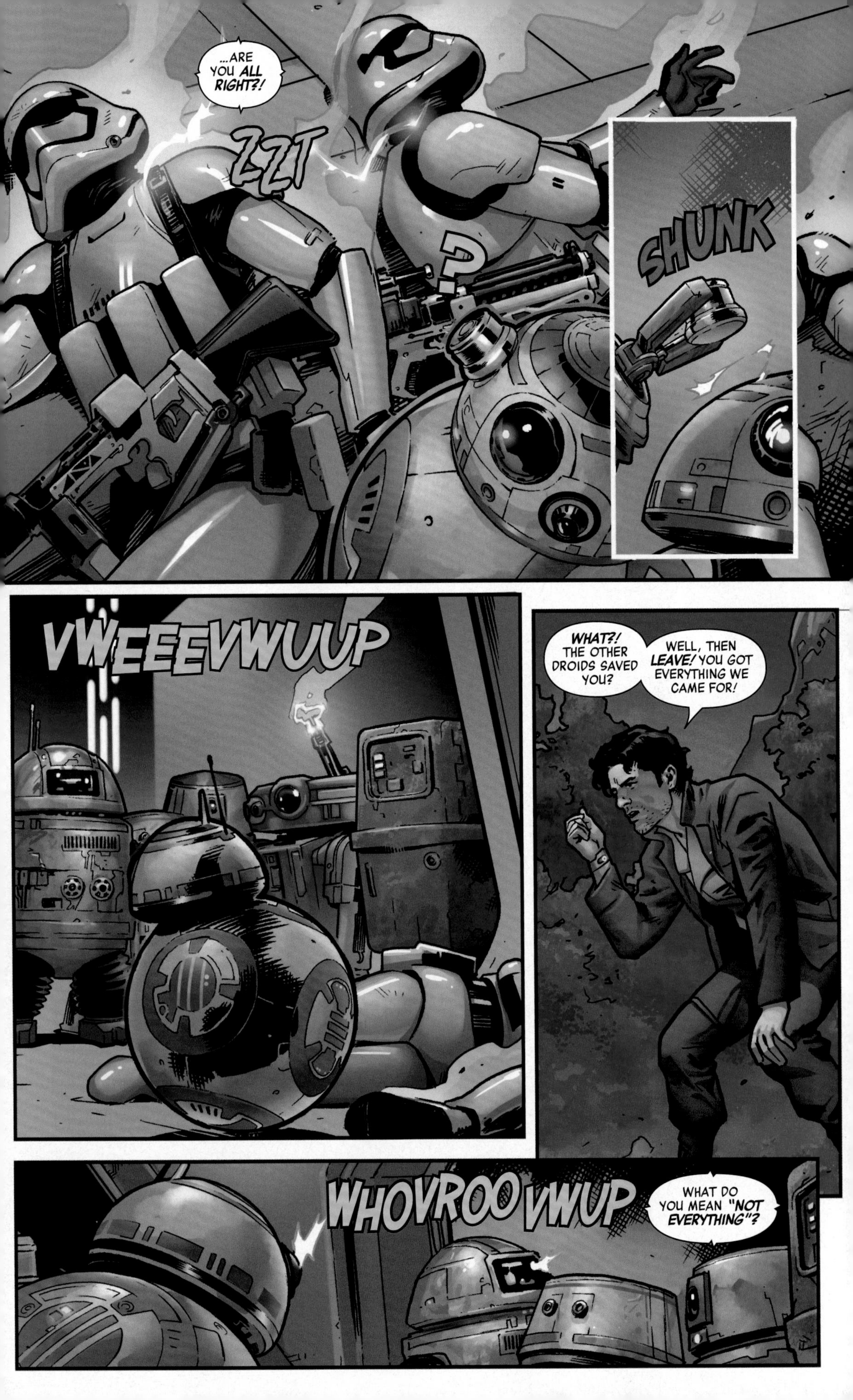

...ARE YOU ALL RIGHT?!
ZZT
?
SHUNK
VWEEEVWUUP
WHAT?! THE OTHER DROIDS SAVED YOU?
WELL, THEN LEAVE! YOU GOT EVERYTHING WE CAME FOR!
WHOVROO VWUP
WHAT DO YOU MEAN "NOT EVERYTHING"?

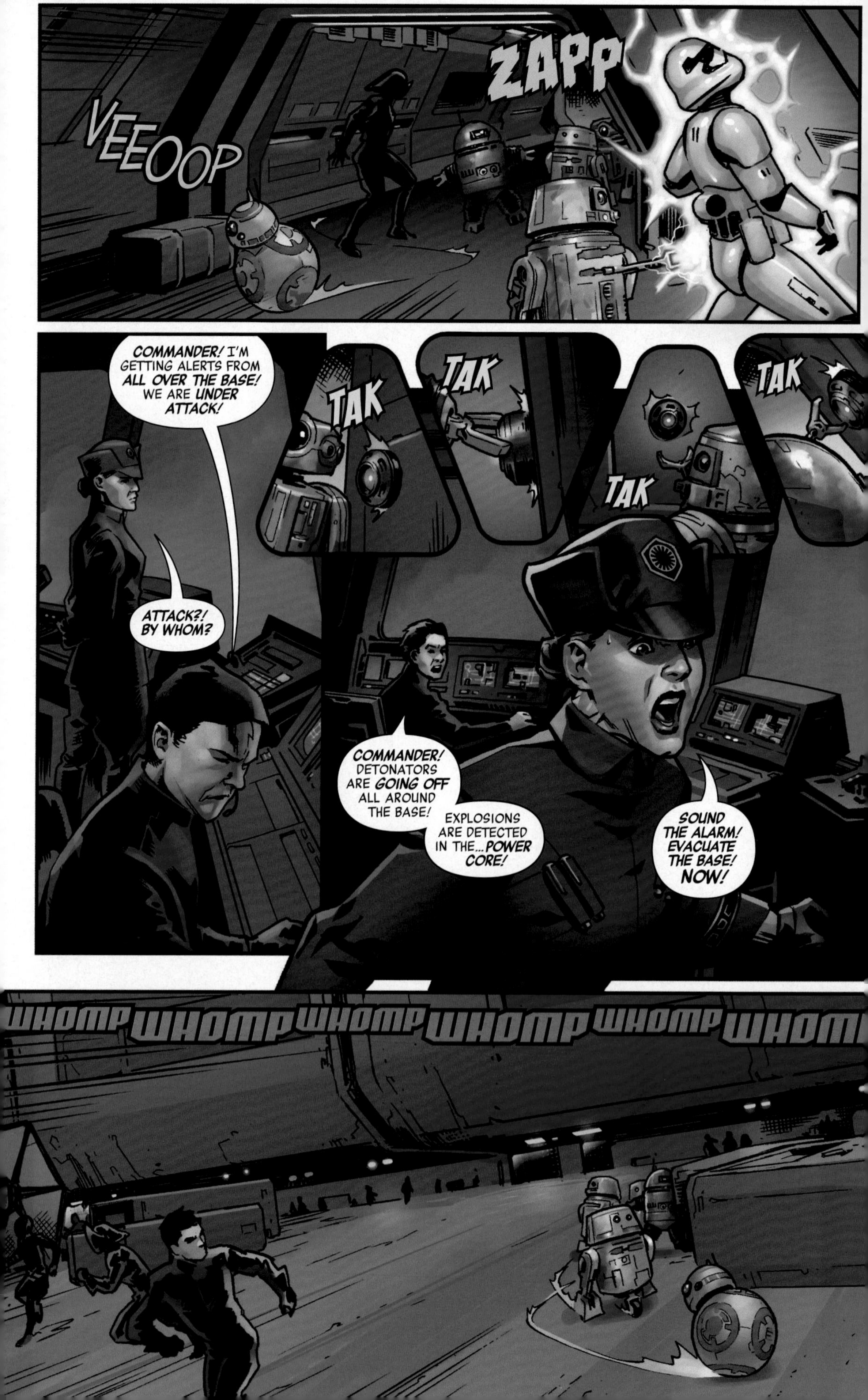
VEEOOP
ZAPP
COMMANDER! I'M GETTING ALERTS FROM ALL OVER THE BASE! WE ARE UNDER ATTACK!
ATTACK?! BY WHOM?
TAK
TAK
TAK
TAK
COMMANDER! DETONATORS ARE GOING OFF ALL AROUND THE BASE!
EXPLOSIONS ARE DETECTED IN THE... POWER CORE!
SOUND THE ALARM! EVACUATE THE BASE! NOW!
WHOMP WHOMP WHOMP WHOMP WHOMP WHOMP

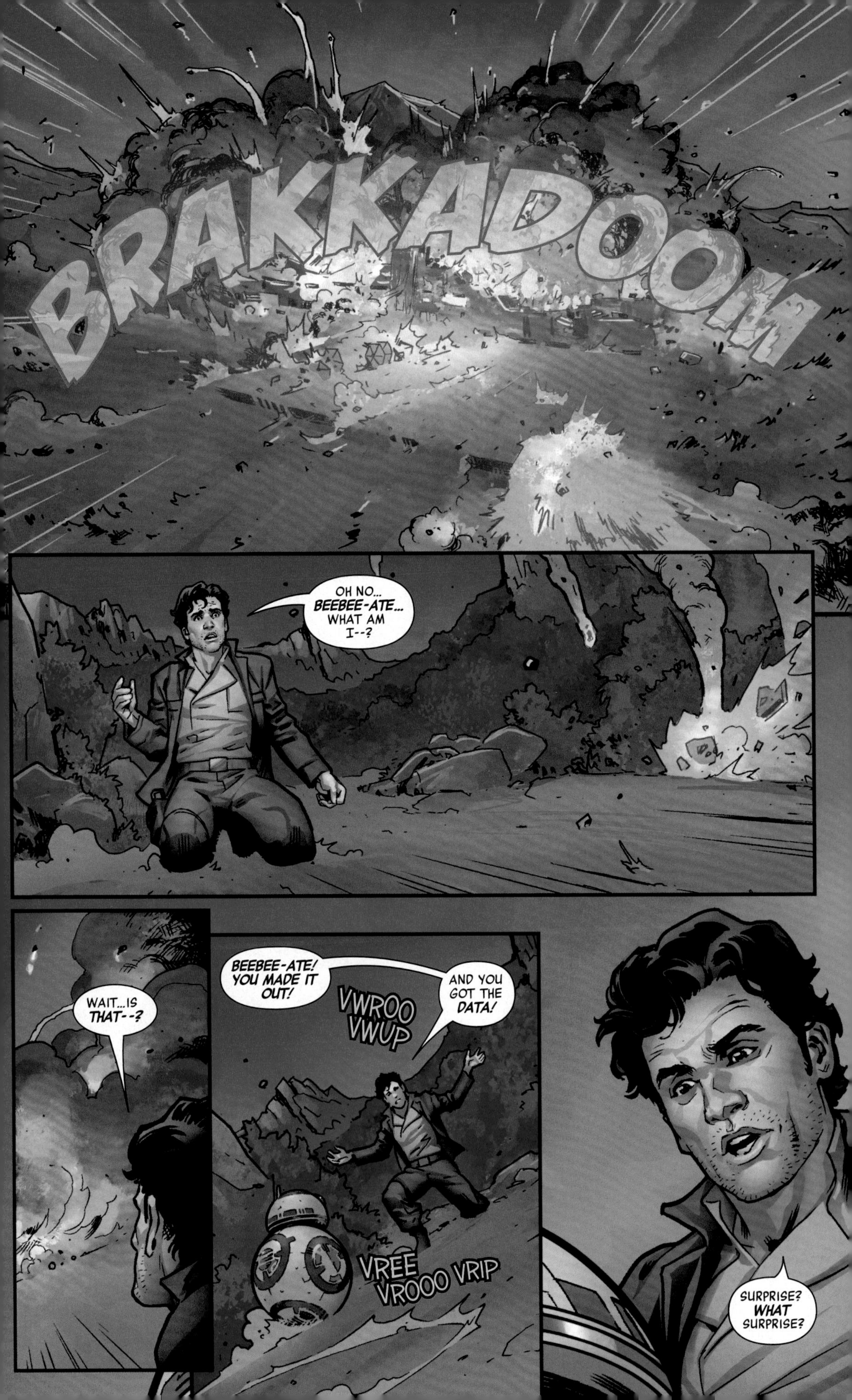
BRAKKADOOM
OH NO... BEEBEE-ATE... WHAT AM I--?
WAIT...IS THAT--?
BEEBEE-ATE! YOU MADE IT OUT!
VWROO VWUP
AND YOU GOT THE DATA!
VREE VROOO VRIP
SURPRISE? WHAT SURPRISE?

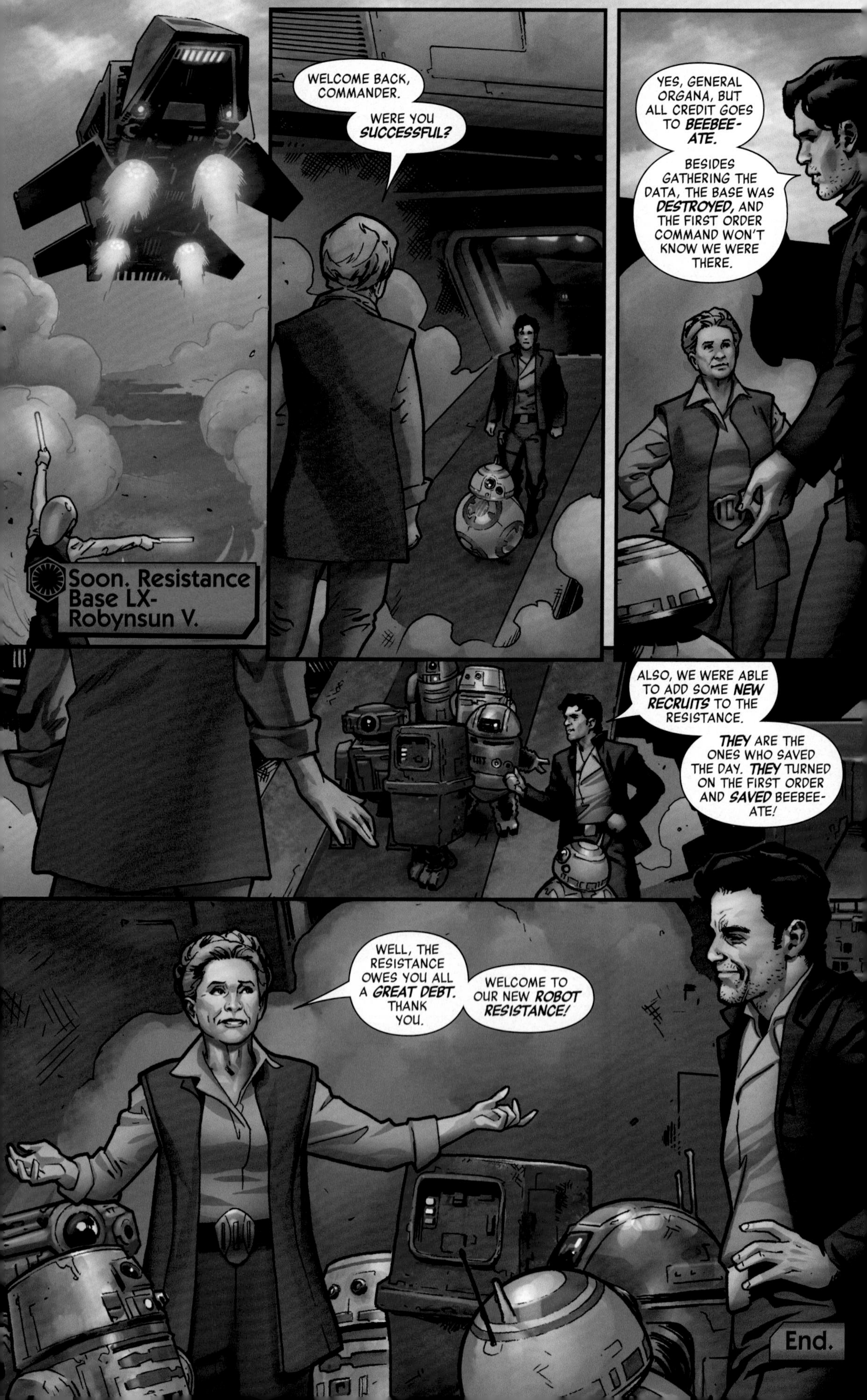
Soon. Resistance Base LX-Robynsun V.
WELCOME BACK, COMMANDER.
WERE YOU SUCCESSFUL?
YES, GENERAL ORGANA, BUT ALL CREDIT GOES TO BEEBEE-ATE.
BESIDES GATHERING THE DATA, THE BASE WAS DESTROYED, AND THE FIRST ORDER COMMAND WON'T KNOW WE WERE THERE.
ALSO, WE WERE ABLE TO ADD SOME NEW RECRUITS TO THE RESISTANCE.
THEY ARE THE ONES WHO SAVED THE DAY. THEY TURNED ON THE FIRST ORDER AND SAVED BEEBEE-ATE!
WELL, THE RESISTANCE OWES YOU ALL A GREAT DEBT. THANK YOU.
WELCOME TO OUR NEW ROBOT RESISTANCE!
End.

AR WARS

AGE OF RESISTANCE

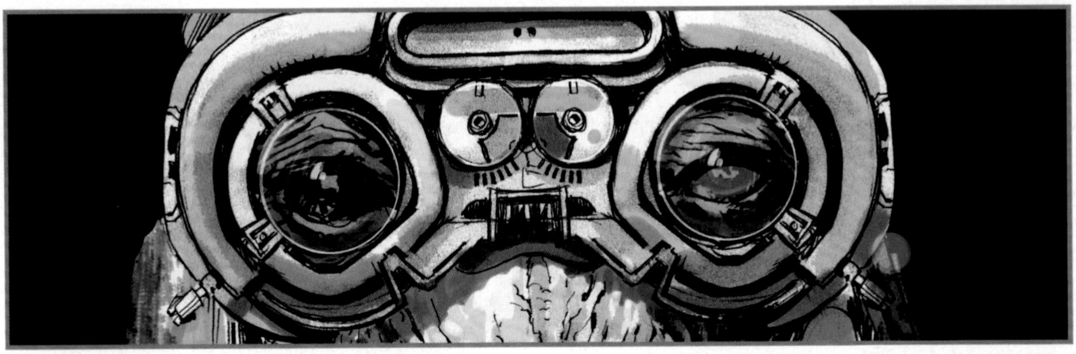

Art by Glyn Dillon

AGE OF RESISTANCE SPECIAL

By Bria LaVorgna

BB-8: ROLLING PERFECTION

There is one simple truth in life: BB-8 is better than all of us. That little droid has it all. He's a first-rate copilot, experienced at prison breaks, an excellent judge of character and extremely huggable. What more could you possibly want from a droid?

From the moment he rolled by in the first teaser trailer for *The Force Awakens*, BB-8 captured the love of *Star Wars* fans everywhere. His design both invoked the astromechs we were already familiar with and brought something completely new to the table, an apt description of the movie itself too. To this day, he continues to be one of the most instantly recognizable aspects of the sequel trilogy.

Bringing the BB-8 puppet to life was very much a team effort. "Matt [Denton] made the brain, Josh [Lee] built the body and, hopefully, Dave [Chapman] and I gave it heart and soul," said puppeteer Brian Herring in an interview with StarWars.com. During filming, Chapman and Herring worked together to bring the little round droid to life, with the former standing offscreen controlling his head and the latter donning a green-screen outfit and running the droid's body around the sets. The puppeteering pair used seven different versions of BB-8 during the filming of *The Force Awakens*, each with a different purpose, and that's not even counting the version that eventually rolled down the red carpet!

It's the droid's personality just as much as his design that makes him so beloved. In another interview with StarWars.com, Herring said, "He's very loyal, but he's a biter, you know, he's feisty. And he's clever, you know, so he gets what he wants. He's tenacious and mischievous and he's tough as well." We saw all of that as BB-8 first struggled to get off of Jakku and then again on his mission with Finn and Rose and even with his partnership with Kaz Xiono in *Star Wars Resistance*. However, nothing can ever top the love and devotion between BB-8 and Poe Dameron. Who doesn't want a friendship like that in their life?

Round and determined, BB-8 is a hero of the Resistance, the best of friends and a true icon for the ages.

ADMIRAL HOLDO: EXPECT THE UNEXPECTED

How to render movie audiences speechless in two easy steps: 1) Take the helm of an MC85 Star Cruiser and be the only one on board. 2) Make the jump to lightspeed through Supreme Leader Snoke's flagship, breaking it in two.

Initially introduced to *Star Wars* fans in Claudia Gray's novel *Leia, Princess of Alderaan,* Vice Admiral Amilyn Holdo excels at the unexpected. Poe Dameron was more than a bit surprised that the woman in front of him was *the* Admiral Holdo from the Battle of Chyron Belt. Amid a sea of drab olive uniforms and orange flight suits, she stood out with her form-fitting dusty purple dress with jewelry that evoked the stars above her homeworld of Gatalenta. Only General Organa dressed in a similar fancy fashion, and even she deemed Holdo "a little odd" when they first met in the Apprentice Legislature decades earlier when the Empire was still the major threat to the galaxy.

Clothes and hair color aside, Holdo also stood out in terms of leadership style. Poe was particularly caught off-balance by how close to the chest she kept things in comparison to Resistance leaders he knew better, like Leia and Ackbar. In an interview with the *Los Angeles Times*, actress Laura Dern said director Rian Johnson initially described Holdo to her as "someone who is so steadfast that you don't know what side they're on because they don't need the rest of the world to know their plans."

After the explosive Holdo Maneuver that buys what little is left of the Resistance the time they desperately need to get to Crait, Leia sums up the Vice Admiral best to Poe: "She was more interested in protecting the light than seeming like a hero." Said Dern in the same interview with the *Los Angeles Times*, "I do think the idea of willing sacrifice, and someone's silent intent to not need to be a hero but to save everyone, is just profound... It's a deep spiritual question, in many religions too, this idea of not needing to prove who you are, but knowing it." While the personality conflicts between Holdo and Poe may have been an issue, Amilyn's willingness to do precisely that is what makes her a hero in the end, even if her methods are a bit unorthodox. But then again...this is Amilyn Holdo we're talking about. Always expect the unexpected.

MAZ KANATA: MORE THAN MEETS THE EYE

The eyes have it when it comes to Maz Kanata. That's just one of the many surprises the diminutive alien has up her sleeve, and given that she's over a thousand years old, she had the opportunity to acquire quite a lot. She's got the friendship of Chewbacca, more flags hanging over her castle than most people can identify and the Skywalker lightsaber in a box in her basement.

All very normal things, of course, when you're the smuggler queen of Takodana.

For all the centuries that Maz has lived, we still don't know much about her. Even the name of her species remains an enigma. However, what we do know about her says a lot. After all, she's someone whom Han Solo trusts, and that list can't be very long. Even more fascinatingly, Maz knows about the ways of the Force even if she isn't a Jedi (or a Sith). A person can learn a heck of a lot over a millennium, and discovering how and where Maz picked up her knowledge and collections will be just as interesting as learning how far that knowledge stretches and what else she may have been hiding in the castle's storage room.

For actress Lupita Nyong'o, the part of Maz was a welcome challenge after her role as Patsey in *12 Years a Slave*. The actress not only provided the voice for Maz but also did the motion capture performance, which involved wearing a gray bodysuit, having her face completely covered in small dots and wearing a camera rig, all vastly different from her Oscar-winning role. "It was about an opportunity to do something that wasn't limited by my body," Nyong'o said in an interview on *Good Morning America*. "It's an opportunity to play in a different playing field because you get to be a different thing."

While certainly not one to cross, Maz Kanata just might be one of the best people to have in your corner. She has connections across the galaxy and is even ready to offer a little tough love to a certain Corellian smuggler when it's most needed. But she'll also, if she sees the potential in your eyes, tell you what you need to hear to help you along your journey because sometimes even the best of us need a little push toward becoming the hero they were meant to be.

Art by Jake Lunt Davies

Art by Christian Alzmann

Art by Robert Rowley

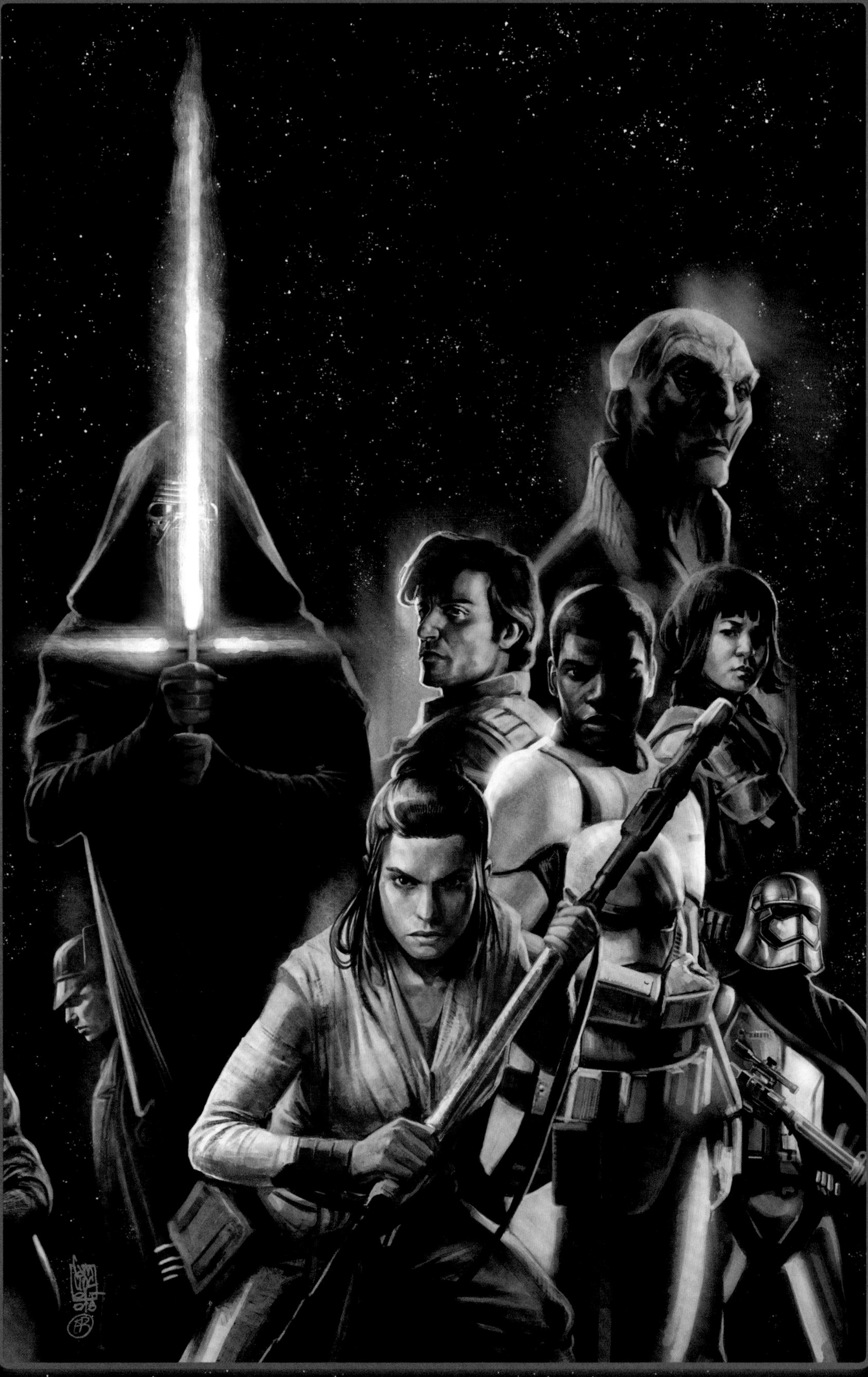

***STAR WARS: AGE OF RESISTANCE* — *FINN* Variant by**
GIUSEPPE CAMUNCOLI & ELIA BONETTI

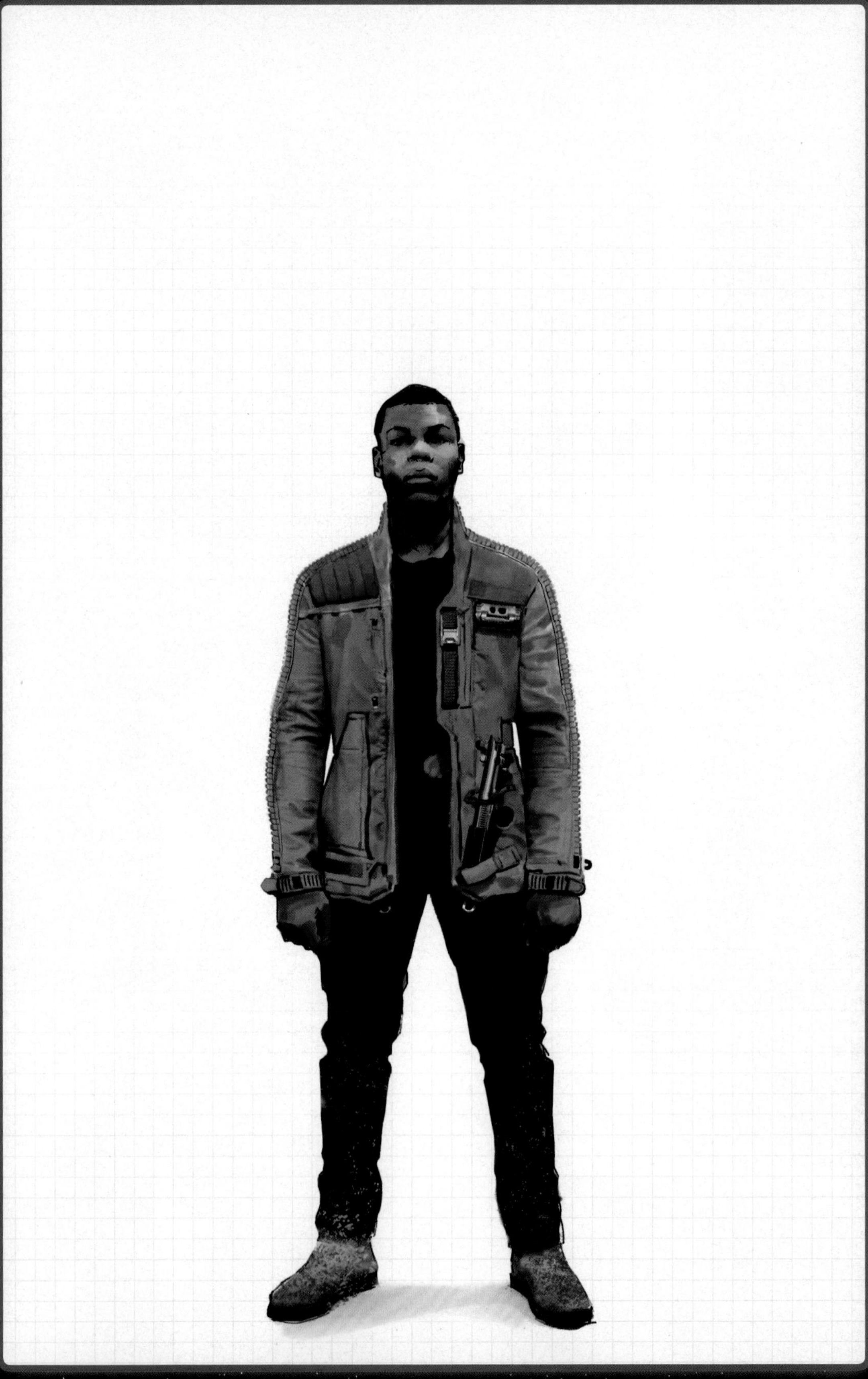

***STAR WARS: AGE OF RESISTANCE* — *FINN* Concept Variant by**
GLYN DILLON

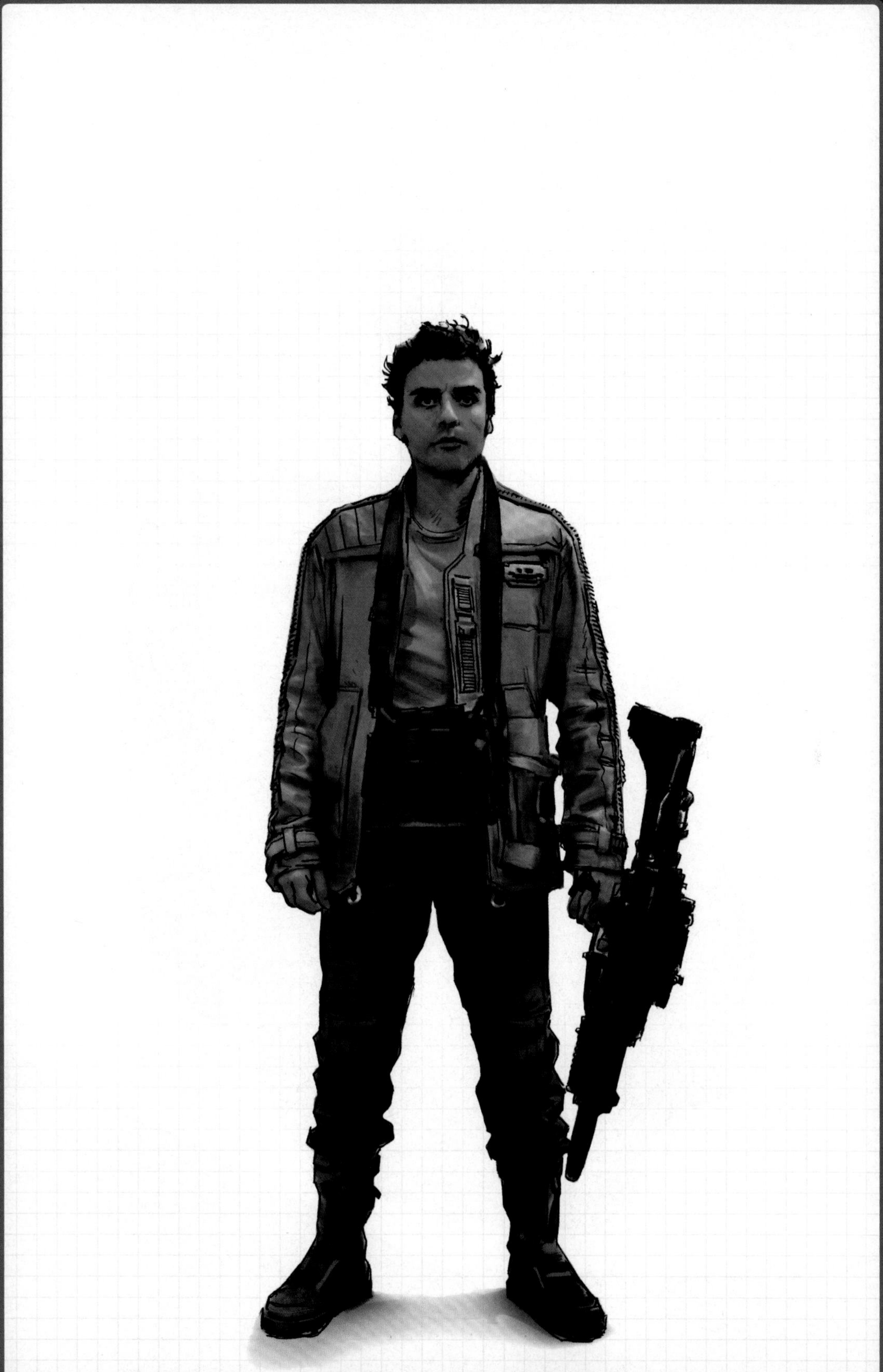

STAR WARS: AGE OF RESISTANCE — POE DAMERON Concept Variant by
GLYN DILLON

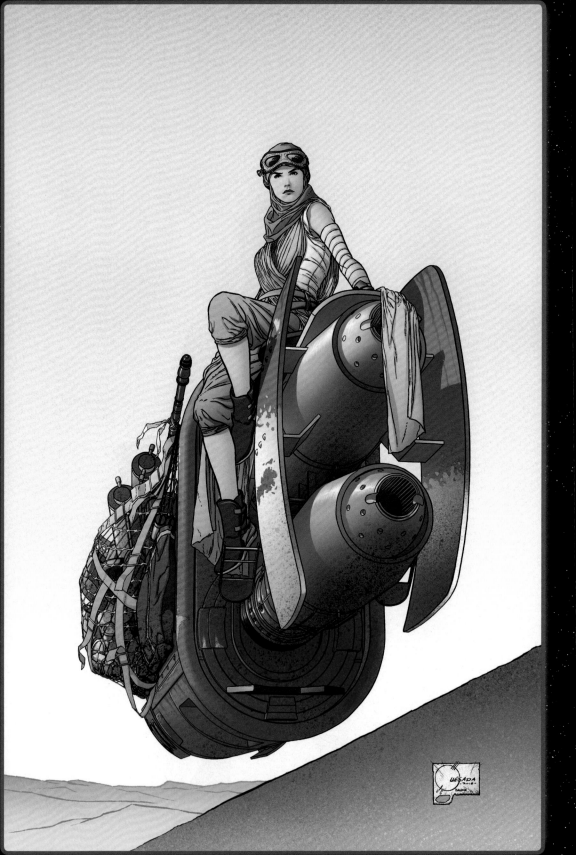

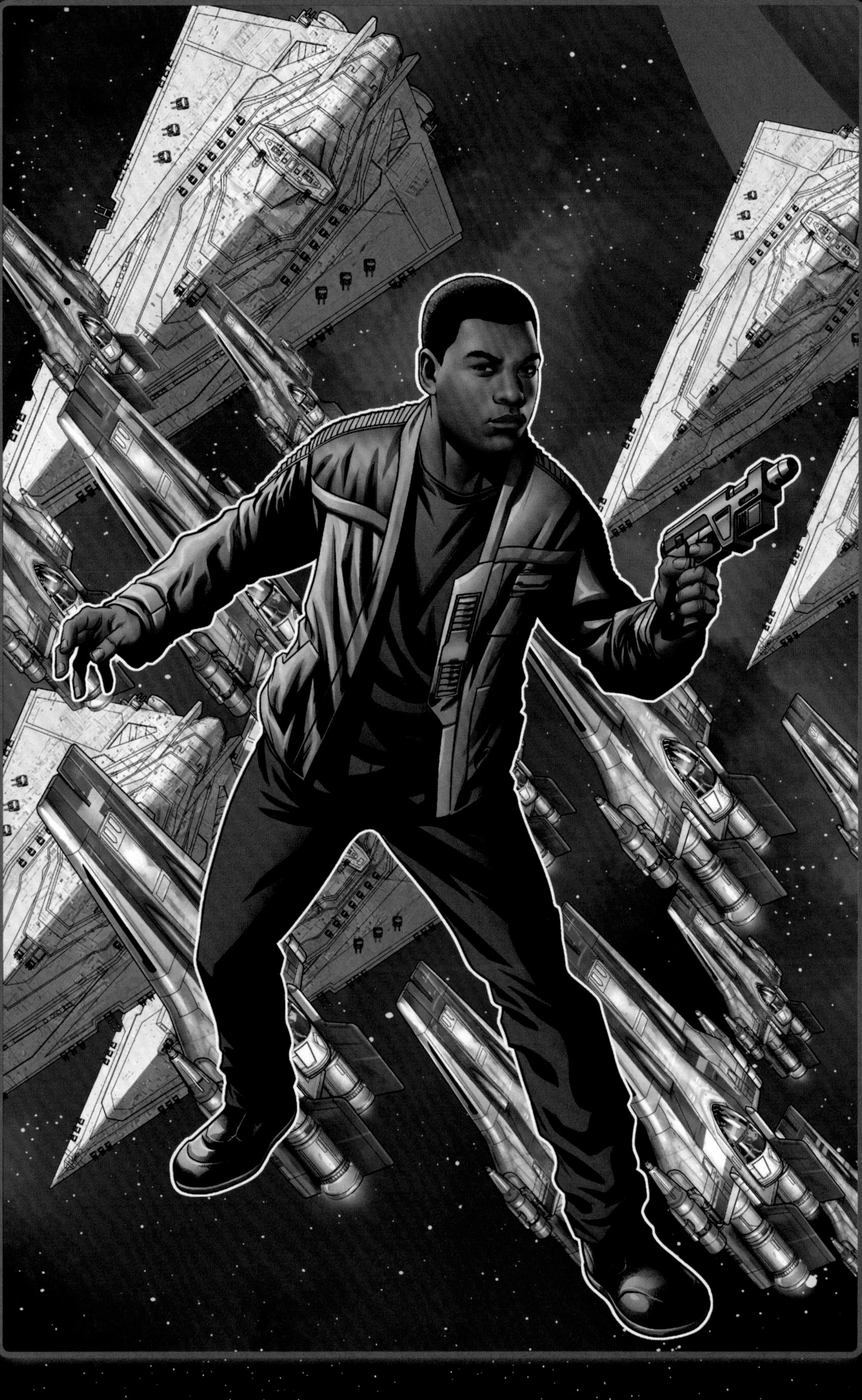

STAR WARS: AGE OF RESISTANCE — *FINN* **Puzzle Piece Variant by**
MIKE McKONE & GURU-eFX

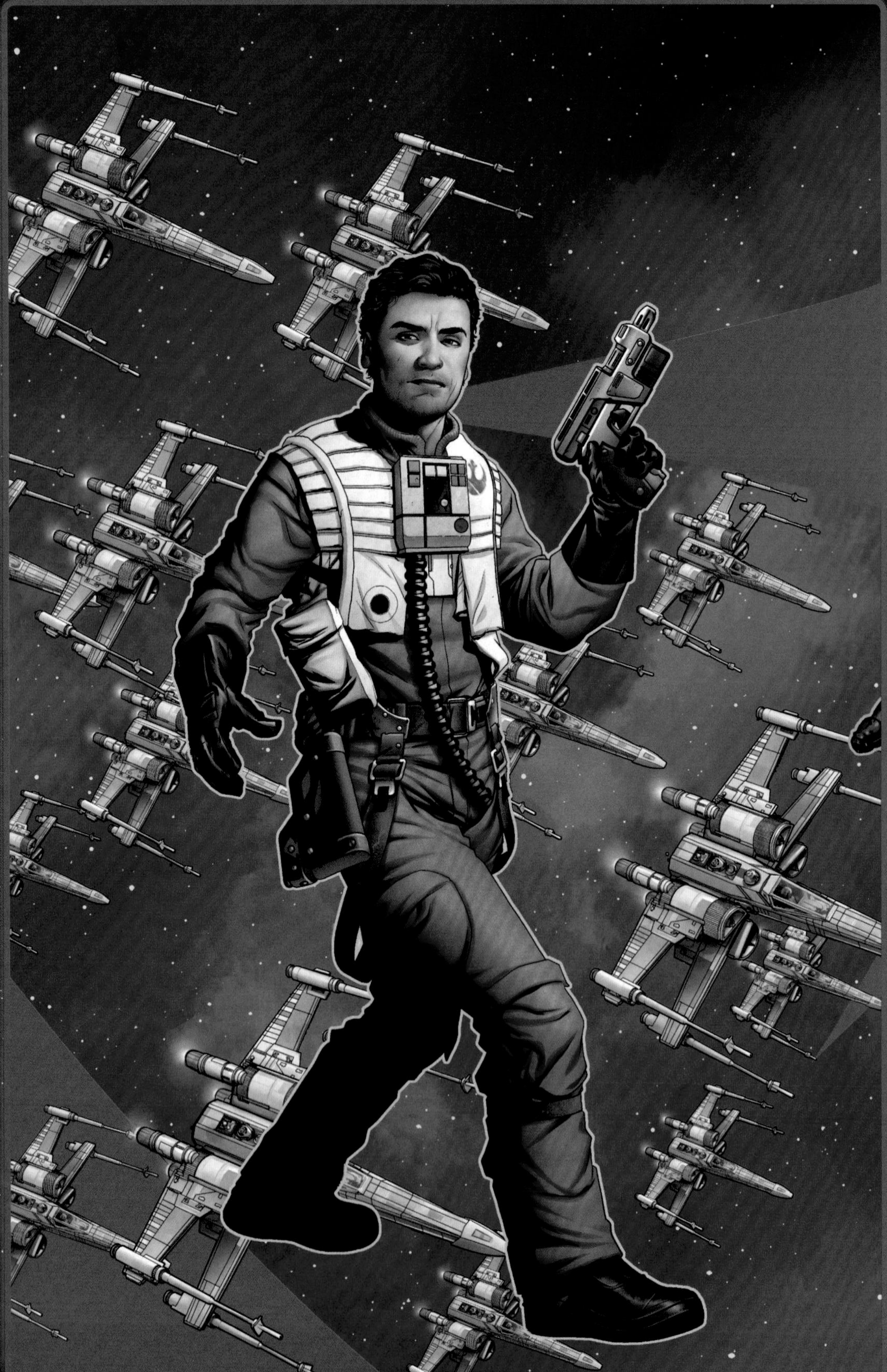

STAR WARS: AGE OF RESISTANCE — POE DAMERON **Puzzle Piece Variant by**
MIKE McKONE & GURU-eFX

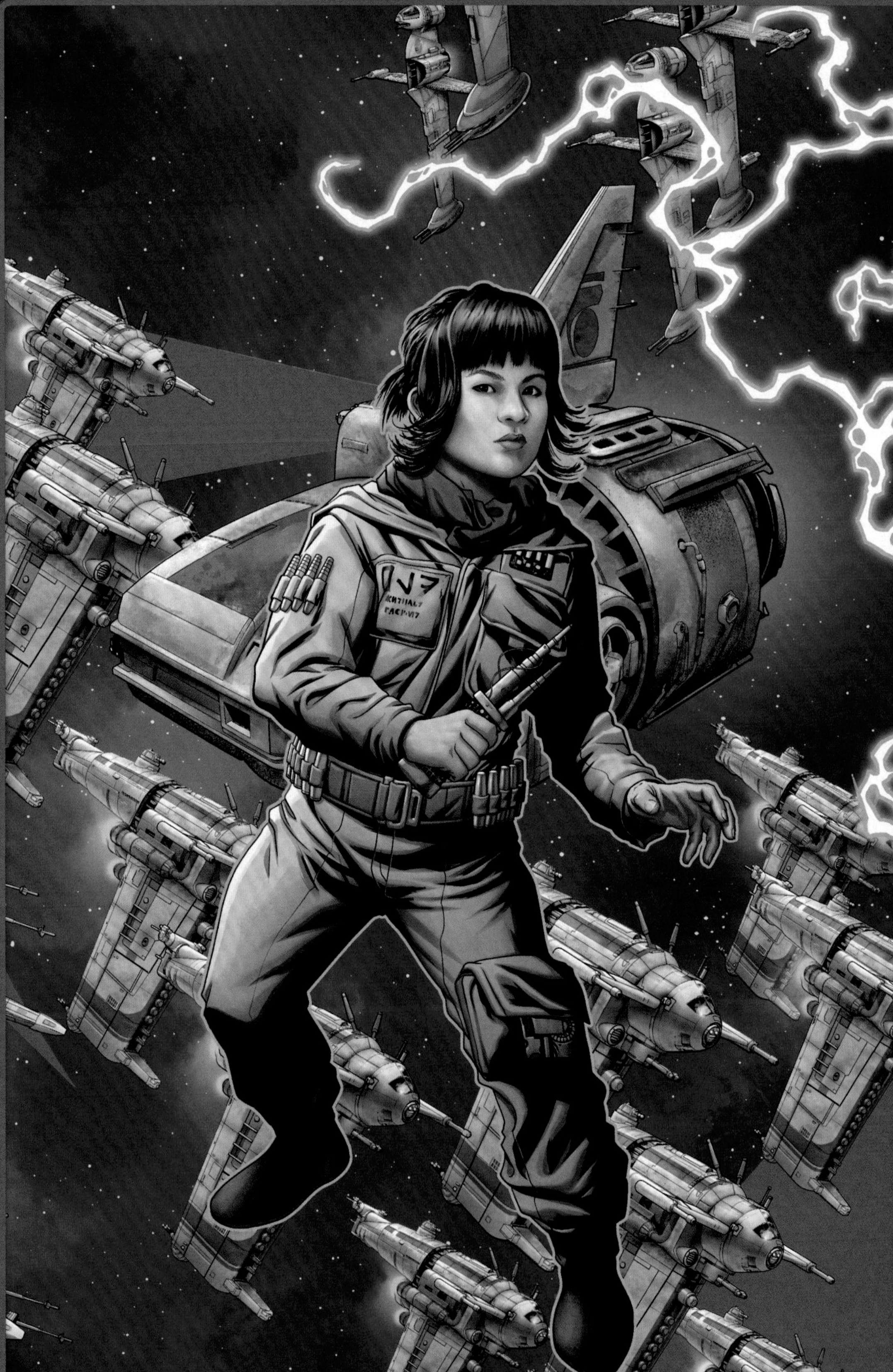

STAR WARS: AGE OF RESISTANCE — ROSE TICO Puzzle Piece Variant by
MIKE McKONE & GURU-eFX

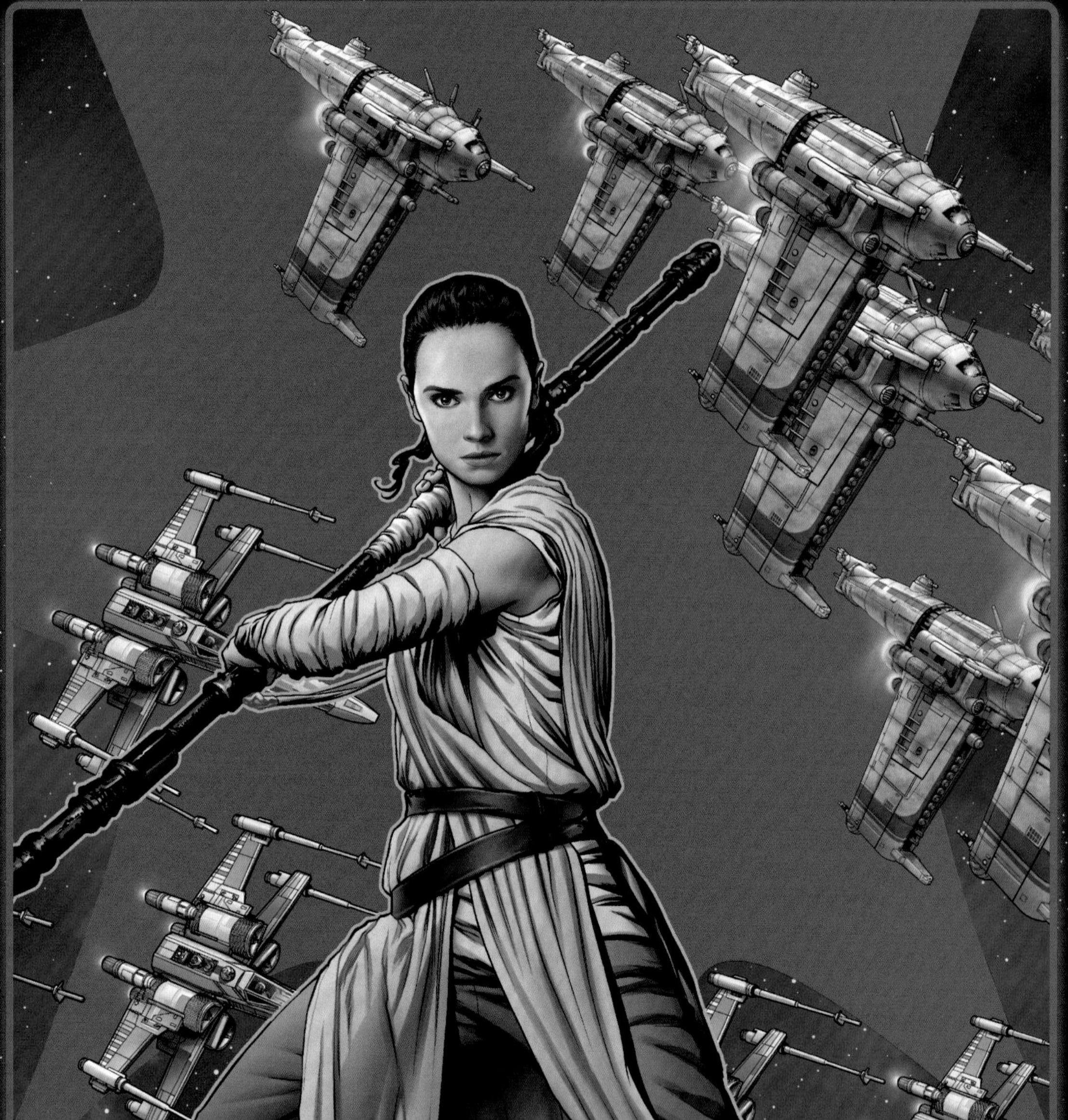

***STAR WARS: AGE OF RESISTANCE* — *REY* Puzzle Piece Variant by**
MIKE McKONE & GURU-eFX

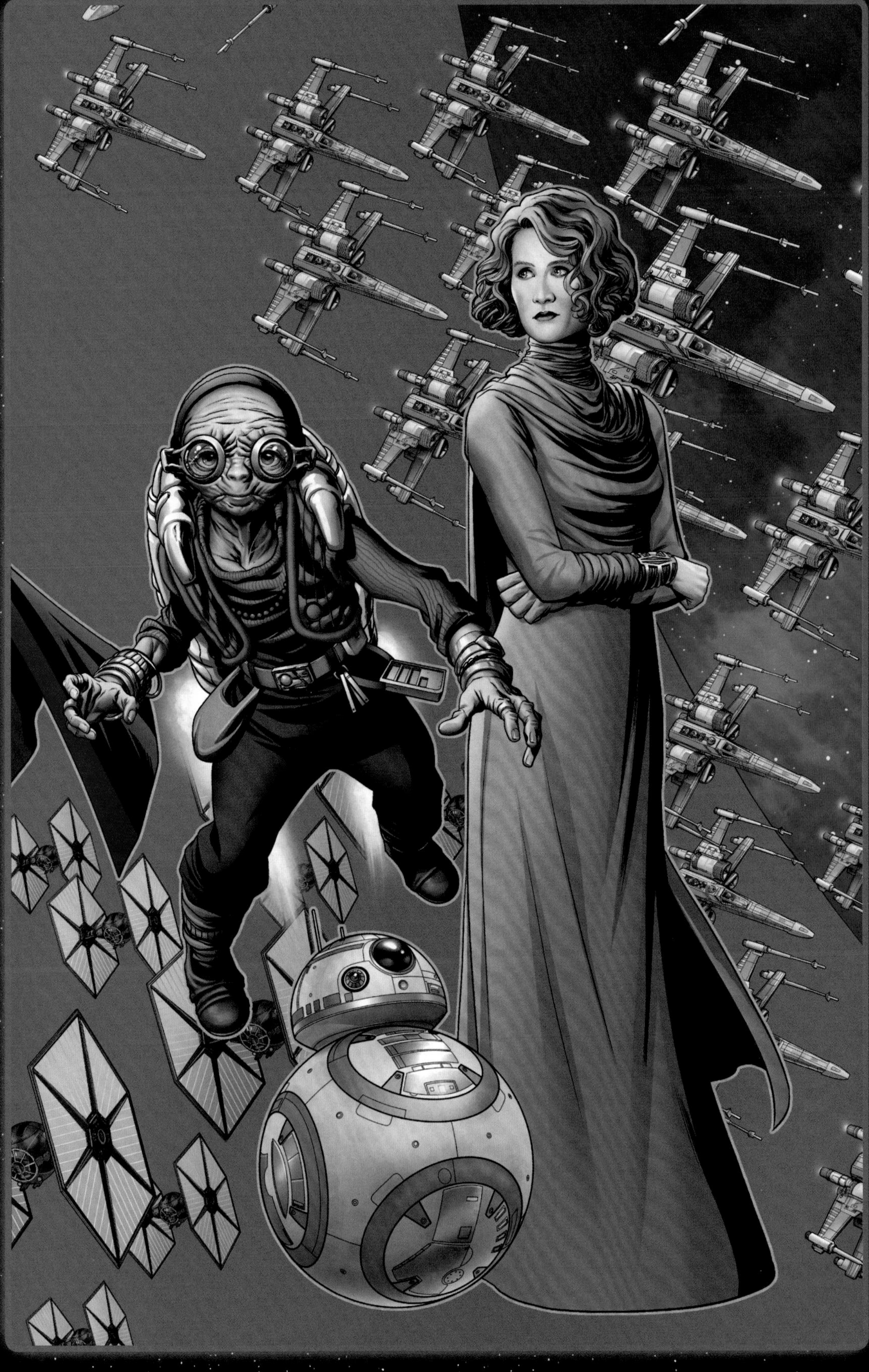

STAR WARS: AGE OF RESISTANCE SPECIAL Puzzle Piece Variant by
MIKE McKONE & GURU-eFX

STAR WARS™

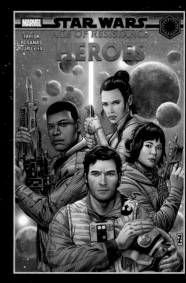
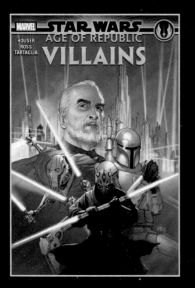
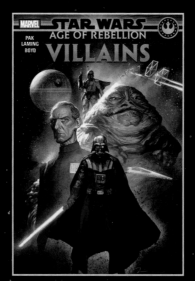